ROADMAP

to

SUCCESS

TABLE OF CONTENTS

A Message from the Publisher

I've done a lot of driving in my life and one thing I have been smart enough to have is a dependable road map. If you don't have a good plan to get from where you are to where you want to go, you will get lost.

I've known many people who have started out in business and thought they had a good plan, but did not achieve the success they wanted. A major problem for many of these people was that they had not sought good advice from people who had achieved success. If you don't learn from the experience of others, you might achieve success but you will probably get there the hard way. You might get lost down many side roads before you find the right one.

Roadmap to Success, is a mini-seminar on how to plan for your success. The successful people in this book have the experience that will help you find what you need to create your road map to success. These perceptive businesspeople were fascinating as they unfolded their own personal road maps and told me about their various success journeys.

I invite you to set aside some quiet time and learn from these exceptional authors. I assure you that your time won't be wasted. It's not often that you can access such a large quantity of quality information that will either get you started or help you get further along on your road to success. This book is an investment in your future—your successful future!

Interviews Conducted by:
David E. Wright, President
Insight Publishing & International Speakers Network

CHAPTER 1

An interview with…

Barbara Boden

SOULMAP—

THE SECRET TO SUCCESS FOR WOMEN

David Wright (Wright)

Today we're talking with Barbara Boden, educator, entrepreneur, and success coach. Barbara has a passion for awakening the spirit of leadership in women. She is Founder and President of Leading Attitudes, Inc., an educational enterprise that provides coaching, consulting, learning environments, and resources for leaders and their teams. An educator and collaborative leader at heart, she is committed to awakening the full potential in people and their organizations. Her firm is celebrating nineteen years of serving public and private sector clients, including recognized mega and micro organizations.

An intrepid seeker, Barbara has explored many paths and countless learning environments in search of universal truth. Personal leadership development and spiritual awakening are her passion—and her profession. She is inspired by the fresh perspectives and transformational possibilities available as the new sciences and spirituality converge.

She knows at her core that the feminine spirit is the key to a new worldview, and she believes that awakening the spirit of personal leadership in women is vital for the wellbeing of our global family. "Outmoded success maps and traditional approaches will not work for navigating this chaotic time," she says. "If we think we can rely on them, we become confused. We need a map with new dimensions."

To explore new directions and collaboratively create new success maps, she is calling forth "The Global Partnership for Awakening Women Leaders." This dynamic visionary entity is a beacon of hope, inspiration, and learning for women as they navigate turbulent new leadership territory. The partners are gifted, adventurous, passionate women who are responding to the calling of their soul and co-creating an empowering impactful presence. Barbara and her professional team are committed to providing wise counsel, treasured resources, and empowering environments to women striving to create healthy, successful, fulfilling lives, and positively impact the quality of life on the planet.

Barbara, welcome to *Roadmap to Success!*

Barbara Boden (Boden)

Thank you so much, David. It is a pleasure to be here with you today.

Wright

Barbara, why did you say yes to our invitation to be in this book?

Boden

My intuition recognized that this is a valuable opportunity to deliver an important message to women around the world.

Wright

And what is the message?

Boden

As a woman, by definition, you are naturally a leader. Often, without recognizing it, you hold the dreams for the children, the community, and the world. But often you forget the value of your role.

The world needs you! It needs leaders like you who see our common ground as sacred ground. The universe is calling for our collaborative wisdom to transcend the current mind-set of separation, defensiveness, and war to reveal a New Earth consciousness of compassion, inclusiveness, and peace.

Our definitions of success are changing, and you can expand your impact. The world is transformed by your presence, your energy, and your spirit-inspired leadership. When you lead your life and your organization from a place of deep connection and authenticity, you are en route to success. Your work *can* be the forum for your personal evolution. You *can* leave a legacy inspired by your soul.

It is time for enlightened responsibility to lead your life. Beyond old guilt, blame, and fear, there is a field of possibility waiting to be experienced—a world where we can know who we truly are and what we have come to do. As an educator and certified coach, I specialize in coaching women who seek to reach their highest potential, to access untapped capabilities, and skillfully navigate their lives. I am honored to champion women to stretch beyond their comfort zone and transform their worlds.

I invite you read this chapter from the core of your being.

It is time to awaken to that which we are! It is a time to remember that we are more than we have recognized. Beyond the "not-good-enough" ego voice that holds us back is the truth of our being. In our deep heart, we carry the map of transformation for our life and for humanity. We are the map! And we are the sojourners.

We have witnessed the twentieth century driven by the intellect, by information, technology, and science. This has spawned thoughts of scarcity, defensiveness, anxiety, and has led to physical, financial, and emotional devastation. Driven chiefly by the mind and consumed by analysis and fear, we as a society have lost perspective and forgotten our grander identity.

I see many women disheartened, giving up on their dreams, settling for less, and abandoning hope of success—wondering, "Who am I becoming? What am I doing with my one precious life?"

Success now is not about learning more information or relaying on other people's plans. It is about honoring our inner wisdom as an expression of Universal Knowing. On my own journey, I have come to understand that we carry the question—and the answer. We know the way. We are the light we've been told about since childhood. We long to awaken to that light.

Some early women's road maps contained directions and warnings: "Go here. Don't go here. Watch out for this." They contained enough knowledge to inspire some women to dare their own heroine's journeys.

Years ago my mother-in-law, who lived in Massachusetts, described how the twisty roads in Boston came to be. "They were originally cow paths," she said. "As society changed, these well-worn paths evolved into roads." Many extraordinary women have ventured success paths and inspired others. Masses of us have trod those rutty paths through hierarchical organizations with a single focus—climb the ladder— only to find the ladder leaning on the wrong wall. We struggled to maintain our passion and our self-worth as we were overcome by values and voices that were not our own.

Others lost our way in relationships. We signed away our inner voices and long to reclaim them. What looked like success was an illusion as we gave up ourselves in the process.

Today, we long to be excited about our life again. We seek a new dimension of personal inspiration and new a view of success. We are finding our own path.

Wright

So, Barbara, what do you think women mean by success?

Boden

In the hearts of the women I know, success is discovering their true identity and living their life on purpose. It is finding value, vision, and voice, not from the outer world, but from the True Self within. It is accessing the ability to break free from the internal disempowering dialogue to discover our courage and untapped capability—and live passionately with full responsibility for our lives.

Women tell me they feel successful when they know their True Self and trust their inner wisdom, when they see that their path is aligned with their destiny, and they can leave a legacy inspired by their soul.

Wright

What do you mean by "True Self"?

Boden

When I say "True Self," I mean the organizing and all-sustaining life force of the universe that is our Essence—the Spirit in us that is Infinite intelligence and Divine love. As we awaken to this Presence, we can experience God-realization and discover our unbridled capacity.

Wright

How does this relate to success?

Boden

Guided and sustained by our True Self we can confidently persevere on our path. We can find safety and creativity in our spiritual core, and we can hold perspectives that support us through our human challenges.

Today, as global citizens, we find personal success is intrinsically linked to each other and to the quality of life on the planet. Daily we see that our priceless feminine spirit is being called forth.

Margaret Wheatley, renowned researcher, teacher, and author of *Leadership and the New Science*, advocates, "It's time to realize that we will never cope with this new world using our old maps. It is our fundamental way of interpreting the world—our worldview—that must change. Only such a shift can give us the capacity to understand what's going on, and to respond wisely."

Wright

What is the role of women in this shift?

Boden

Everywhere, women are called to step up and inspire this shift. Women's dynamic role is the key. I believe the catalyst for the new worldview is the awakened spirit of leadership in women of all ages and backgrounds, from all over the world, from all religions and no religion. Collectively, women carry new visions, new definitions of success, and new maps for our journey. In our hearts, women hold the solutions to our global problems—and must bring them forth.

I've learned that there is in each of us a yearning, a Calling of the Ages, to know who we are, to remember the truth of our Being, to bring forth the holy qualities that lie dormant in us, and to express these gifts to create a more perfect and peaceful world. Our role is to listen attentively and respond to that universal Call from the place deep within that knows truth and longs to be heard. It is time to stop looking outside ourselves for answers—time to look inward and discover our Soulmaps, drawn in our hearts eons ago by our Creator.

It is time to unfold each Soulmap, shine the light on it, and set out on our heroines' journeys to awaken to the truth of who we are and who God is. As each of us awakens to the True Self, we'll be a light that inspires others to find their own grander identity. Each one of us has students waiting for our message. With a collective shift in our worldview we'll save time in creating a brighter future—one that is currently beyond belief—but not beyond accomplishment!

Wright

Are women hearing this Call, and are they responding?

Boden

Yes, David. Many women are responding to the Call to finally listen to their inner voice and choose environments and paths that honor their value and fulfill their life purpose.

But, sadly, I hear many women longing to respond and frustrated that they are not. They feel stuck in their busy worlds. They yearn for guidance to find a more meaningful life, but haven't known where to turn. Today's intense and stressful environments exhaust women at every level. Many "successful" women know that they are not thriving. They want to contribute meaningfully, but, overcome by circumstance and feeling overwhelmed, they feel trapped in their ordinary lives, longing to do extraordinary things.

In confidence, many tell me that they are not only overwhelmed with their busy lives and frustrated by the glass ceiling, but also stifled by those disempowering secret conversations that stop them from saying "no" to the demands of the world and "yes!" to the calling of their soul. That ego voice demands, "Who are *you* to think you are a leader? What makes you think *you* can make a difference?"

That incessant "not-good-enough" voice nags at us, shuts down our visions, and demands to know who we think we are. It stops us in our tracks en route to our dreams so that just when we are about to launch, we don't. We don't start a business. We don't go for the grant. We don't pick up the phone. We don't change careers. We don't forgive ourselves. We procrastinate. We watch our self-worth spiraling down and don't know how to stop it.

We imagine having the resources and the freedom to make the kind of difference we know we can make, but here we are again, standing on the shore, looking at the opportunity, capable yet vacillating . . . hesitating to launch into the uncertain future . . . still on the verge. Deep down, we know that we carry an untapped wealth of wisdom and energy waiting to be released to the world, yet we don't know how to reach it. We long for guidance.

Wright

So what do you tell them?

Boden

"Just where you are right now is perfect. Here you can realize your truth and start on your path to success."

I remind them: *As a woman, by definition, you are naturally a leader. You are more capable than you know at this moment.*

If you are hearing the Call to be more, it is time to respond to the urgings of your soul. It is time to know your True Self and your purpose, and time to step into the vision you have been given. It is time to make the difference you know in your emerging leader's heart that you are called to make. Your world is waiting for you to say, "Yes!"

So much of your energy has gone to trying to achieve, become, and learn. So much of your time is spent acquiring new information, exploring trainings, and experiencing something that you hope will make you feel ready to step into what you desire for your life.

It is time for your wisdom to be honored, first by yourself and then by the world. It can no longer be overlooked, overcome by circumstance, or silenced by your own inner critic. It is time to go beyond the stories you have told yourself about who you are—time to abandon old external expectations and outdated road maps.

You can open your own Soulmap in a nurturing environment where you are honored in your wisdom and held capable of knowing your path. You can stop searching outside yourself and look inward to know and express your magnificent identity.

Wright

Why is there a Soulmap for women? And what is it?

Boden

The Soulmap is valuable for men and women, David, but I think our language is different. My purpose here is to inspire the heart of emerging women leaders so that they find the confidence to begin their own heroine's journey to a deeply meaningful life.

From the male perspective, a hero's journey has traditionally begun as an external quest. I believe a heroine's journey is an extraordinary *internal* voyage of discovery to unearth our invisible sacred treasures and gift those to the world. I've found that when we transcend the layers of our being, we can touch the Secret and experience the power of our True Self.

It is both a powerful individual and shared journey as we discover that, like an island, deep under the ocean, we are one with the core. We emerge from that deep exploratory dive transformed—and naturally experience a consciousness shift. With our new worldview, our life is transformed.

The balance of the twenty-first century offers an astonishing opportunity to transform our society—to initiate an evolved global consciousness inspired and crafted by awakening feminine wisdom.

We are not alone. We see significant progressive thinkers assessing old organizational paradigms seeking new approaches to success. Might this awakening parallel the shift in worldview among the scientific community? Newtonian physics assumes that there is an external world separate from us. Its focus on objective information, measurement, and analysis parallels many stagnant organizations and lives. The new physics—quantum mechanics—with its focus on dynamic possibility and our impact on world, tells us that it is not possible to observe reality without changing it. We co-create it. Our presence matters!

In *The Dancing Wu Li Masters: An Overview of the New Physics* Gary Zukav says, "Quantum mechanics resulted from the study of the subatomic realm, that invisible universe underlying, embedded in, and forming the fabric of everything around us ... There is no such thing as objectivity. We cannot eliminate ourselves from the picture. We are part of nature, and when we study nature there is no way around the fact that nature is studying itself. . . . Physics has become a branch of psychology, or perhaps the other way around.

". . . Philosophically . . . the implications of quantum mechanics are psychedelic. Not only do we influence our reality, but, in some degree, we actually *create* it . . ."

If the Swiss psychologist, Carl Jung and Nobel Prize-winning physicist, Wolfgang Pauli, are correct, Zukav says, ". . . then physics is the study of the structure of consciousness." *We* are this consciousness! We dwell in a world that co-evolves as we interact with it!

What an empowering gift the new sciences have given us! It astonishes us—awakens us out of old ideas of what is real. The unseen connections between what were previously thought to be separate entities are the elemental ingredient of all creation. As the languages of Eastern mystics and Western physicists become similar, I wonder . . . if things change merely by observing them from our perspective, what then is possible? What might change in our lives when our viewpoint changes or when the view of ourselves changes?

At the subatomic level, mass and energy change unceasingly into each other. Most often, we are so preoccupied with our human experience that we forget the unseen spiritual energy that we are. What is possible if we connect more fully with the energy of our True Self?

I invite you to consider the emotional impact of this perspective framed by my associate, Julie, and notice, as you read the questions how your energy shifts. Imagine . . .

What if it were as simple as opening to the wisdom and presence that are always here? What would then be available to you? How would you be? Who would you be?

What if everything you ever needed was and is here, right now? Everything you need to be the leader you are. Everything you need to succeed. What if it is all here, right now? Who is the leader within you? What is she saying? What is the impact of your awakened leader's heart?

Wright

How can this Soulmap change one's perspective, Barbara?

Boden

It can be significant, David. The Soulmap to Success is a courageous metaphorical passage through the layers of our humanity to embrace our spirituality where we glean the treasures of that unseen dimension of our existence. With this knowledge, we have access to abundant internal and external resources and can live a more authentic, courageous, and inspired life.

One of my significant spiritual teachers illustrates this exploration with the "Layers of the Heart" drawing. He also says, "He who knows himself knows his God." What if "She who knows herself knows her God"?

Wright

What do you mean when you say "Layers of the Heart"? And does it help you know yourself?

Boden

Much of the depth and breadth of our identity is beyond our awareness. This heart is a simple metaphor for complex dimensions of our being.

For more than two decades, since my husband passed away, I have been a seeker—on a quest for universal truth and my own identity. I have explored many spiritual paths and innumerable personal and professional development programs, and traveled thousands of miles in search of unifying principles.

One memorable day in the fall of 2005, I attended a program that introduced what I now call a Soulmap. The seminar was given by two gifted Sufi teachers. As one of them—Salima—drew the "Layers of the Heart" on a flipchart and explained each one, I at once saw a way to harmonize the various aspects of our being and recognized what I was striving to reach. I hope this concept will be valuable to our readers.

My understanding is that these four concentric hearts describe the pathway we walk to touch the True Self that we each carry at our core. (See diagram.) This is based on the teachings of the Guide of the Shadhiliyya Sufis, Shaykh Muhammad Sa'id al-Jamal ar-Rifa'i as-Shadhuli, who lives in Jerusalem. The full explanation can be found in his book, *Music of the Soul*, published by Sidi Muhammad Press. Sidi, as he is affectionately called, has dedicated his life to bringing peace, love, justice, and mercy to the world through teachings of unity.

The Layers of the Heart—Dimensions of Our Being

I view this wisdom as a gift for our time. Its universality can interface with many paths. This chapter contains my own interpretation of his enlightening concept. With each step on this purifying path, we get closer to knowing the Secret of our True Self. It does not require adding something to who we are but instead encourages us to penetrate the veils to experience our true identity.

I encourage you to give yourself this gift, and start on your heroine's journey now by doing the Pathwork Enquiries in each section. If you take time to draw your own heart and write your unique descriptors in the drawing, I am certain you will gain insight. Using a full sheet of paper allows space to write in each section. You might title it "Layers of My Heart" or "Dimensions of My Being" or a title of your own choosing.

There are no right or wrong answers—just discovery. To encourage your exploration and to clarify some points, I have included a few of my own private disclosures.

The self

The outside layer of this heart—number one—is called *The self* (small s). Sometimes, to clarify, I call it the rational self. This facet carries the collection of elements of the three-dimensional world, the reactive mind, the body, judgments, physical experiences, worldly relationships, behaviors, ego, "our story," busyness, intellect, and incessant mind chatter—thoughts—that stop us from hearing the still small voice and hides our True Self.

In his book, *A New Earth, Awakening to Your Life's Purpose,* Eckhart Tolle clarifies: "More fundamental than the external forms—things and bodies—are the thought forms that continuously arise in the field of consciousness. They are finer and less dense than matter, but they are forms nonetheless. What you may be aware of as a voice in your head that never stops speaking is the stream of incessant and compulsive thinking. When every thought absorbs your attention completely, when you are so identified with the voice in your head and the emotions that accompany it that you lose yourself in every thought and emotion, then you are totally identified with form and therefore in the grip of ego. Ego is a conglomerate of recurring thought forms and conditioned mental-emotional patterns that are invested in a sense of I and a sense of self."

Many people live only in this aspect, unaware that we are more. When we are committed to transformation and breakthrough success, our "stuff" comes up to be recognized and cleared.

Most of us—men and women—find embedded in this layer a lingering message about ourselves that originated somewhere in our early childhood. This childhood decision arose from our interpretation of the events of our young lives and was reinforced as we grew. Some messages are empowering; others are not. Carol McCall, author of *The Empowerment of Listening* course, with whom I trained years ago, has researched this process and the resulting disempowering messages. Major ones are: "not enough," "not good enough," "not worthy," "stupid," "not important," "not wanted," "people can't be trusted," "loser," "truth doesn't work," and "nobody cares." It seems we each carry a primary thought form that unconsciously drives our choices. Our early decision becomes the filter through which we experience the world. Each has its own flavor—and impact—sending us into an internal drama and generating inner critic messages that de-motivate us if unchecked. Recognizing them can reduce their control. Transcending them will get us back on course toward our true self and real success.

Would you like to identify yours?

Pathwork Enquiries:

- In layer one, what words best describe this physical and mental dimension of your life? Consider your quality of life, your relations, surroundings, health, finances, etc.

- What do you intuit is your early childhood decision? It shows up as the primary recurring core message of your inner critic. Capture that—and write it in the outside layer. My own ego voice insists, "Not good enough!" It drives me crazy, makes me doubt my ability, and causes me to strive for perfection. She certainly objected as I said yes to this book! What is the drama yours creates?

- What name would you give *your* inner critic? And how would you describe her? Some programs call your inner critic your imposter or mask because it is not the truth. I sometimes call mine Perfecta because she nags about everything needing to be perfect. It is never good enough! She's formal and perfectly dressed—lookin' good all the time. It is hard to hide from her scrutinizing gaze. She constantly whispers in my ear. When I can see the bigger picture and appreciate the humor, I call her Lucy—for *I Love Lucy.*

The Heart

Layer number two, *The Heart* carries the unseen world, our feelings and emotions—our happiness, sadness, anger, excitement, fears, guilt, and anxieties. These are the fluctuating up and down emotions, mostly triggered by our thoughts and experiences in the external world—the outside layer.

Pathwork Enquiries:

- In layer two, what are the words for your primary emotions—those that are most familiar? What are the feelings you experience frequently?

- Can you notice what triggers your emotions and where you get stuck? Again, no judgment. Capture the primary ones.

- My big trigger is that "not-good-enough" early childhood decision. It shows up in my fear of what I think someone thinks.

- Having my adult children live with me for a year with a sweet dog, a new huge energetic lab-mix puppy, and our wonderful vocal new baby girl at the same time that I was trying to run a business from home, learn to be a writer, develop a Web site, and start the Global Partnership, surfaced undeniable awareness of that inner critic—and placed her boldly before my eyes. The effects were overwhelming and damaging to our relationships. The judgments that I felt coming from the kids were magnified by the judgments I placed on myself and then reverberated in our relationship. *A Course in Miracles* has excellent teachings on this dynamic.

I now see that these fearful disempowering thoughts were to be exposed—and cleared—like the rays of sun burning away fog to reveal a magnificent landscape. Reflecting on our lives in safe environments can enlighten us, reduce the emotional charge, and release the ego-pictures we hold in our minds. For those reasons, I love our virtual Collaborative Wisdom Circles and the safety of a coaching relationship.

- What drama energy do you bring into your environment? How do your feelings affect your actions and your ability to relate to yourself and others? The cycle may be beyond your awareness right now; at first, it was for me. It had me shut down and strive harder to focus on work. Many months later, I was relieved and blessed to discover that a significant contributor to my feeling of being overwhelmed and my inability to stay focused was due to an undetected case of Lyme disease. It took a long time to realize that the diverse, seemingly unrelated symptoms were all caused by the bite of a minute deer tick.
The diverse and demanding projects and circumstances that I had committed to turned out to be more than my mind and body could comfortably handle, and the stress impacted my immune system.
In my heart of hearts, I know that this situation was a gift to my personal walk through the human challenges of life to reach a deeper understanding of Spirit. What happens for you?

Wright

Barbara, how do these thoughts and feelings relate to success?

Boden

Years ago, I learned about the early childhood decision and the resulting disempowering drama cycle but could not see beyond it. I believe that the Soulmap can take us through the drama to awareness, empowerment, and success.

Have you noticed that many professional development programs that promise to teach success stop with the mind and emotions? I've learned that in order to experience *true* success, we must go deeper and encompass the core of our being. This success map takes us through the self and the feelings into our soul and the unity that is The Secret of our true identity.

The Soul

Layer number three is The Soul. Before this "Layers of the Heart" concept, I rarely used the word "soul" because I could not comprehend it. Now, I understand it as our unique individual expression of the Divine—the set of holy qualities that makes up our treasured essence. Our embodiment of these qualities is like the colors on a palette. We each have our custom hues with which we paint the world. This soul is not about religion. It is about our innate spiritual capacity and essence.

Examples of these refined qualities are joy, mercy, love, compassion, wisdom, healing, truth, generosity, graciousness, power, creativity, and many more. We each carry a distinctive encoded cluster. Knowing your holy qualities may give your life new meaning and re-inspire your passion. If you take time to notice, you'll surely recognize holy qualities in your friends and associates—and yourself.

Pathwork Enquiries:

- What are your unique holy qualities? Be truthful with yourself, not modest. Write them in this layer of your heart map. You'll find a rich selection. Close your eyes and check with your heart, *not* your mind for these, because the ego will have much to say if you go there! Two of mine are light and mercy, or merciful light. You may want feedback to find yours.

- What is a symbol for your qualities? You'll be amazed at the power of your symbol, so I encourage you to give yourself the gift of discovery. You'll find value in drawing your symbol. It can help you to remember and relate to it at a deeper energy level. You'll have something vivid to hold onto as you navigate your path to success.

- Light has long been a symbol for me. Others often told me what they experienced. My deceased husband and more than one friend over time have given me the nickname of "Sunshine" and even gifted me with golden sun necklaces. I encourage you to find your symbol, treasure it— and live into it.

Our holy qualities also provide clues about our Soul Mission. Generally, when instructors teach people to look for mission or purpose, they teach us to search in our mind and the three-dimensional world—the outside layer in this model. What are we supposed to "do" in the world? We get frustrated and bewildered because we have to figure it out.

Our true mission is more subtle—and powerful—than that. I've discovered that our Soul Mission is purely to express the unique Being we were designed to be—our flavor of ice cream. I believe that knowing our Soul Mission is a primary key to real success.

Why? Because we don't realize that we are already being our Mission! Until we wake up to who we authentically are, we can stay on our gerbil wheel, entangled in our drama, entwined in our thoughts and emotions.

When we say "yes" to the Call to experience our authentic Soul Mission, our path is prepared for us. We need only recognize it. Everything is in Divine order. We can navigate with our Soulmap, so we can live a spirit-guided life and enjoy "beyond-belief" success! Wisely, then we can make choices that align with our True Self and we can knowingly decide at each fork in the road.

Amazingly, I've also learned that this Mission—the deeper thing we came to experience—is the *remedy* for whatever particular concern, anxiety, or fear we carry. *The gift that we feel called to give to others is actually the gift we are called to give to ourselves!* We already have the answer. No wonder some teachings say, "Give to yourself first." We can then overflow to the world.

How does this work? On my quest I've found that my life purpose is to "Be the Light that shines in your Soul—and reawakens you to your magnificent Being." That Divine light has always been there. How natural then to become a coach for awakening people to their value—and what a challenge it is to accept this for myself! I now understand that this tonic for my distress is already present—in my own nature. I just need to remember and embrace my Mission.

In the circumstance of my beloved adult children living with me, I knew at my core that there was a profound purpose in the situation, but did not initially recognize it. I had said yes to a number of challenging commitments, all at once, terrifying my limited human self, who doubted that I was capable. Eventually, I began to understand that this overwhelming feeling was the answer to my deep desire to clear that disempowering "not good enough" belief from my life. I said "yes" at the deepest level—and the circumstances were beautifully crafted for me to break through the old belief system that had run my life for decades. It was time to do the deep internal cocoon work of transformation, to break free from limiting beliefs, and fly. And so laboriously, I did the work. In discomfort and in the dark I struggled through the self-doubt to awaken to my true self.

What did I learn? When I lose my own light in the smokescreen of the inner critic, I don't experience my gifts—and others don't. When I welcome light and mercy, that dissipates the "not-good-enough" smokescreen and my countenance shines again—worthy of the essence God placed in me and the nickname people have given me for years. In that light, people around me again experience their own radiance.

With this deeper insight, we can choose to open to The Holy Secret and receive the Light that reveals the truth. We can awaken to the lesson and to new thoughts. We can begin to sort truth from our own fiction.

The cocoon perspective is dominated by the thought that I am still not good enough. There is more "work" to do to become my True Self. The Guide says of this process, "Break your tomb!" Break through the human limitations. Now is time to let go of the lie. The butterfly viewpoint sees that we are already complete—just fly!

As a Coach-Partner, I will support *you* to experience an extraordinary breakthrough—and reach a level of success beyond your dreams.

This may be the most significant work you do in your life! Identifying the childhood decision that stops you from your victory and awakening to your innate Soul Mission (that existed before that limiting belief) will set you on your path to success.

With that in mind, I invite you to conscientiously explore:

Pathwork Enquiries:

- Who are you—*really*? Who are you called to Be? What people come to you for, or describe you as, are clues to your Soul Mission. What do they seek from you? What contributions do you make—just with your Being? What happens in your Presence? What is the legacy you leave? I encourage you to take time to let this inherent Mission be revealed to you. Live in this important inquiry—and and see what comes to you. It can change your life!

- How does this relate to what you are deeply passionate about?

- Will you capture the insights? Will you begin to draft your Soul Mission without editing? Just breathe love into your heart—and listen. Open to receive whatever comes. It will be revealed. It may come in pictures or sounds or colors. Capture it all and edit later. Call for support if you wish.

- You may find that your inner Mission gives rise to an outer expression— a "to-do mission" in the world. Recently, I found a paper from twenty years ago that said my mission was to bring spiritual values to the workplace. What do you know of your worldly mission?

Here in layer three, you'll also begin to see glimpses of another significant aspect of your real map to success—your Life Vision. Awakened from Soul, not just generated from your mind, that, too, will be aligned with the universal plan—and ready to unfold organically.

I still have what I affectionately call "my refrigerator drawing" from twenty years ago. Nearly everything in it has come true—most of it in three years. Being a beacon of light on a mountain, a light-filled welcoming new home with an amazing view; happy people coming and going, just the right space for kids, airy office, light wood, cathedral ceiling; a new life partner—with the airplane that I had drawn in the picture; sanctuary. And now, I am awed by the number of children and grandchildren whose happy faces appear in the drawing.

Often, people tell me that they don't have a vision or known how to create one. What I've learned is that as we engage more fully with the inner aspects of our self and embrace our true nature, we find vision, wisdom, and power beyond our mind's comprehension.

It may be fulfilling work we can do together. You will find it richly rewarding to experience this essential part of your Soulmap. It may be valuable to have a guide. In *The Reinvention of Work: A New Vision of Livelihood for Our Time,* Matthew Fox admonishes that our Vision is not big enough. I believe your personal Vision is a vital contribution to our global Vision.

The Secret

Layer number four, The Heart of Hearts, contains—The Secret—the deeply-held essential truth of who we are—Spirit, God, The One, the Light, Divine Love, Higher Power, Allah (Arabic word for God), Unity Consciousness, Universal Energy, Chi, HaShem, Tao, quantum field, to name a few descriptors. To arrive here is often a challenge. It means walking through the "stuff" of our lives.

This is the real Secret! This abiding Holy Presence is in all of us, even if we are unaware of it. There is nothing we can do to erase it. From this still small voice comes the reverberating *Call to Remember.* Here is our yearning to come "home." As we respond to this deep desire, our heroine's journey brings us eventually to our heart of hearts where we find the holy treasure—the truth of our being, The Secret of our existence—our True Self. A place of wisdom, confidence, and infinite resources where there is no separation. All is One.

This Secret inside you is waiting to be revealed. Are you experienced it?

The Bible says, "Be ye not conformed to this world, but be ye transformed by the renewing of your mind." When mind is transformed by Spirit in our heart of hearts, everything is transformed. At any moment, we may experience a quantum shift. When Remembrance is complete in our being, we glimpse the Secret. There is only God. We begin to know our True Self. We are blessed and encouraged as we sense the Divine Presence. Here light meets Light—and we are one with Source.

We begin to see that we can no longer hide our light because it is The Light. When we commit to self-actualization, we become the attraction that opens us to everything we need to be and all that we already are. "You think you are just a small star when, in fact, you contain the whole world," says Guide Sidi.

Here, we access the attributes and qualities we need at each moment. We are infinitely resourceful. We are wise. We can discern and act wisely. From here, we know true success—and the path to reach it. We can bring the gift of our True Self to our daily life and work.

We can use the logical mind to make the highest choices to care for and nourish our physical body and rely on our deep-seated inner knowing to help us navigate the more challenging passages on our path. The Truth we carry in the depths of our being is accessible as the compass for our Soul, providing direction and timeless wisdom through our challenges. In her book, *Science and Health with Key to the Scriptures,* Mary Baker Eddy writes, "Spirit, God, gathers unformed thoughts into their proper channels and unfolds these thoughts, even as He opens the petals of a holy purpose in order that the purpose may appear." Guided by Inner Wisdom, we are perfectly attuned to the Divine plan for our lives. The skills we need to access our guidance are not learned, for we already know them. What is needed is the courage to allow what is programmed within to surface.

Let's explore more deeply this part of your map.

Pathwork Enquiries:

- How do you connect with the Holy Presence? Are you aware of this Presence in yourself?
- What do you long to know of your True Self? What do you already know?
- What do you long to discover?
- Can you recall your own experiences of Oneness? What meaning do they have for your today?
- Does your current community enhance your awakening to your True Self? What else is possible? What resources might you want to explore?

Wright

Barbara, can you help women put this concept into perspective?

Boden

Yes, David. Self-actualization, as we progress through the layers, will inspire a new worldview and reveal new fields of possibility for our success. An increased level of trust and confidence may result in career transitions or family and relationship re-formations. A commitment to release what is no longer true for us may be reflected in something as small as cleaning out a closet or as large as leaving a confining job. In each case we will have demonstrated to ourselves that we trust Spirit's wisdom to provide what is next—and perfect—for our spiritual evolution and human success.

Many women are being called to step up even beyond self-actualization into a new dimension of spiritual leadership and contribution—to transcendence where we do not see our interests as separate from others—where we find our work is to support others to self-actualize as we expand our own learning. For me, a symbol that represents this collaborative energy is the infinity sign; it illustrates our reciprocal releasing habitual nature and awakening to true empowerment.

What I have shared here is merely an overview of the Layers of the Heart. As we answer from our deeper nature, we are increasingly guided by Divine inner wisdom and less by the external voices of world. "Sometimes we're in the 'fire' and sometimes in the 'garden' as we make this journey," one teacher says. "It is all holy. Keep walking." Funny, I just heard the voice of Dori in the movie, *Nemo*, "Keep swimming. Keep swimming."

Whether you are walking or swimming on your journey, know that we at Leading Attitudes are committed to providing wise counsel, treasured resources, and empowering environments to you as you strive to create your healthy, successful, fulfilling life and become the contribution you long to be.

The light is dawning on a new earth consciousness. This is an unprecedented time in history where many of us are integrating our personal calling with creating mission-driven businesses and choosing more meaningful careers. Many feel compelled to contribute to the transformation. Our life is truly becoming our enlightened work.

As you listen to your soul's desire, know that it is responding to humanity's hunger for your wisdom and your emerging leadership.

Your success is on the horizon. When you hear the calling of your soul, know you are ready to answer. The response is already in the call. As you embrace the fullness of your Being that already knows your answers, you are surely on your path to success.

As you engage your compass and survey your map, remember that you are ready for your journey. Where you answer from is where you land. Shift your attention from your mind to the eye of your heart. Your Heart knows Spirit's Truth and your mind knows the world. Use both. Trust your deeply encoded Soulmap. Hold your expanded vision. Notice what is already happening. As you wake up to the signs revealing themselves on your way; stay open to Spirit everywhere—especially in your deep heart.

Be patient with yourself. Your thriving is crucial to your endurance and your continuing contribution. Care for yourself first, and use the maps and empowering global networks to support you.

If you are reading this, know that it is not an accident. Individuals and organizations that integrate meaning and mission into business are the ones that can succeed in the new economy and have a profound positive impact on our global family. Many entrepreneurial women are learning that the more they integrate their spiritual nature and their work, the easier and more profitable business becomes.

You are not alone. As Patricia Aburdene writes in *Megatrends 2010: The Rise of Conscious Capitalism,* the most critical factor to this major trend of conscious capitalism is the quest for Spirit and meaning. "Business owners have shifted from a desire to make money to a desire to make a difference and have a meaningful life. At first glance, you may think that focusing on meaning excludes money; but the reality is the complete opposite."

In our shared commitment to awaken and contribute, I believe the Universe has crossed our paths. Together, we can open your Soulmap, discover your amazing gifts, and expand your spiritual capacity to make an extraordinary difference and experience true success.

Increasing our self-worth as women will increase our net worth—and our impact. And as we venture on our journey home to our heart of hearts, we are blessed with a gift more profound and powerful than self-worth—self-love. Here, we can be still *and* move mountains.

You are the light of the world and humanity needs your Holy Light. It is time to wake up!

Wright

What do you encourage women to do now?

Boden

I'd say, partner with us to create your success. It is time to gather "mighty companions." *A Course in Miracles, Manual for Teachers* says, "[We] will not go on from here alone." Together, let's engage our collective capacity to courageously craft a future that inspires millions of women and girls to create a new reality *for all*.

Join us to banish self-doubts and overcome fear. Let us support you to reclaim your True Self and answer the Call to contribute from your essence, so you experience extraordinary fulfillment.

I encourage you to take time to develop your layers of the heart description and discover your personal leadership qualities—some of the dimensions that will determine your Soulmap to Success. I invite you to fill out the short survey at the end of this chapter, and when you are ready, contact us. Send your ideas to Leading Attitudes via fax or e-mail, being sure to identify yourself. Together we can create your Soulmap and start you on your heroine's journey to success. It may seem beyond belief right now, but is not beyond accomplishment!

As we each recommit to our journey to authentic success, I offer a gift that has reassured me when I have traversed unfamiliar territory. It is a quote from W. H. Murray, who led the Scottish Himalayan Expedition in 1951. While the quote is not new, the wisdom is timeless and may inspire Remembrance of the Guiding Spirit of the Universe.

> Until one is committed there is hesitancy, the chance to draw back, always ineffectiveness. Concerning all acts of initiative and creation, there is one elementary truth that kills countless ideas and splendid plans: that the moment one definitely commits oneself, then Providence moves, too.

> All sorts of things occur to help one that would have never occurred. A whole stream of events issues from the decision, raising in one's favor all manner of unforeseen incidents and meetings and material assistance, which no one could have dreamt would have come one's way. I have learned deep respect for one of Goethe's couplets:

> Whatever you can do, or dream you can, begin it.
> Boldness has genius, power, and magic in it.

Wright

This has been a great conversation. I really appreciate the time you've spent with me this afternoon answering all these questions. I have certainly learned a lot, Barbara. You have given me a lot to think about.

Boden

David, it is a pleasure to talk with you. I sincerely appreciate the invitation to be part of *Roadmap to Success.*

Success Survey

We truly want to understand. What does "success" mean to you? Does it relate to:

- Building the business of your dreams?
- Achieving financial success?
- Providing unlimited opportunities for your family?
- Becoming the leader that you know deep down you are meant to be?
- Being a great mom or spouse?
- Discovering your Soul Mission and living into it?
- Expanding a Vision?
- Enjoying personal freedom to be authentically you?
- Getting past your internal critic?
- Giving back to the community?
- Experiencing a quantum leap in your confidence?
- Increasing your energy level and mental focus by aligning your physical and spiritual life?

Include your name, address, telephone number, and e-mail address. Send your answers to the above questions to me. My contact information is on the next page. We will be happy to share the results when you participate.

ABOUT THE AUTHOR

BARBARA BODEN, catalyst and transformation coach, is founder and CEO of Leading Attitudes, Inc.™ a coaching and consulting firm that specializes in empowering women to develop their inherent leadership qualities in order to make a significant difference, fulfill their destiny, and leave a soul-inspired legacy.

Barbara and her partners guide and coach emerging women leaders to explore the depths of their Being, discover their true wisdom, capitalize on their inherent capabilities, engage their inner power, and lead their lives with grace and confidence.

A Certified Professional Co-Active Coach, she is co-leader of the Women as Leaders Community for The Coach's Training Institute, and is credentialed by the International Coach Federation. She holds myriad certifications and a master's degree in Organizational transformation and transformational leadership. She believes that the true meaning of "educate" comes from its root Latin word, *ducere,* meaning to draw or lead. The prefix "e" means "out of." Therefore, educate means to bring forth what is within.

Barbara is an educator and entrepreneur and has been a religious educator and co-owner of an acclaimed Vermont country inn. She has served as Executive Director of an international association, and a Professional Partnering and Team development facilitator on $7 billion of design and construction projects. She is a franchise holder for Leadership Management, Inc. and for twenty years she has facilitated adult learning in businesses, academic, and government settings. She has been honored a number of years by *Cambridge Who's Who of Executives, Professionals, and Entrepreneurs.*

She is Mom to three wonderful adult children, Scott, Kristine, and Kathie, who are committed to making a difference in the world, Mom II to their terrific spouses, Mark, and Silvana, and "Grammy" to two precious granddaughters, Ryley Erin, Fiona Kaitlyn, and grandson, baby Michael who is to arrive soon. She lives on a mountain where she shares the meadow with deer, wild turkeys, and red foxes. Unique travels include China, sacred Inca sites in Peru, and Buddhist monasteries in Tibet.

She is active in her community interfaith council and enjoys participating in drumming circles with her djembe drum.

Barbara Boden

Leading Attitudes, Inc
2317 Michael Road
Myersville, MD 21773
Phone: 800-281-TEAM (8326)
301-293-3004
E-mail: Barbara@LeadingAttitudes.com
www.LeadingAttitudes.com

CHAPTER

2

An interview with…

Stephen Covey

A VALUES-BASED APPROACH

David Wright (Wright)

We're talking today with Dr. Stephen R. Covey, cofounder and vice-chairman of Franklin Covey Company, the largest management company and leadership development organization in the world. Dr. Covey is perhaps best known as author of *The 7 Habits of Highly Effective People,* which is ranked as a number one best-seller by the *New York Times,* having sold more than fourteen million copies in thirty-eight languages throughout the world. Dr. Covey is an internationally respected leadership authority, family expert, teacher, and organizational consultant. He has made teaching principle-centered living and principle-centered leadership his life's work. Dr. Covey is the recipient of the Thomas More College Medallion for Continuing Service to Humanity and has been awarded four honorary doctorate degrees. Other awards given Dr. Covey include the Sikh's 1989 International Man of Peace award, the 1994 International Entrepreneur of the Year award, *Inc.* magazine's Services Entrepreneur of the Year award, and in 1996 the National Entrepreneur of the Year Lifetime Achievement award for Entrepreneurial leadership. He has also been recognized as one of *Time* magazine's twenty-five most influential Americans and one of *Sales and Marketing Management's* top twenty-five power brokers. As the father of nine and grandfather of forty-four, Dr. Covey received the 2003 National Fatherhood Award, which he says is the most meaningful award he has ever received. Dr. Covey earned his undergraduate degree from the University of Utah, his MBA from Harvard, and completed his doctorate at Brigham Young University. While at Brigham Young he served as assistant to the President and was also a professor of Business Management and Organizational Behavior.

Dr. Covey, welcome to *Roadmap to Success.*

Dr. Stephen Covey (Covey)

Thank you.

Wright

Dr. Covey, most companies make decisions and filter them down through their organization. You, however, state that no company can succeed until individuals within it succeed. Are the goals of the company the result of the combined goals of the individuals?

Covey

Absolutely—if people aren't on the same page, they're going to be pulling in different directions. To teach this concept, I frequently ask large audiences to close their eyes and point north, and then to keep pointing and open their eyes. They find themselves pointing all over the place. I say to them, "Tomorrow morning if you want a similar experience, ask the first ten people you meet in your organization what the purpose of your organization is and you'll find it's a very similar experience. They'll point all over the place." When people have a different sense of purpose and values, every decision that is made from then on is governed by those. There's no question that this is one of the fundamental causes of misalignment, low trust, interpersonal conflict, interdepartmental rivalry, people operating on personal agendas, and so forth.

Wright

Is that primarily a result of an inability to communicate from the top?

Covey

That's one aspect, but I think it's more fundamental. There's an inability to involve people—an unwillingness. Leaders may communicate what their mission and their strategy is, but that doesn't mean there's any emotional connection to it. Mission statements that are rushed and then announced are soon forgotten. They become nothing more than just a bunch of platitudes on the wall that mean essentially nothing and even create a source of cynicism and a sense of hypocrisy inside the culture of an organization.

Wright

How do companies ensure survival and prosperity in these tumultuous times of technological advances, mergers, downsizing, and change?

Covey

I think that it takes a lot of high trust in a culture that has something that doesn't change—principles—at its core. There are principles that people agree upon that are valued. It gives a sense of stability. Then you have the power to adapt and be flexible when you experience these kinds of disruptive new economic models or technologies that come in and sideswipe you. You don't know how to handle them unless you have something you can depend upon.

If people have not agreed to a common set of principles that guide them and a common purpose, then they get their security from the outside and they tend to freeze the structure, systems, and processes inside and they cease becoming adaptable. They don't change with the changing realities of the new marketplace out there and gradually they become obsolete.

Wright

I was interested in one portion of your book, *The 7 Habits of Highly Effective People*, where you talk about behaviors. How does an individual go about the process of replacing ineffective behaviors with effective ones?

Covey

I think that for most people it usually requires a crisis that humbles them to become aware of their ineffective behaviors. If there's not a crisis the tendency is to perpetuate those behaviors and not change.

You don't have to wait until the marketplace creates the crisis for you. Have everyone accountable on a 360-degree basis to everyone else they interact with—with feedback either formal or informal—where they are getting data as to what's happening. They will then start to realize that the consequences of their ineffective behavior require them to be humble enough to look at that behavior and to adopt new, more effective ways of doing things.

Sometimes people can be stirred up to this if you just appeal to their conscience—to their inward sense of what is right and wrong. A lot of people sometimes know inwardly they're doing wrong, but the culture doesn't necessarily discourage them from continuing that. They either need feedback from people or they need feedback from the marketplace or they need feedback from their conscience. Then they can begin to develop a step-by-step process of replacing old habits with new, better habits.

Wright

It's almost like saying, "Let's make all the mistakes in the laboratory before we put this thing in the air."

Covey

Right; and I also think what is necessary is a paradigm shift, which is analogous to having a correct map, say of a city or of a country. If people have an inaccurate paradigm of life, of other people, and of themselves it really doesn't make much difference what their behavior or habits or attitudes are. What they need is a correct paradigm—a correct map—that describes what's going on.

For instance, in the Middle Ages they used to heal people through bloodletting. It wasn't until Samuel Weiss and Pasteur and other empirical scientists discovered the germ theory that they realized for the first time they weren't dealing with the real issue. They realized why women preferred to use midwives who washed rather than doctors who didn't wash. They gradually got a new paradigm. Once you've got a new paradigm then your behavior and your attitude flow directly from it. If you have a bad paradigm or a bad map, let's say of a city, there's no way, no matter what your behavior or your habits or your attitudes are—how positive they are—you'll never be able to find the location you're looking for. This is why I believe that to change paradigms is far more fundamental than to work on attitude and behavior.

Wright

One of your seven habits of highly effective people is to "begin with the end in mind." If circumstances change and hardships or miscalculations occur, how does one view the end with clarity?

Covey

Many people think to begin with the end in mind means that you have some fixed definition of a goal that's accomplished and if changes come about you're not going to adapt to them. Instead, the "end in mind" you begin with is that you are going to create a flexible culture of high trust so that no matter what comes along you are going to do whatever it takes to accommodate that new change or that new reality and maintain a culture of high performance and high trust. You're talking more in terms of values and overall purposes that don't change, rather than specific strategies or programs that will have to change to accommodate the changing realities in the marketplace.

Wright

In this time of mistrust among people, corporations, and nations, for that matter, how do we create high levels of trust?

Covey

That's a great question and it's complicated because there are so many elements that go into the creating of a culture of trust. Obviously the most fundamental one is just to have trustworthy people. But that is not sufficient because what if the organization itself is misaligned?

For instance, what if you say you value cooperation but you really reward people for internal competition? Then you have a systemic or a structure problem that creates low trust inside the culture even though the people themselves are trustworthy. This is one of the insights of Edward Demming and the work he did. That's why he said that most problems are not personal—they're systemic. They're common caused. That's why you have to work on structure, systems, and processes to make sure that they institutionalize principle-centered values. Otherwise you could have good people with bad systems and you'll get bad results.

When it comes to developing interpersonal trust between people, it is made up of many, many elements such as taking the time to listen to other people, to understand them, and to see what is important to them. What we think is important to another may only be important to us, not to another. It takes empathy. You have to make and keep promises to them. You have to treat people with kindness and courtesy. You have to be completely honest and open. You have to live up to your commitments. You can't betray people behind their back. You can't badmouth them behind their back and sweet-talk them to their face. That will send out vibes of hypocrisy and it will be detected.

You have to learn to apologize when you make mistakes, to admit mistakes, and to also get feedback going in every direction as much as possible. It doesn't necessarily require formal forums—it requires trust between people who will be open with each other and give each other feedback.

Wright

My mother told me to do a lot of what you're saying now, but it seems that when I got in business I simply forgot.

Covey

Sometimes we forget, but sometimes culture doesn't nurture it. That's why I say unless you work with the institutionalizing—that means formalizing into structure, systems, and processing the values—you will not have a nurturing culture. You have to constantly work on that.

This is one of the big mistakes organizations make. They think trust is simply a function of being honest. That's only one small aspect. It's an important aspect, obviously, but there are so many other elements that go into the creation of a high-trust culture.

Wright

"Seek first to understand then to be understood" is another of your seven habits. Do you find that people try to communicate without really understanding what other people want?

Covey

Absolutely. The tendency is to project out of our own autobiography—our own life, our own value system—onto other people, thinking we know what they want. So we don't really listen to them. We pretend to listen, but we really don't listen from within their frame of reference. We listen from within our own frame of reference and we're really preparing our reply rather than seeking to understand. This is a very common thing. In fact, very few people have had any training in seriously listening. They're trained in how to read, write, and speak, but not to listen.

Reading, writing, speaking, and listening are the four modes of communication and they represent about two-thirds to three-fourths of our waking hours. About half of that time is spent listening, but it's the one skill people have not been trained in. People have had all this training in the other forms of communication. In a large audience of 1,000 people you wouldn't have more than twenty people who have had more than two weeks of training in listening. Listening is more than a skill or technique; you must listen within another's frame of reference. It takes tremendous courage to listen because you're at risk when you listen. You don't know what's going to happen; you're vulnerable.

Wright

Sales gurus always tell me that the number one skill in selling is listening.

Covey

Yes—listening from within the customer's frame of reference. That is so true. You can see that it takes some security to do that because you don't know what's going to happen.

Wright

With this book we're trying to encourage people to be better, to live better, and be more fulfilled by listening to the examples of our guest authors. Is there anything or anyone in your life that has made a difference for you and helped you to become a better person?

Covey

I think the most influential people in my life have been my parents. I think that what they modeled was not to make comparisons and harbor jealousy or to seek recognition. They were humble people.

I remember one time when my mother and I were going up in an elevator and the most prominent person in the state was also in the elevator. She knew him, but she spent her time talking to the elevator operator. I was just a little kid and I was so awed by the famous person. I said to her, "Why didn't you talk to the important person?" She said, "I was. I had never met him."

My parents were really humble, modest people who were focused on service and other people rather than on themselves. I think they were very inspiring models to me.

Wright

In almost every research paper I've ever read, those who write about people who have influenced their lives include three teachers in their top-five picks. My seventh-grade English teacher was the greatest teacher I ever had and she influenced me to no end.

Covey

Would it be correct to say that she saw in you probably some qualities of greatness you didn't even see in yourself?

Wright

Absolutely.

Covey

That's been my general experience—the key aspect of a mentor or a teacher is someone who sees in you potential that you don't even see in yourself. Those teachers/mentors treat you accordingly and eventually you come to see it in yourself. That's my definition of leadership or influence—communicating people's worth and potential so clearly that they are inspired to see it in themselves.

Wright

Most of my teachers treated me as a student, but she treated me with much more respect than that. As a matter of fact, she called me Mr. Wright, and I was in the seventh grade at the time. I'd never been addressed by anything but a nickname. I stood a little taller; she just made a tremendous difference.

Do you think there are other characteristics that mentors seem to have in common?

Covey

I think they are first of all good examples in their own personal lives. Their personal lives and their family lives are not all messed up—they come from a base of good character. They also are usually very confident and they take the time to do what your teacher did to you—to treat you with uncommon respect and courtesy.

They also, I think, explicitly teach principles rather than practices so that rules don't take the place of human judgment. You gradually come to have faith in your own judgment in making decisions because of the affirmation of such a mentor. Good mentors care about you—you can feel the sincerity of their caring. It's like the expression, "I don't care how much you know until I know how much you care."

Wright

Most people are fascinated with the new television shows about being a survivor. What has been the greatest comeback that you've made from adversity in your career or your life?

Covey

When I was in grade school I experienced a disease in my legs. It caused me to use crutches for a while. I tried to get off them fast and get back. The disease wasn't corrected yet so I went back on crutches for another year. The disease went to the other leg and I went on for another year. It essentially took me out of my favorite thing—athletics—and it took me more into being a student. So that was a life-defining experience, which at the time seemed very negative, but has proven to be the basis on which I've focused my life—being more of a learner.

Wright

Principle-centered learning is basically what you do that's different from anybody I've read or listened to.

Covey

The concept is embodied in the Far Eastern expression, "Give a man a fish, you feed him for the day; teach him how to fish, you feed him for a lifetime." When you teach principles that are universal and timeless, they don't belong to just any one person's religion or to a particular culture or geography. They seem to be timeless and universal like the ones we've been talking about here: trustworthiness, honesty, caring, service, growth, and development. These are universal principles. If you focus on these things, then little by little people become independent of you and then they start to believe in themselves and their own judgment becomes better. You don't need as many rules. You don't need as much bureaucracy and as many controls and you can empower people.

The problem in most business operations today—and not just business but non-business—is that they're using the industrial model in an information age. Arnold Toynbee, the great historian, said, "You can pretty well summarize all of history in four words: nothing fails like success." The industrial model was based on the asset of the machine. The information model is based on the asset of the person—the knowledge worker. It's an altogether different model. But the machine model was the main asset of the twentieth century. It enabled productivity to increase fifty times. The new asset is intellectual and social capital—the qualities of people and the quality of the relationship they have with each other. Like Toynbee said, "Nothing fails like success." The industrial model does not work in an information age. It requires a focus on the new wealth, not capital and material things.

A good illustration that demonstrates how much we were into the industrial model, and still are, is to notice where people are on the balance sheet. They're not found there. Machines are found there. Machines become investments. People are on the profit-and-loss statement and people are expenses. Think of that—if that isn't bloodletting.

Wright

It sure is.

When you consider the choices you've made down through the years, has faith played an important role in your life?

Covey

It has played an extremely important role. I believe deeply that we should put principles at the center of our lives, but I believe that God is the source of those principles. I did not invent them. I get credit sometimes for some of the Seven Habits material and some of the other things I've done, but it's really all based on principles that have been given by God to all of His children from the beginning of time. You'll find that you can teach these same principles from the sacred texts and the wisdom literature of almost any tradition. I think the ultimate source of that is God and that is one thing you can absolutely depend upon—"in God we trust."

Wright

If you could have a platform and tell our audience something you feel would help them or encourage them, what would you say?

Covey

I think I would say to put God at the center of your life and then prioritize your family. No one on their deathbed ever wished they had spent more time at the office.

Wright

That's right. We have come down to the end of our program and I know you're a busy person. I could talk with you all day, Dr. Covey.

Covey

It's good to talk with you as well and to be a part of this program. It looks like an excellent one that you've got going on here.

Wright

Thank you.

We have been talking today with Dr. Stephen R. Covey, cofounder and vice-chairman of Franklin Covey Company. He's also the author of *The 7 Habits of Highly Effective People,* which has been ranked as a number one bestseller by the *New York Times*, selling more than fourteen million copies in thirty-eight languages.

Dr. Covey, thank you so much for being with us today.

Covey

Thank you for the honor of participating.

ABOUT THE AUTHOR

STEPHEN R. COVEY WAS RECOGNIZED in 1996 as one of *Time* magazine's twenty-five most influential Americans and one of *Sales and Marketing Management's* top twenty-five power brokers. Dr. Covey is the author of several acclaimed books, including the international bestseller, *The 7 Habits of Highly Effective People,* named the number one Most Influential Business Book of the Twentieth Century, and other best sellers that include *First Things First, Principle-Centered Leadership,* (with sales exceeding one million) and *The 7 Habits of Highly Effective Families.*

Dr. Covey's newest book, *The 8th Habit: From Effectiveness to Greatness*, which was released in November 2004, rose to the top of several bestseller lists, including *New York Times, Wall Street Journal, USA Today, Money, Business Week*, Amazon.com, and Barnes & Noble.

Dr. Covey earned his undergraduate degree from the University of Utah, his MBA from Harvard, and completed his doctorate at Brigham Young University. While at Brigham Young University, he served as assistant to the President and was also a professor of Business Management and Organizational Behavior. He received the National Fatherhood Award in 2003, which, as the father of nine and grandfather of forty-four, he says is the most meaningful award he has ever received.

Dr. Covey currently serves on the board of directors for the Points of Light Foundation. Based in Washington, D.C., the Foundation, through its partnership with the Volunteer Center National Network, engages and mobilizes millions of volunteers from all walks of life—businesses, nonprofits, faith-based organizations, low-income communities, families, youth, and older adults—to help solve serious social problems in thousands of communities.

Dr. Stephen R. Covey

www.stephencovey.com

CHAPTER

3

An interview with…

John Santangelo

MASTERING INFLUENCE & COMMUNICATION

David Wright (Wright)

Today we're talking with John James Santangelo, nationally acclaimed speaker, author, seminar leader, and success coach. He has been a guiding force in empowering individuals, businesses, and corporations to achieve their highest potential. John is a foremost authority in success strategies and an expert in the field of communication. He is a clinical hypnotherapist and a neuro-linguistic programming (NLP) master trainer. He has utilized NLP success strategies and communication skills with companies such as The Learning Annex, Mary Kay Inc., Well Point, Make-A-Wish Foundation, Xerox, Re/Max Realtors, the Teamsters Union, and post 9/11 as head trainer teaching lie-detection skills to the U.S. Army Counterintelligence Team. Whether you're looking to fulfill your short- or long-term goals, increase your sales performance, or conduct corporate sales and communication trainings, John's knowledge, experience, and expertise can help you achieve the next level of your success.

John, welcome to this powerful collection of chapters in *Roadmap to Success.*

John Santangelo (Santangelo)

Thanks so much David, it's an absolute pleasure to be a part of such an outstanding book project.

Wright

Would you tell our readers what NLP is and how it was developed?

Santangelo

Absolutely. NLP, or neuro-linguistic programming, began as a modeling project or structure of excellence! It reveals how people do what they do to produce positive results in their lives. It was originally developed by Richard Bandler, John Grinder, and others. It became a model of structure that explains how we process the information that comes to us from our outside world. The definition is: neuro (meaning the mind) linguistic (the language we utilize to communicate with ourselves and others) and programming (the strategies we run to produce the results in our lives). The belief is that "the map is not the territory."

And so the internal representations we create inside our minds about an outside event are not necessarily the event itself—it is only a representation of our outside world. Hey, my mom still asks me what I do, and it's still a challenge having it make sense to her.

The developers stated it's "an attitude and a methodology that leave behind a trail of techniques." Typically, what happens is that there is an external event, which is anything coming in through our five senses. We run that event through our internal processing filters. Then we make an Internal Representation (I/R) of that event. Those I/R's of the event combine with a physiology, which creates a state of mind. "State" refers to the internal emotional state of the individual (e.g., a happy state, a sad state, a motivated state, and so on). Our I/R includes our internal pictures, sounds, dialogue, and our feelings—whether we feel motivated, challenged, pleased, excited, and so on. A given state is the result of the combination of an internal representation and a physiology.

We experience events coming in through our five sensory input channels, which includes:

1. Visual—including the sights we see or the way someone looks at us.
2. Auditory—including sounds, words we hear and words spoken to us.
3. Kinesthetic—internal/external feelings, touch of someone/something.
4. Olfactory—the sense of smell, and
5. Gustatory—the sense of taste.

Neuro—The nervous system, through which our experience is processed via our five senses:

- Visual
- Auditory
- Kinesthetic

- Olfactory
- Gustatory

Linguistics—Language and other non-verbal communication through which our neural reps are coded, ordered, and given meaning:

- Pictures
- Sounds
- Feelings
- Tastes
- Smells
- Words (self-talk)

Programming—The ability to discover and utilize programs we run (the communication to ourselves and others) in our neurological systems to achieve our desired outcomes.

Let me try to explain it more simply for our readers. In our real world experience, it means the ability to shift our focus and our perceptions at any given moment—to alter our state of mind (i.e., emotions and/or feelings) from which we make decisions that definitively shape our lives. When we shift our focus and the meaning we place upon the events in our lives, we behave differently. NLP gives us the ability to utilize practical tools, methods, and exercises by which change happens at a conscious and unconscious level. NLP is the basis of how we operate and use our brains to effect change. So in a sentence: it's the ability to utilize our internal pictures, sounds, feelings, and internal dialogue to produce extraordinary results on a daily basis.

Today, NLP has developed into much more. It has progressed into the marketing arena, parenting roles, finances and wealth-building strategies, and into the educational system, where I believe it is needed most. It literally became a so-called "road map to success"!

Wright

So, isn't the technology of NLP similar to Anthony Robbins' methods?

Santangelo

Actually, it's exactly what Tony has been teaching for the last thirty years. In fact, Tony was taught by Richard Bandler, John Grinder, Robert Dilts, and Judith Delozier in the beginning of his career. These were the same amazing individuals I had trained under.

Tony's first book, *Unlimited Power*, was all about the pure technology of NLP. Tony ended up changing the name from NLP to NAC to re-brand himself, although the technology and methods still remain the powerful change techniques behind his illustrious career.

Accolades to Tony because he's been a guiding force within the NLP community and many wonderful trainers have followed in his footsteps.

Wright

So if NLP is a model of excellence, what do you believe are the three most important reasons why people do not succeed?

Santangelo

I believe for most individuals, and at least the people I've had the opportunity to interview and coach over the last ten years, that the first thing is, *people don't really know what they want* from their lives. This is clarity! In Napoleon Hill's ground-breaking book, *Think and Grow Rich*, published in 1937, he interviewed five hundred of the most successful men in America. He called this concept "a definiteness of purpose!"

The second thing is they *don't ever develop the necessary skills,* which I believe are communication skills, not just with themselves, but also with other people. As Zig Ziglar once said, *"You can have everything in life you want, if you will just help enough other people get what they want."*

The third thing that I know to be a most important factor is they *don't have the ability to get out of their own way* due to *fear.* Fear holds more people back from accomplishing the things they desire most in their lives than any other obstacle. It stops them before they even begin to dream and set goals.

> *"Fear kills more people than death; death kills us but once and we don't even know it, but fear kills us over and over again, suddenly at times and brutally at others."*—General George Patton.

Most of our obstacles come in the form of negative beliefs or limiting decisions about ourselves—thoughts like: *"I can't do this," "I'm not good enough," "I don't have enough money," "I don't have enough knowledge," "I'm not worthy."* Limiting decisions about who we are include: *"I'm too old," "I'm too fat," "I'm too lazy"* (which by the way, I believed for a long time). Most of these have been programmed into our subconscious when we were very young, before the age of ten years old, because at that age we don't have the ability to filter such beliefs. These "programs," usually downloaded from our primary caretakers—our parents—even though sometimes well meaning, can have such a negative impact later on in our adult lives. One of my sayings is, "We spend our first ten years learning this and the next sixty years unlearning it!"

Most of us learn through the trial-and-error process of life. The challenge is that we end up repeating the same negative mistakes over and over again. So to become successful you need to find what *is* working and model that particular behavior or skill to produce the results you *do* want!

Wright

So, the three most important reasons that people are not successful are: lack of clarity, no skills, and inaction. What, then, is success?

Santangelo

That's a great question, although a very subjective one. It's like asking you what reality is—it's all just a perception. Everyone has a completely different perspective or representation of what success is for themselves. From what I've seen in the people I've worked with over the years, it's two simple, but not easy, concepts.

The first one is: *Know exactly what it is you want*—as I said before, a clarity of purpose!

Secondly, *eliminate self-imposed roadblocks* to your success. It is always a challenge for people to hear "self-imposed," which is by far the most difficult thing for people to do—get out of their own way! It took me about twelve years to figure out what success would be for me. Then it became just a matter of moving toward it on a consistent basis.

At a very young age I was reading a lot of books, listening to self-development programs, and attending many seminars. I was curious about "how" some people seemed to effortlessly succeed while others struggled throughout their entire lives.

Once I made the decision to discover my purpose and get clear about what success was for me, I was able to recognize two things about who I was: I loved to teach and I loved to entertain. Then a frightening thought popped in my head, *"Okay, but what are you going to do with that?"* Well, I'd been watching professional speakers and I had learned from watching my father speak and lead individuals and companies for many years. So, I decided I would focus my energy on speaking!

I put together an action plan of what I wanted it to look like and what I needed to do, be, and have in order to make this happen. From there I knew I had to go back to school, get a formal education, get the degrees and certifications I needed in this specific field to become more credible, and then stick with it—persistence—doing whatever it took to get myself to take action every day. When I look back on those beginning days I thought I knew so much! Being naive can be so enlightening!

Wright

Will you share some significant stories about your experience working with NLP and others?

Santangelo

Yes, I'd love to! There are so many wonderful and amazing individuals and companies that I've had the pleasure to work with!

One specific student, Valerie, pops into my head. She attended one of our twelve-day NLP certification programs last year. I remember her first day. She showed up as a very quiet, reserved, and certainly a not self-confident individual. At that time, she was living with someone; she was in a very bad relationship, and in a job she hated. During the workshop we also discovered that she had been diagnosed with cancer. It was a very tough time in her life, to say the least. During the twelve-day course we offered each individual fourteen new empowering beliefs that would have a huge impact on how each of them viewed the world and coupled that with specific exercises to help change their views of past events and then re-program the limitations they come to class with.

Immediately after she completed the six-weekend course, Valerie called me to say she finally left her abusive relationship, quit her job, and found out that she was cancer-free. She said she attributed these remarkable changes in her life by utilizing the NLP tools she had learned. She graduated from the course feeling more confident in herself and knowing that she's worthy of anything she desires in her life. Oh, and one more piece of great news about her—after she had quit, her boss offered her more money and a better opportunity at the company! She is currently with that same company and is now traveling the world teaching impoverished children the English language. She is living her dream and experiencing success.

Presently, David, we're training with a lot of Realtors and people who work in mortgage companies, especially in this crazy economy where Real Estate and financial markets are experiencing so much chaos. We're teaching and helping them develop lasting business relationships because with any successful business you don't just want customers, you want raving fans!

For many people, selling and sales have such a negative connotation. Successful product sales are really about building relationships and understanding clients' buying strategies. Think about that—do you ever want to feel as though you're being *sold to*? No, but people love to *buy!* Statistically people buy more from people they like than from anyone else. Eighty percent of all products and services sold are based upon the relationship created, not necessarily the product or service.

In our presentations and workshops we teach salespeople how to effectively communicate and build rapport with people through mirroring and matching another person's energy. *"People like each other when they tend to be like each other."* The rule we create for our students is: Like, Trust, Buy! If people like you, they'll begin to trust you and then buy from you. We teach a very simple and specific formula or strategy for this type of selling process and it's easy for them to learn. After taking our program, most people discover that they can immediately apply the attitude and methodologies

NLP offers. We simply just teach them to tap into their own personal power to achieve outstanding results. And the stories could go on.

Wright

How can NLP benefit me in making positive changes in my life?

Santangelo

The term "positive changes" makes the assumption that you know what is positive for you. The first thing I would ask you, David, is what do you focus on from moment to moment? Your focus determines your perceptions of your world. Ralph Waldo Emerson said, *"You become what you think about all day long."* That summarizes our lives in a nutshell. What you place your attention upon shows up. This is called the Law of Attraction. The entire movie *The Secret* was based upon this simple concept.

When working with my clients and students, the one thing I continually point out to them is what are they focusing on in the present moment and what is working or what is not working? When you focus on what's not working in your life, that is exactly what will show up. We actually end up creating more of what is not working. The same holds true about success in your life. If you focus upon what *is* working, more of that will manifest into your life.

The second thing you can do is ask yourself, "What meaning am I placing upon this event I'm creating?" The meanings produce for you a specific state and physiology that determine our behavior. The decisions we make in life shape our future, and each decision we make is bathed in an emotional state when we're deciding. So, the state of mind you're in at the moment you're making decisions shapes your destiny.

The next time you experience any kind of fear, a bad feeling, or a negative state of mind, ask yourself this question, "What feeling would I like instead?" This question immediately gives the unconscious mind something else to focus upon; it also creates a more empowering state of mind. NLP offers us the ability to step into any particular state of mind at any given moment. It's called an anchor. It's a trigger to fire off an emotional state, such as a state of confidence, focus, or calm, because in those specific states, you're more effective.

Wright

You talked of simplicity earlier. Can anyone easily learn the methods and apply them in their lives immediately?

Santangelo

Yes, there are actually no prerequisites to learning and practicing NLP—no previous knowledge or study at all. We have a lot of students, parents, and salespeople who show up; there are even therapists who attend. We have extraordinary individuals who want to climb to the next level by learning "how" to operate the "owner's manual" to their brain.

Basically, our brain functions like a computer, and if we knew how to manipulate the software, or more importantly, the operating system, we would be able to alter the results we produce on any given day.

Essentially, there are three different skill levels that we offer. One is a basic practitioner level (originally one hundred and twenty hours), where students are literally immersed in this amazing technology. This is not just another weekend workshop where you teach a little information and then hope the students retain some of the content to use when they leave the program. Because we teach in many different learning styles, conscious and unconscious learning, most students are able to retain up to 90 percent of the material we cover. Remember learning to drive your first car? How did you do that? You learned, by *doing!* Over and over again, we immerse students in harmonized strategies and concepts by presenting them in class repeatedly. Modeling—that's how you've learned everything!

The second program is the master's level program, where you receive advanced techniques of how to communicate with yourself and other people.

The third level is to become a presenter or trainer. You become artful in your abilities to deliver information to groups and/or workshops. Many people want to become better sales trainers or to overcome their fears so they can get up and speak in front of people. Teachers come to learn to teach more effectively.

I have personally gone through all three of these programs. I have gone through them several times with different instructors in order to gain new insights and new perspectives to become a better trainer of NLP.

We also have professional speakers who take our certifications. The one thing that makes a great and qualified NLP trainer is competency—period! So if you decide you want to learn all about NLP and its methodologies, and how it can help you become and have more of what you want, make sure you learn from instructors who have actual real world experience applying their NLP skills. Be sure that they have utilized their NLP skills in the outside corporate or coaching arena. Or give us a call and we can direct you to one of our programs or to someone who has become an outstanding and competent NLP trainer.

Wright

How have some of the companies you've worked with benefited from these strategies?

Santangelo

You may have read on my Web site that I had an amazing opportunity to train with the U.S. Army Counterintelligence Team post 9/11. On December 12, 2001, we began working with the Counterintelligence Team. We spent an entire week at Fort

Bragg, North Carolina, teaching them basic NLP skills customized to suit the need and demand for critical information. There were forty amazing individuals taking our training, having to learn how to apply these skills to interrogate terrorists, fundamentally for the safety for our country.

Being on the base was absolutely amazing. We had to be fingerprinted and ID'd, and went through three machine gun guarded checkpoints to even get on the base. Wow, did it shift my perspective on how, operationally, we do politics.

I remember having dinner one particular night on base and hearing some very loud thunderous booms, one after another. I immediately jumped up and asked the captain what the hell it was.

He said, "Oh, it's just the artillery battalion shelling the range."

"Oh, is that all it is?" I asked.

He said it as though it happened every day. It did for him, but not for me! Again, everything in our lives is just a matter of perspective—our own!

One of the things I am most proud of from that experience is the statement the captain of the team made to me on their last day of the training. *"John,"* he said, *"this was by far the most important training that I've ever put my guys through in forty years that I've been working with the Army."* I'm proud to say that NLP and the skills that I've learned over the years were being put to use for incredible service to our magnificent country.

Wright

You mentioned financial and wealth-building strategies. I'm sure many of our readers would love to know how you have used NLP to create more wealth and abundance in your own life.

Santangelo

I'm sure they would because that was the original question I continually asked myself many years ago—how can I learn to do what other high-achievers do so successfully? The biggest shift for me occurred when I finally made the decision to *become successful* and do whatever it took! I got serious about creating abundance in my life. I immediately instilled two beliefs about money and wealth: a) that money is a reflection of the value I place upon myself; and b) it's not how much I make but how well I manage it!

The first thing I did was to sit down and write out my one-year, ten-year, and twenty-year goals. Let me tell you, that in itself was a challenge. I finally figured out what I wanted but had no idea how to implement a plan for obtaining it. The thing to overcome was that every time I got stuck (meaning I felt bad or procrastinated or starting blaming myself and/or others for my failures), I learned to consistently shift my focus to what I did want and got myself to act! That's true personal power!

I actually utilized the tools NLP offered to get out of my own way and alter my states so I could immediately feel better about what I was focusing on at that moment. From there I was able to make significant decisions that would eventually shape my life's direction. As I've said before, making better decisions shapes your future! You cannot possibly make important decisions when you're in the midst of emotional drama. Have I said that enough?

I believe that's the biggest challenge people face on a daily basis. They may actually know what they want and they're moving toward it, but something shows up in their life that stops them dead in their tracks, and the only thing—the *only* thing— that can do this is an emotion or a feeling! There is nothing outside of you that can ever stop you. It's the negative feelings in life that prevent you from doing, being, and having the things you desire. If this resonates with any of you then your opportunity to move beyond any negative emotions lies in discovering how we can help you do that and then you can go beyond your wildest expectations!

NLP is based on a therapeutic model of change, studying three of the very best therapists over the course of many years, how their clients made significant progress in their lives, and how these therapists helped them achieve that. They also studied high achievers and extracted a very specific formula of their successes:

1. Outcome—what do you want?
2. Action—what are you doing on a daily basis?
3. Awareness—is it working, or not?
4. Flexibility—are you flexible in your approach to do something different?

There's a wonderful story about Thomas Edison inventing the incandescent lightbulb. He failed over ten thousand times attempting to rectify the problem. I cannot even imagine failing ten thousand times. Imagine people nowadays—most wouldn't even try one hundred times and many probably not even ten! This man did it over ten thousand times! What kind of flexibility did he have to have within him? He knew it was eventually going to work, and it was just a matter of moving forward every single day until something changed. In fact, the story was that after five thousand attempts, a young reporter said to him, "Mr. Edison, you've failed five thousand times trying to invent this lightbulb. The world wasn't meant to be lit by electrical light." Edison, clearly determined, replied, "Son, you don't understand how the world works. I haven't failed five thousand times, I found five thousand ways it wasn't going to work."

Wow, what a completely different perspective on a problem. This is what NLP allows us to do—shift our perspectives on any challenge that arises.

I believe our future—destiny, fate, whatever you want to call it—is determined by one thing in life: our decisions! We make our decisions through our emotional states. At any given moment in time, we're able to control (some people have an issue with that word "control") which state of mind we would like to be in, in order to make better decisions. When you're in a negative state, you're going to make a negative decision. When you're in a confident state, you're going to make a more confident decision. When you're in an empowering state, you're going to make an empowering decision. When people find themselves in a negative state, that's when they have to make a decision. A decision could be go left or right, choose this or that, go forward or backward, take this path or that one. Every decision we make, no matter how small, shapes our lives, and when we're in a better state of mind we make better decisions, thus producing a better quality of life at the end of our years.

You know, David, a very old gentleman once said to me, "Do you know the one thing that I have at this last stage of my life?" From my young perspective, I couldn't even answer that question. I couldn't imagine being there at that point in my life. He said, "Memories! It's the memories that I've created over the course of my life. That's the one thing that I have right in this moment that I can feel good about."

So, I ask everyone I work with, "What memories are you creating on a daily basis? Are they memories that you'll feel good about when you look back on your life?" I truly believe that is what it's all about for us and what our time here reflects for each of us. What do you focus on? Are you living in your past or creating your future?

The techniques I've learned and the strategies that we teach to individuals, companies, and corporations is simply to focus on more of what they do want rather than what they do not. One of my quotes that represent this is, "Life is precious and way too short! How many of you truly live how you want to live, and act how you want to be remembered? Remind yourself each day that you matter and can make a difference!"—John James Santangelo.

Wright

Do you think NLP can be used to assist people to become more motivated in their job or maybe in their social life and in their relationships?

Santangelo

Yes. That is a simple answer to such complicated questions, which I believe are: What motivates you? What motivates you as a partner in a relationship? What motivates you on a daily basis as an employee?

Many employers never take the time to discover what truly drives their employees to do the work that they've been given.

This brings up another issue altogether: are employees even well suited for the particular jobs they do? We often offer a technique to companies called "profiling." We use a very practical and simple survey called the Language And Behavioral profile (LAB). It determines what particularly motivates an individual in a particular context (e.g., work, relationship, school, etc.). We use it to determine how well suited people are for a particular job description. LAB profiling is a psychometric tool that will give our clients practical insights into human behaviors. This tool:

- Is a model that is flexible and creative,

- Is an incredibly effective coaching model,
- Gives precise information on what motivates individuals and groups, and
- Gives a procedure for empirically improving sales and marketing results.

The LAB Profile predicts one's behavior based on one's use of certain types of language patterns that reflect the thinking styles of a person and indicates his or her motivation and attitude. With this information you can advertise for a very specific employee, predict job performance, assign tasks efficiently, and you can influence behavior. The LAB Profile is a systematic way of gathering information about a person and it is a set of clear-cut procedures to help you utilize that person's talents.

There are fourteen traits in the LAB Profile—six motivation traits and eight working traits. The motivation traits show how people trigger their motivation and behavior in a given work context.

The working traits identify what sustains their motivation. There is nothing good or bad about a particular trait—it is a matter of understanding which trait is the most appropriate in a particular context.

We're finalizing the implementation of this profile system and developing a whole new workshop around it this year. We're expecting a huge response from employers and employees alike.

According to many national statistics, this is one of the biggest challenges companies face in today's marketplace—job satisfaction! People feel unsettled and move from one job to the next without any feeling of pride or loyalty. Again, it comes back to a feeling—feeling you're part of something, just as you would feel that you're part of a family.

There are some companies that do create this sort of corporate culture, and I can tell you they are the ones who efficiently succeed in today's economic whirlwind. That's the way it was twenty-five years ago (here I go getting nostalgic). People were dedicated and had internal pride about doing their job. That's not so prevalent anymore. There is no gold watch and fanfare after many years of dedicated service. There are no feelings of contributing back to society and leaving a part of your legacy behind. Head hunters are stealing employees, vice presidents, and CEOs from companies left and right for just a few more dollars a year (okay, millions of dollars a year). Is that what we have become—a nation of takers? At some point, we have to give back. You cannot make withdrawals without making enough deposits! Okay, I'm done! I'll get down off my soapbox now!

So to answer your question, we need to understand what drives each individual. What motivates you in your specific job as an employee? What do you need in order to feel worthy and proud of what you do?

The answer isn't so much how to get motivated but in answering the question *when* was the last time you felt completely motivated? With NLP, we can replicate that experience at any given moment in time. We can take people back into their past and help them find a specific event in which they felt completely and totally motivated. Then we can set what we call a "resource anchor"—"Pavlovian conditioning," which is a unique trigger set during a peak emotional state to elicit a specific response like motivation. With proper anchoring techniques, we can link up any emotion to bring back that feeling at any time.

Imagine being able to feel motivated and confident at any time you desire. How positively would that impact your current lifestyle? When you feel more motivated, you're going to work smarter, you're going to give your job and the company you're working for more energy. Your salary could benefit immensely, even in this chaotic market.

Wright

Wow, John, you are a wealth of success strategies and principles that each one of us should practice daily to help us consistently move forward in our lives. One last question about your work: how does our spirituality play a part in our in our success?

Santangelo

Well, first, it depends upon if you do believe in God—the Creator, the Universe—whatever you want to call Him. We are all part of that same consciousness of thought. There's a universal law called divine reciprocity—you give and the universe gives in return. When you plant a seed, the ground yields a harvest. That is a reciprocal relationship. The ground can only give to you as you give to the ground. You put money in the bank and the bank returns interest. That is reciprocity. When we give, we create a vacuum, which attracts even more than what you have given away.

The guideline for our giving to God and His work is found in 2 Corinthians 9:6–7: *"Now this I say, he who sows sparingly shall also reap sparingly; and he who sows bountifully shall also reap bountifully. Let each one do just as he has purposed in his heart; not grudgingly or under compulsion; for God loves a cheerful giver."*

Giving or tithing can be one of the important lessons you choose to learn in your life. So why give? When you learn to let go of the "things" you think you own, they no longer own you. Begin to give back for all you do have and you'll draw upon that vacuum to attract abundance in your life. Think about it—how can you desire "more" in your life if you do not make room for more to grow within it?

There is unlimited abundance in the world to go around, and yet some people actually believe there is only so much wealth and prosperity to be had. By tithing or giving back, you ensure your prosperity in God's eyes, as well as everyone around you. All the relationships you create will be a direct reflection of this idea of giving back—even the relationship you have with yourself!

It matters not where you give or tithe or whether you give of your time or money. It's not important! It only matters that you give out of love! Operate from your heart not your head. It is your intent that is of most importance. When you give for the highest good for all involved, we all win. We all share in this abundant universe. If I win, you win! Plant good seeds! Everyone deserves all this world has to offer, so practice recycling your abundance and ask yourself this question daily: "Am I planting good seeds?"

There's an even more powerful spiritual sutra I'll leave you with. It's about gratitude! Gratitude is giving thanks to "All That Is!" So many of us focus on the 10 percent we don't have rather than the 90 percent we do have! Rarely are we thankful for everything that shows up in our lives, and consequently we're always complaining that life never gives us a break. You see, when we focus upon the "lack" in our life (what is missing), our unconscious mind will move us in that direction; but when we focus our attention on our abundance (all that you do have), it will consequently produce more of that. "As you sow, so shall you reap." Gratitude is simply giving thanks for all that we do have.

When your heart and soul is filled with gratitude, you cannot possibly focus on what is missing. Nothing can be a greater expression of gratitude than to thank the universe and God for all that has been provided to you for all that you ask of it. An "attitude of gratitude" is a wide open channel for any and all that is good to come your way. It opens the floodgates to your success, good health, and abundance. By keeping this channel open, you clear the path for abundance to consistently flow to you at all times. Conversely, when the channel is closed, it seems that nothing good comes your way.

There's another wonderful quote on my desk I've repeated over the years, "There's no such thing as luck, only opportunity meeting preparedness." When you are present in the moment and aware that the universe does provide for you, saying "thank you" is the way to bless all that was, all that is, and all that will be!

I challenge each one of you listening or reading this to try it for thirty days. Every morning say "thank you" for everything in your life—everything! Be thankful for the bad as well as the good. After all, lessons come in all forms. By choosing to acknowledge only the good, you'll miss out on some of the most valuable lessons of all. Be thankful for *all* of it because it's all yours! Get in the daily habit of expressing gratitude for all things, and watch how your life expands and grows beyond your expectations. Then begin to notice, every day, how your blessings continue to just "show up!"

Wright

Thank you for that, John. I'm sure that many individuals and companies will be interested in working with you, so what will you offer them as far as support and/or information about your services?

Santangelo

Our support comes in a variety of different methods. One is on an individual or corporate coaching level, where we work personally with you over a specified period of time to produce very specific results.

Another would be our keynotes and speeches, which we deliver to organizations and associations.

We also offer training workshops and seminars that give groups the viable working knowledge of effective communication and success strategies.

I believe people and companies are tired of just getting the "what to do," in today's economic turmoil. They now need the strategies of *"How to do it"!* That is the important distinction we offer our clients—*Results!*

Wright

So if companies wanted to have you come and speak to them, what's the best way to reach you for your speeches, trainings, and professional coaching that we've been talking about?

Santangelo

The easiest would be through one of our two Web sites. The first is our corporate site: www.JohnSantangelo.com, and the other one is for our NLP training programs we present to individuals and corporations. We do many two- and seven-day NLP trainings for companies in which we'll present for a designated time and train the entire staff in sales or communication skills. That Web site address is www.LANLP.com. Our toll-free number is 888-NLP-Coach or contact us through one of the e-mail addresses listed on each site.

Wright

Wow, what a great conversation, John. Just to let you know, I've read a lot about NLP in the past—though it's never been explained to me this easily—and how I can directly apply it to my life to achieve more of what I want right now! I really have learned a lot today.

Santangelo

Thank you, David. I truly appreciate your feedback and comments!

Wright

Today we've been talking with John James Santangelo. He is a dynamic speaker, author, seminar leader, and success coach, and, as we have learned today, John is an authority in success principles, and an expert in the field of communications. John is an NLP master trainer and clinical hypnotherapist.

John, thank you so much for being with us today on *Roadmap to Success.*

ABOUT THE AUTHOR

JOHN JAMES SANTANGELO C.Ht., nationally acclaimed speaker, author, seminar leader, and success coach, has been a guiding force in empowering individuals, businesses, and corporations to excel at peak performance. John is a foremost authority in success principles and an expert in the field of communication. He is an NLP master trainer and clinical hypnotherapist. He has worked with companies such as The Learning Annex, Mary Kay Inc, Well-Point, Xerox, RE/MAX Realtors, the Teamsters Union, and the U.S. Army Counter-intelligence Team. Whether you're looking to  fulfill short- or long-term goals, increase your sales performance, or conduct corporate sales/communication trainings, John can help you achieve the next level of success! For more information on how to develop successful business strategies please phone or visit the Web sites listed below.

John James Santangelo

5699 Kanan Rd. Suite #188
Agoura Hills, CA 91301
818.879.2000 / 888.NLP.Coach
www.JohnSantangelo.com
www.LANLP.com
www.UltimateLifeChallenge.com

CHAPTER 4

An interview with…

Joe Colletti

A STRATEGY OF SUCCESS

David Wright (Wright)

Today we're talking with Joe Colletti. Joe is a keynote speaker, a sales skills trainer and consultant, and has been in sales, sales management, marketing, and training for over thirty years. He's taken his decades of experience to formulate his fundamental and exciting approach to increasing sales and management effectiveness. His results-oriented methodology and personal style have been well received by clients nationwide. Joe delivers world-class personal sales development and company growth programs. He accomplishes these objectives via his Power Training Programs, his "Where Your Feet Hit the Road Workshops," his high level educational and motivational keynotes and his Sales and Management Coaching, Consulting Expertise . Joe has written articles for *Real Estate Today Magazine,* (The Name Has changed) as well as *Sales + Marketing Ideas Magazine* to name a few. Additionally, he has been quoted in *Professional Builder, Atlanta Building News, St. Petersburg Times*, and more, and is a regular, much in-demand speaker at the International Builders' Show.

Joe has been responsible for the sales management of over 8,000 home sales and has a strong background in master planned golf courses and new home neighborhoods. His real life experience as a salesperson, a vice president of corporate sales, and international sales consultant serve to provide his clients with practical solutions to selling new homes in today's highly competitive marketplace.

Joe, welcome to *Roadmap to Success.*

Joe Colletti (Colletti)

Thank you very much, I'm glad to be here.

Wright

You speak about desire being the catalyst to your success, so how do you define desire?

Colletti

Well, to me, desire is a real hunger to succeed. What I can relate it to basically is a pain deep in my belly (if I can say it that way) of wanting to succeed at whatever I try. I really have the philosophy that whatever I take on, I need to at least succeed at it before I make a decision that it's not something that I need to continue with. So desire to me is something that is inherent—it's in there, it's a hunger to be successful, to accomplish whatever I set out to accomplish, and if I do not accomplish what I set out to do, then I have a very difficult time living with myself. I have a need to succeed at whatever I try before I move on to something else.

Wright

I understand that you've determined three areas that drive all people's desire for success. Would you explain those to our readers?

Colletti

Yes I will. The three areas that drive all success came to me years ago when managing commission salespeople. There are three areas that drive people's desires to be successful and help them accomplish what they want to accomplish in life. They're not listed here in any specific order—the order is determined by who you are.

First there is the ego. Specifically, I'm referring to a positive self-image where people feel good about themselves, they're happy at what they've accomplished, and they're successful. I'm not referring the popular definition of ego where people think they are better than anyone else. I'm not talking about that kind of ego at all. I'm talking about self-satisfaction of accomplishments.

The second is money. Money is another driving force for desire. For some people it's money that drives them to be successful. Money has a tendency to be number one on many people's list, but regardless of what position it is on your list, it still is one of the determining factors. Money helps everyone reach the goals and the direction that they want to achieve.

The third involves proving something to yourself or to someone else. I've found that a lot of people have to prove something to themselves—they have the ability to succeed or ability to accomplish whatever task they seek to accomplish. Many people have to prove something to someone else—perhaps they're trying to prove to a spouse or a friend or somebody who is very close to them that they have the ability to be successful.

I find that all three of these desires come into play with everyone's success. Everybody has them in different order—the order of their highest desires provides the pain in the belly.

To some people, money is number one on their list. It drives them to be successful. For others it's ego—the satisfaction of receiving awards and plaques and recognition. For others it's proving something to themselves or someone else. Everyone has a different priority. It's interesting—when people find out what the order is for them, they can focus on the desires that will propel them to capitalize on those strengths whenever they need to.

Wright

Will you tell our readers about how you apply self-visualization to help you in accomplishing your successes?

Colletti

Self-visualization is something I've used for as long as I can remember when first starting in business. When I was a lot younger, I would do self-visualization—I would actually visualize myself in a particular situation I would be going into. For example, if I was going to be doing a presentation, I would visualize myself walking into that presentation. I would visualize myself sitting down at a conference table and choosing the place I felt would be the best place for me to sit. I would visualize people sitting around that table, even though I might not have met all of them yet. I would visualize what my tactics would be, the first things I would say and do at the start of my presentation. I would visualize what my conversation would be like. Would it be building confidence or building trust? I would then get into the meat of the actual presentation. I would actually visualize myself going through that process completely. I now practice visualization every time, in every situation. I've learned to do it quickly now because I've been doing it for so many years.

When the time comes and I actually walk into the conference room, my confidence level is so much greater because I am already prepared on what I'm going to do. I even go so far as to have an idea of where I'm going to sit, if possible. I know because I've already been through it in my mind.

Wright

I know you're a true believer in self-visualization, but you also practice self-talk as well. Would you tell our readers how and why it makes a difference?

Colletti

We all have obstacles that get in our way to be successful. There are outside sources that pull against us—the day-to-day lifestyles that we have and challenges that are ahead. We hear voices in our head that are either negative or positive.

When you are actually in a situation to do self-talk, the key is to actually talk to yourself and program yourself for what you want to have happen. So self-talk is actually programming yourself, or retraining yourself, to be positive about whatever challenge is in your way. You've heard the saying "we are what we think." I truthfully believe that—if we think that we can't do something, we never will. If we think we can do it, we will find a way to make it happen. We have so many challenges that prevent us from doing that. We need to do self-talk to actually help program ourselves to do the right thing and stay moving in the right direction.

Self-talk to me is vital because there are times when those outside sources tug on you. You feel that maybe what you want is not going to work; but if you turn around and do self-talk, you might get the results you want. I talk to myself and go over my qualities, my character, my abilities, and successes, and my skills level. This reinforces that I in fact have the ability to accomplish what I set out to do.

There's a story that I have used for years. It appears in the book, *A Second Helping of Chicken Soup* by Jack Canfield and Mark Victor Hansen. The story is told of Major James Nesmith who was a POW during the Vietnam War. Before he went to Vietnam he was an avid golfer—he loved to play golf—he regularly scored in the 90s. Unfortunately, he was captured and became a POW. He was in a POW camp for almost seven years. He was one of the lucky ones—he came home. People wanted to know how he was able to survive in those conditions, and he said that he survived because of a desire to live. Every day, in his mind, he designed a new golf course, with dogleg to the left, par threes, par fives. Each day the course he designed was more complicated and more challenging. In his mind, he actually visualized himself playing the course, picking the correct club, seeing the club in his hands, adjusting his grip, and seeing his swing and follow through. He would watch the ball go through the air and land. He played his new course every day in his mind. So what do you think one of the first things he wanted to do when he was back in the States?

Wright

I'd say play golf.

Colletti

Yes, he wanted to play golf. The first time he played golf in over seven years, he shot a seventy-two! It was all due to self-visualization—he practiced on different courses in his mind and made them more and more difficult, so when he actually picked up the club in his hands and went out on the course, it was as though he had been there before.

Wright

How important is it to balance success in your life?

Colletti

When it comes to business, it's one of the number one things you have to do. I learned the hard way that balancing business and balancing family is something that needs to be done. Too many of us have a tendency to lean one way or the other. The majority of successful people lean heavily on their business and they shortchange their personal life.

I tended to do that when I was younger. I found myself not taking vacations because I was too busy. I wasn't just hurting myself, I was hurting my family, but I didn't realize it at that time. The tendency is that you get so wrapped up in becoming successful and reaching your goals that you feel if you don't completely concentrate on your business you're going to lose out. Well I found out, as I got older and more mature, that it wouldn't have made a difference. If I had continued to do what I'd been doing but taken some time off and spent a little more time with my family, I still would have been exactly where I am today. Unfortunately, too many of us get into that routine.

Through the years, I would tell people who worked for me my story. I'd say, "Look, I want you to work hard. I want you to be successful, *but* you need to balance your successes with your home life—you need to enjoy your family." There's the old saying that you need to work hard and you need to play hard; but balance is vital for total success.

Wright

So how do you do it?

Colletti

Well, the way that I try to do it, is basically to work real hard but to never forget that my family is there. I never forget that I've got to pay attention to them. I never forget to take my wife somewhere and I never forget to pay attention to my daughter and let her know I love her.

What we need to do is to balance our life. Spending a lot of time away from home is difficult if you're in that type of a business, but when you do come home you have to make it good quality time; you've got to make sure that you're touching somebody in your family every day in, even if you're away.

Wright

A wise man told me a long, long time ago that if I were ever walking down a road and saw a turtle sitting on a fencepost, I could bet that he didn't get up there by himself. So who in your life were role models and played a big part in your success?

Colletti

Well the person I would say played the biggest part in my success was my father. My father was born in Italy, and he came over to the United States with his parents and his brothers. He came here when he was young man of about seven years old or so. He came to a new country, he had to learn a language, he had to put up with the difficulties of being a stranger in a new land; but with only an eighth grade education, he still became successful. He had abilities and talents, but he didn't have education—he had to do it strictly from his desires and his hard work.

Wright

I understand that you have a saying: never compromise who you are. Sounds like a great saying, but would you tell our readers a little bit more about what you mean?

Colletti

People tend to exhibit what I call "the willow branch syndrome." They blow in the wind. Whatever way the wind blows, the willow branch will follow; many people would just as soon be a chameleon and adapt to whatever is needed to achieve the success they desire. If you do that, you're shortchanging yourself. What's really important to me is to not compromise who you are. If you do, you will never feel that you've arrived. When you feel that you've arrived you will fall backward because you're not truly successful. People will compromise their knowledge, their skills, their character, their ability, just to get one step further ahead, whether it means obtaining a new client or getting that new promotion or whatever it may be in life.

To me, when people compromise they are actually prostituting themselves because all they're worried about is getting what they want, getting a new sale, accomplishing that new opportunity. This will come back to bite you big time because who you are makes you the person that people want to work with. You want people to feel they can trust you and that what you say is the truth. You want them to know that you don't bend in the wind like a willow branch. This is integrity and it is what makes people want to work with you.

Wright

So what do you think are the biggest obstacles people face in trying to be successful?

Colletti

I find that the biggest obstacles are basically that they give up before they succeed. There is no set timetable that states you will be successful within a certain period of time. Just because success doesn't come as fast as you anticipate is no reason to give up. There are so many things that we're doing and juggling at one time to make success happen. Too many people think that it's easy and when it doesn't happen fast enough, they quit too soon.

Today everybody thinks that success should be easy. I have a quote on my Web site: "If success were so easy to obtain, there would be no such words as failure." And the reason for this is that success isn't easy, and that's why there are so many benefits for people who become successful. It takes hard work, it takes desire, and it takes balancing your life between your career and your family.

Also I won't give up or change my direction until I have succeeded at whatever I set out to achieve. What I mean by that is, I don't have to achieve it at 100 percent, but as long as I achieve it above a 75 percent range, I have succeeded, in my opinion. Then I can make the decision about whether or not I want to adjust, change, or move in another direction.

Wright

So what message do you want our readers to take away or to hear so that they can learn from your success?

Colletti

The message I'd like to give everyone is to associate with those who are the best at what they do and focus on how you can learn and grow by association. I've always tried to do that. I believe that if you get involved in organizations and in different careers, find out who the people are who are respected and who are successful, and get to know who those people are. I think it's important to introduce ourselves to those individuals and when we see them again we go back and reintroduce ourselves until they know who we are. I think that is so important. I think it's very similar to what you mentioned earlier, David, about associating with those you actually are doing business with. Whether those writing chapters in a book or leaders in companies or businesses or whatever it might be. I really think that is the key—to associate with those who are the best at what they do and focus on how you can learn and grow by associating with them.

Wright

Well, what a great conversation, Joe. I really do appreciate your discussing this important subject. I want to thank you for taking all this time to answer these questions this morning.

Colletti

Thank you very much for the opportunity, David, I appreciate it.

Wright

Today we've been talking with Joe Colletti. Joe is a speaker, trainer, and consultant. He delivers world-class personal sales development and company growth programs through his "Power Training" programs and his "Where Your Feet Hit the Road Workshops." He's written several articles about the subject of Real Estate, and he is a much sought-after speaker in the building industry. I don't know about you, but I'm going to listen to what he says. It sounds like he knows what he's talking about.

Joe, thank you so much for being with us today on *Roadmap to Success.*

Colletti

Thank you, David.

ABOUT THE AUTHOR

JOE COLLETTI, KEYNOTE SPEAKER, Sales Skills Trainer and Consultant has over 30 years of experience in Sales, Management, Marketing and Training. He has taken his decades of experience to formulate his fundamental and exciting approach to increasing sales and management effectiveness. His results- oriented methodology and personnel style have been well received by clients nationwide. Joe delivers world class Strategies and Solutions for Personal Sales Development and Company Growth.

Joe Colletti

225 Kendemere Point
Roswell, GA
770.641.3080
Joe@JoeCollettiandAssociates.com
www.JoeCollettiandAssociates.com

CHAPTER 5

An interview with…

Denise Federer

BREAKTHROUGH TO UNLIMITED SUCCESS

David Wright (Wright)

Today we are talking with Denise Federer, PhD. She is founder and principal of Federer Performance Management Group. Dr. Federer's twenty-four years of experience of working with key executives, business leaders, and Fortune 500 companies as a clinical psychologist, consultant, coach, and trainer lend her a unique perspective on leadership and success. She is an expert in the psychology of money, wealth management, performance enhancement and business consulting. Her goal in working with clients is to help them realize their extraordinary potential to achieve significant change.

Dr. Federer, welcome to *Roadmap to Success.*

Denise Federer (Federer)

Thank you, David. I appreciate that.

Wright

So in your coaching work, how have most individuals you've worked with defined success?

Federer

Although definitions of success may vary in the context of my work, a successful individual or star performer is defined as someone who excels at being at the top of his or her game as measured both qualitatively (the person is ethical and respected) as well as quantitatively (the person might be a top producer in his or her respective field). Additionally, another factor I look at is people's ability to maintain success over time.

Wright

What does it mean to be ready for success?

Federer

The key question that I have attempted to answer in my close to thirty years in the areas of behavioral change, motivation, and peak performance is "What makes so many of us resistant to making changes in our behavior if we intuitively know it could lead to greater success in our lives?"

Think about it—quitting smoking, losing weight, exercising, earning additional educational credits, developing better relationships with friends, family, colleagues—all of these behaviors, if we are willing to work on them logically, will lead to greater health, success, and happiness. Yet, most of us are resistant to making the necessary changes we need to make to achieve these goals. My key question is why is that? I think it boils down to being ready to accept success and all that success implies.

Wright

Would you tell our readers about the concept of "Peak Performance" and describe how it relates to the program you developed, "Working in the Zone"©?

Federer

The concept of Peak Performance originated in the world of elite athletes. These athletes, such as Tiger Woods, Roger Federer, and Lance Armstrong have long strived to experience this feeling of Peak Performance, or what psychologists call *Flow* or *Being in the Zone.*

"Being in the zone" is defined as being completely one with what you are doing and being able to control your destiny for at least one moment. It is a state of consciousness where you become totally absorbed in what you are doing to the exclusion of all other thoughts and emotions. In other words, it is your mind and your body working effortlessly together. Baseball players have described being in the zone or achieving peak performance as seeing a pitch perfectly and as the ball was coming toward them it almost looked the size of a grapefruit. It's that moment where everything else is tuned out and you are so focused on what you are doing and intensely enjoying the moment you are experiencing.

The key to achieving this level of success is in finding joy in the work, not just focusing solely on outcome. My goal is to help individuals realize that the desired outcome will happen naturally if you shift your energies to the process.

I have developed a program for helping individuals achieve this feeling of Peak Performance called "Working in the Zone." The focus is to help individuals shift their thinking and discover incredible feelings of power and joy during the process of doing the work.

Wright

What is the relationship between success, challenge and change?

Federer

What elite athletes have taught to the rest of us who want to be at the top of our game is that you must create challenges for yourself and move beyond your comfort zone to achieve the next level of success. I always think about Tiger Woods and how he stopped and retooled in the middle of his tour, trying to get a different swing. Most people would have said, "Why would he stop? He was doing so great." What elite athletes understand is that the first requisite for being in the zone is striking a balance between the challenges they face and the skills they have. So challenge leads to flow or being in the zone. Therefore, you need to create a challenge and move out of your comfort zone in order to get to the next level of success in your life.

Wright

Why is it so difficult to commit to changes in our life, especially if we know how positive it will be for our personal and professional success?

Federer

Well, to put it simply, it is because change is hard and learning and maintaining the behavior is even harder. In fact, I believe many people don't make many changes until they are uncomfortable enough or are even miserable enough. I often joke that I need to write a book titled *You're Just Not Miserable Enough Yet.*

Added to that is the fact that even when we attend an inspiring program, and we get motivated to change, the laws of retention work against us. Ninety percent of what we learn is forgotten after seven days. My role in the change process is to be a thinking partner and help my clients get out of their comfort zones by challenging their thinking, creating some discomfort, and helping them stay motivated in the behavioral change process.

Wright

What are the three D's that you believe make it difficult for most of us to commit to these changes?

Federer

As I said, most of us are resistant to making the necessary changes we need to achieve our goals. I believe there are three main reasons why people resist change; I call them the three D's:

1. **Lack of desire**—you don't see the need for it. You really have to care about the outcome and it has to be worth it to you. Of course, I just said that it is a lot of work to make a behavior change, so you have to have that desire.
2. **Lack of determination**—you don't think you can make the necessary changes. It's just too hard. For example, if you ask someone to commit to running a marathon, for many people who have never run any distance, that concept is just too overwhelming. So the person won't put the effort in to achieve that goal because he or she just doesn't feel it can be done; it is just too hard.
3. **Lack of dedication**—you don't have the commitment to make the consistent changes that will stick long-term.

So when you think about something that you should do but you don't do it, chances are the reasons are due to one of the deficits in one of these three D's—desire, determination, or dedication. In reality, it often only takes one or two small changes in thought and behavior to have a significant impact and help shift you in the direction of these new goals.

Wright

What are the four critical obstacles that you believe interfere with the change process?

Federer

There are four main areas that sum up the critical obstacles that interfere with a successful change process. The first one is *inertia*. I think this is the main factor that impacts our willingness and desire to make changes and embrace new concepts. It can be summed up by the familiar phrase, "If it's not broken, don't fix it." We all have behavioral patterns and established routines that have contributed to our success. As I said before, we get comfortable. However, successful people eventually hit the wall or a plateau. A common response to experiencing a plateau in our work or success level is to work harder and faster, doing what we have always done. The problem, of course, is that it rarely achieves the hoped for breakthrough.

The second area that I think is an obstacle for people in the change process is *pain tolerance*. As I said earlier, in order to overcome the inertia you have to make changes, and change can produce painful anxiety. Most people do anything to avoid pain. So, your current situation has to be uncomfortable enough to challenge your pain tolerance. This concept relates to what I said earlier, people are just not miserable enough to make the necessary changes to achieve the next level of success.

The third obstacle to change is *life cycle stage.* Where you are in the life cycle of your career and developmental stage in your life will often determine your priorities or how stuck or inspired you might be to get out of your comfort zone and make changes. At every stage of life we have different challenges, as we do in every stage of our work life. So, depending on where you are in life determines whether or not change is a priority.

Finally, the fourth obstacle that interferes with change is unproductive thoughts and emotions. Negative thoughts and feelings can play a significant role in contributing to someone's inertia and resistance to make changes. Research continuously confirms the power of our positive thoughts in impacting our feelings of behavior. The good news is that behavior is easier to change than feelings and there are ways to combat negative thinking, which is all a part of the work I do in coaching.

Wright

What role does understanding your motivation, values, and where you are in the change process play in an individual's willingness to make the necessary changes for desired success?

Federer

That's a good question. I believe the more you understand about where you are in the change process, what motivates you, and what your core values are, the sooner you can begin to feel empowered to make the necessary changes to achieve your goals. Briefly, according Prochaska's Model of Change, there are six stages for change.

There are three stages that allow you to begin the change process:

1. The first stage is contemplation. What you are saying in this stage is: "Maybe I need to change." There is a raising of consciousness—you are aware you need to change. You're beginning to feel the pain. You're beginning to struggle with the question of, "Should I make a change in my behavior or life?"
2. The next stage is preparation. You're convinced you need to make a change and you are committed to taking the necessary actions. At this stage you are gathering resources and support.
3. Action is the third stage and here you are really ready to initiate.

So I think that it's important to figure out where you are in all of this. As you begin to think, "Where I am is no longer comfortable, I need to do something different," you are ready to overcome some of your resistance to change and achieve your desired goals.

Values and motivation play a key role in understanding your resistance to this change. Often the anxiety we feel embarking upon change results from the perceived conflict between our current values and achieving success. For example, many of my clients initially might hold some misconceptions of what it means to be successful and they feel uncomfortable with the anticipated changes in their life that they believe they will have to make to achieve their desired outcome. They may be asking themselves, "Is it too big a price to pay to be successful?" However, there are some important things to keep in mind. Values change over time in response to changing life experiences and our values influence our motivation. What we desired and made us comfortable in our twenties may not be the same in our forties. So, knowing what makes us tick and what matters gives us powerful information about ourselves and helps facilitate the change process.

Also, in order to get out of your comfort zone and learn new behavior, the potential outcome of your effort has to have meaning for you.

You are only going to be motivated to accept the challenge of change and work toward a new level of success if the payoff is worth it. I think that how motivated we are to engage in these new behaviors and make changes is dependant on three main factors:

1. How strong and consistent are our needs?
2. What are our expectations of the outcome?
3. How badly do we want the payoff? For example, if I want to stop smoking, I have to really feel motivated that my health may be at risk for me to stop. There are a lot of factors working to make me decide that I am going to take this next step and make some changes in my life.

Wright

You used smoking as an example. You can almost take a blackboard and spend the rest of the day writing down reasons why one shouldn't smoke. Yet, I've been in hospitals where people are on their deathbeds and still smoking. I've even seen them smoking in wards with oxygen.

Federer

Absolutely, and do you know why? It's because when you are looking at what motivates us and why we are willing to change, the outcome has to be worth it. We have to be able to visualize the eventual successful outcome, and unfortunately I think that many people feel that they are victims and unable to change difficult behavior. One of the main goals of my work is to take people out of what I call "the professional victim role" and help them see how empowered they really are. These are choices we make. They are hard choices but they are choices that we consciously make.

One of the things that I often tell people I coach is they can no longer say, "I can't," they have to say, "I won't." One of the key tools for overcoming resistance is learning to shift your thinking—"It's not that I can't stop smoking, it's that I won't stop smoking because it's just not worth it to me. The feeling I get inhaling is just so worth it that I am not willing to anticipate the consequences."

Wright

Will you explain a little more to us about the importance in shifting our thinking and understanding how our beliefs can limit our behavior?

Federer

I think that it's the most important concept in helping people make changes. Shifting our mental framework is a powerful technique. As I said, most of us come to situations with preconceived ideas of "how things should be." But, by moving from certainty to curiosity we allow ourselves to experience the situation from a new perspective and open ourselves up to more possibilities. That's one of the most important concepts I introduce to my coaching clients. I teach them to move from a perspective of, "I know how things have to be," to, "I wonder how things could be."

The next concept is one I just mentioned earlier—understanding the power of not allowing yourself to become a victim and to really embrace the "I can't. I make decisions for myself," versus the "I won't."

I think that the third really important behavioral concept to keep in mind is that behavior is easier to change than feelings. So, if I wait until I feel differently to behave differently, I might wait a long time. But if I can help people find the courage and confidence to engage in new behaviors, even though it sometimes feels fraudulent, eventually those feelings of confidence trail behind. Over time that new behavior becomes a more permanent part of their lifestyle and the way they approach the world.

Wright

In teaching people strategies for change, what are some of the key principles that you address in your SET Program?

Federer

SET is an acronym. I call the program "Getting SET." There are three essential steps to getting set for creating behavioral change and achieving the next level of success in your business or your life:

S—Stating your vision, your mission.
E—Establishing what I call smart goals, which are specific, measurable, action-oriented, realistic, and timely.
T—Taking effective action.

Wright

Why is creating a vision so important?

Federer

This goes back to the original premise of the program I developed to help individuals *be in the zone.* The first step in creating an opportunity to be in the zone or achieving peak performance in your work is to set clear and specific goals. However, the prerequisite for that is to create a powerful vision of where you want to be five years from now. For many people that is not easy and I often take them through a specific visualization process. Having the vision of where you want to be helps you to create the blueprint to begin to set the goals and behavioral steps of how to get there. For many people, as I said, there is resistance to letting go of their inhibitions and allowing themselves to dream and have a vision of the future and what they really want to achieve.

Wright

You've talked about outcome and process, now what role does committing to what you describe as outcome and process goals play to an individual achieving success?

Federer

Research on goal-setting in the world of business has consistently shown that it can lead to enhanced performance and greater long-term success. I think that specifically what the research shows is that it confirms the importance of writing down both our goals and measuring our progress as an essential part of the change process. Often, we overestimate or underestimate when we are left to self-report to our memory. And that's a good example for eating or exercising—we always tend to overestimate or underestimate what we are doing. So it is very important.

There are two aspects of creating an effective goal. The first one is gathering a baseline of your initial behavior and then monitoring your progress over time. When creating your goals, the outcome goals are what you hope to achieve. For example, in the sales world, it might be "Increase my sales by 15 percent." If I am working with someone, that might be one of the behavioral measures of their success.

Process goals are the specific action steps that you take in order to achieve that goal. For example, "Contact ten new prospects weekly" or "Offer a value added seminar to current clients and their guests." The outcome goal is how to measure success and the process goal is the specific behavioral steps to take to achieve that outcome.

Wright

Will you share your theory about what most people need to cope effectively with changes?

Federer

What my experience has taught me is that most people require three things: they need predictability, they need consistency, and they need accountability in order to become comfortable with their own behavior and the behavior of others. In other words, in order for action steps to be meaningful, they have to be straightforward and they have to be repeatable.

Wright

How would you summarize, in a sentence or two, the crux of how you coach people to approach their resistance to change and prepare them to embrace success?

Federer

To sum it up, the main questions I ask individuals I coach is to answer the question, "What can I do differently?" and "What am I willing to do differently to achieve my goals?" The answer to these questions will help clients begin to look at how motivated they are to make the changes that are necessary for the success they would like to achieve. They are often very different. Going back to the example of the smoker, it involves asking, "What I can do and what I am willing to do," which are often on completely different planes.

Wright

How interesting. I appreciate the time you've taken to answer all these questions. What I am coming away with is that almost everything is about decision-making, isn't it?

Federer

Yes, it's about decision points. I think the main goal for people I coach is that they get to choose the decisions they want to make and they are not victims. If they are not willing to make the changes to achieve a certain level of success, they just need to explore that and acknowledge and come to terms with that decision. For many people, some of the reasons why they hold back are based on erroneous assumptions. Exploring those assumptions is a primary focus of the coaching work I do.

For example, a specialty coaching area that I work with is the financial industry. In my initial interviews I often hear financial advisors say, "Well, I am successful enough." When we explore what that means, they reluctantly admit that they either are not comfortable with what they perceive it would take for them to achieve the next level of financial success or they are not comfortable with making more money.

We have often talked about the fact that you can make that money and give it away to charity but don't need to sabotage or stop yourself from achieving the next level of your desired success.

Wright

Today we have been talking with Denise Federer, PhD. She is an expert in the psychology of money, wealth management, performance enhancement, and business consulting. As we have found today, she will probably reach her goal, which is to help her clients realize their extraordinary potential and achieve significant change.

Dr. Federer, thank you so much for being with us today on *Roadmap to Success.*

Federer

Thank you very much for having me. I appreciate it.

ABOUT THE AUTHOR

DR. DENISE P. FEDERER is a speaker, consultant, coach and business coach. She brings over twentyfive years of experience to her work with individual executives and corporations providing performance coaching and consulting. She helps individuals and organizations realize their extraordinary potential and effect significant behavioral change. Her unique perspective as both a clinician and researcher informs the assessment and evaluative feedback on outcome success that she offers to her clients.

Dr. Federer's professional affiliations and involvement over the past twenty years included the American Psychological Association, Florida Psychological Association, and National Register of Health Service Providers in Psychology, National Association of Female Executives, and Society for Psychologists in Management, the International Coaching Federation, and The Family Firm Institute. Dr. Federer has also served on the boards of several non-profit organizations in her local community.

Denise P. Federer, Ph.D.

Federer Performance Management Group, LLC
3641 W. Kennedy Blvd. Suite G
Tampa, Florida 33609
813-876-7191
dfederer@fpmg.info
www.fpmg.info

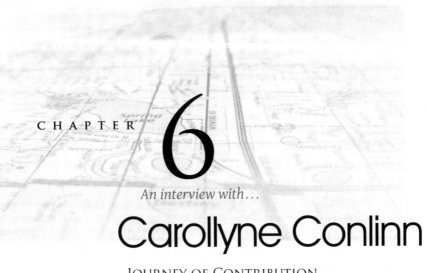

6

An interview with...

Carollyne Conlinn

JOURNEY OF CONTRIBUTION

David Wright (Wright)

Today we're talking to Carollyne Conlinn. Carollyne is the 2009 recipient of the Canadian Coach of the Year Award. She is an international executive coach who integrates entrepreneurial leadership with thirty years of Fortune 500 corporate experience. She has developed programs that create profound change in individuals and organizations. Her Excelerator Coaching System™ has become the core curriculum for the graduate executive coaching program at Royal Roads University. Her Great Question Game™, which introduces groups to coaching, has been very popular with managers and business leaders. In 2009, Carollyne and her partners launched Essential Impact Coaching Inc. to bring systems for coaching cultures into organizations. She currently leads processes for individuals and groups to map their own journey of contribution.

Carollyne, welcome to *Roadmap to Success.*

Carollyne Conlinn (Conlinn)

Thank you, David. I appreciate this opportunity to reflect on my journey from becoming a Corporate Refugee to settling into the new Country of Contribution. I have been surprised by some of the markers on the road to a fulfilling life.

Wright

I haven't heard those terms before. Tell me what you mean by "Corporate Refugee" and the "Country of Contribution."

Conlinn

The key idea behind the Corporate Refugee is that refugees usually leave a place they have considered home and move to somewhere that is new and possibly frightening.

I had been with the same global industry leader for thirty years. Even though the company had three hundred thousand employees, I was one of thirty executives in Canada; and it felt like home. When I chose to leave, there was no next place to go, so I was living in a temporary place in my life not knowing whether I would find another kind of fulfilling work. What I discovered was far more than a new home; it was a new way of living, which includes amazing work. One of the surprises is the realization I am doing exactly what I am meant to do. If we keep with the refugee metaphor, it's as though I have moved into a new home in a new country that is better than I imagined. The Country of Contribution is where everyone longs to live—certain that work and life are worthwhile, and that they are contributing to make a positive difference on the planet.

Wright

It sounds as though you have reinvented yourself as well as your work. What prompted you to leave your successful executive role with all the perks, salary, expense account, travel, etc.? What were the signposts that let you know you were on the right track?

Conlinn

Let me begin with the first signpost that announced it was time to leave my comfortable corporate home. I had a growing feeling that something had to change.

The pull to stay was my loyalty to the company I had grown up in over the course of thirty years. The people felt like my family, and I knew all the managers in my division from coast to coast, even if they hadn't reported to me directly. Many of them were people I had hired or trained in some aspect of their job and nurtured to positions of greater responsibility.

My day-to-day work was still engaging—I was spearheading a new management system in our division, and the approach promised to give more accountability to front line staff. This new initiative matched my belief that work could be meaningful at every level of a system.

The downside was that I had to spend much more time away from home than I liked. My children were entering their teen phase—at eleven and fourteen—and I had always told myself that was the most important parenting time, so I wanted to be closer to home. I was commuting three thousand miles from Vancouver to Toronto, working sixty to eighty hours every week to implement the first big project with the new management system. I couldn't see myself staying in the same role until I retired.

The road ahead was filled with variations on what was familiar. I was already a vice president, and the options were different portfolios, but basically the same kind of work—selling, empowering staff, starting new projects, managing budgets, and creating new approaches. These were all things I had done repeatedly over my years with the company.

Also, I wasn't sure I was up to dealing with new political wrinkles from the parent company. I could see the writing on the wall about centralizing functions, and wasn't sure I wanted to have my autonomy curtailed as much as it would be with a major restructure. This scenario materialized the year after I left, and confirmed my instincts.

What wasn't clear to me was what would be the "right timing." I knew the signpost would need to be very clear to budge me from feeling comfortable, successful, and that I was contributing in a meaningful way to my staff and clients.

One day the sign came from an unexpected source. I was meeting with our key client to review our progress on the project I was leading for them. This time, the client had invited a colleague—someone who had been responsible for the functions we were now managing. This person had a lot to say about what wasn't going right. It sounded as though he had been taking notes for weeks about what was wrong, and had not updated his files with the progress we had made.

Because I took responsibility for leading the project, I heard his criticism as a personal attack. In all my years in the business, I had never had this kind of meeting before and was shocked by the level of negative feedback and disrespect I experienced. I felt my integrity was being challenged as well as my intention to work as a partner with the client.

On the plane home from Toronto that evening, I had time to reflect about the project, my part in not communicating as clearly as I could have, and ways to rectify the situation. Then, from the back of my mind came a thought that was as loud as a paging system in an airport. It was a very simple phrase that would change the course of my life. The voice said: "Enough is enough." I listened again to make sure I heard correctly, and it was still there. In that moment, I knew there was no turning back.

Wright

Sounds like a breakthrough. How did you get from that moment to where you are today?

Conlinn

I took the whole trip home to let that message sink in. I was wrestling with ways to change my approach, lessons to be learned from staying, the challenge of leaving a project when I had not yet trained a successor—yet I realized what I was really doing was planning how to leave, more than how to stay. My heart wasn't in the corporate world anymore, though I had no idea what else I would do.

At first, I didn't tell anyone; I just let the idea simmer. The first person I told was someone in human resources at the end of our annual executive retreat a month later. I sat through the meetings imagining myself not being there—without the people who had mentored me, encouraged me, challenged me, and generally been my companions on the road to success in my profession and company.

After the meeting ended, I stayed behind until everyone had left. Then I sat looking out on the lake at the resort and let my feelings take over. I was sitting sobbing my heart out when I realized someone else was there. Fortunately, she was someone I trusted, and she listened while I poured out my dilemma. She then reflected back that I had already made my decision, and asked how I would manage the transition in a way that would be consistent with my values. It was a great conversation. Even though I hadn't heard the word at that time, looking back, I realize it was my first experience of being coached.

Over the next few months, I struggled with how to support the business in the most responsible way. There were people whom I thought would be able to lead the projects currently underway. I decided I could live with a three-year transition, with diminishing time on my part to ensure everything was handled smoothly. I see now that I was mostly trying to ease myself out of what I knew, because I had no idea where I was going next.

My plan was simply to put one foot in front of the other and see where life took me, and that scared me. Then a friend, who was exploring the new discipline called Executive Coaching, invited me to be her practice client. That was a critical step because, without a thinking partner, my journey could have turned out quite differently.

When I finally met with my CEO, with my letter of resignation in hand, I had a plan and a list of things I wanted as part of a departing package. What made me think I deserved a package is unclear, since I was the one leaving and financial packages were reserved for retirees. However, I reminded myself that I had worked in the company my whole career. With list in hand, I started the meeting. I was emotional, and it took a couple of tries to get out the words—and the reason, which was simply: "I'm done. I accomplished the project you asked me to launch, I can't keep up the commute, and I may not be the best person to take this work to the next level." Then I waited.

What came back was a surprise, and contradicted the part of my mind that was doubtful. He assured me that if there was any part of me that thought I would be treated badly, I could put that fear to rest. True to his word, he included everything on my wish list in my pre-early-retirement package.

For me the most important part of the conversation addressed the meaning of leaving my work family, or more accurately, my struggle with what felt like choosing between two families. He looked at me for a few minutes, then said what I knew was the truth, "You know which is your real family." After that, I was able to relax and move on to the practical steps of handing off my portfolio and moving ahead.

The timeline for transition was closer to three months than three years, as there were competent people already on the team. I was much more "done" than I realized. I struggled to pack my suitcase for those last few trips.

The effect of leaving so quickly was to be jolted out of my comfortable, financially secure life and thrust into the dark unknown without the benefit of the smooth transition I had imagined. I left my career with a feeling of deep gratitude to the many people along the way who had made my work meaningful and the road relatively smooth. I felt generously treated, and the only remaining detail was how to bring closure to thirty years of service. I had read William Bridges' work on transitions, which was just becoming popular at the time. He highlighted the importance of completing the old before embracing the new, so I knew I needed some form of completion. The traditional retirement party wasn't appropriate, since I was leaving at only fifty-two years old. So, I decided a ceremonial leaving party at the Weston Airport Hotel in Toronto would be most fitting. I invited an intimate circle of people for a reception and story-telling time.

I was a little nervous before everyone arrived, sitting in a secluded corner of the piano bar surrounded by trays of beautiful hors d'oeuvres. I wondered if our relationship was as important to them as it was to me. Would anyone even come? Of course they did! It was wonderful to see all the people who had guided and supported me over the years. Some who came had already left the company and we remembered others who were alive only in our memory. We were full of stories and were able to reminisce, laugh, and appreciate the journey.

My parting gift to each of them was *The Four Agreements* by Don Miguel Ruiz. It was part of my own completion to explain to them how they had taught me those agreements in my life, in particular agreement four, "Always do your best."

I got on the airplane that night with a light heart and a sense of readiness for what was next. My question to myself was, "How do I find out what's next when I'm terrified and I don't have a clue where to start?"

Wright

What were some of the speed bumps that slowed you down on your new road to success?

Conlinn

There were several times when I felt stuck. Looking back, I see that those slow periods were essential to moving forward. The first speed bump was staring out the window for six months, watching the two trees that loomed over our community garden emerge from their winter bareness to a glorious showing of white and pink blossoms. I hadn't realized the extent of my depletion from being on planes every week, working eighty-hour weeks without noticing, and having telephone relationships with my husband and children.

When I was doing those things, I told myself that my life was in balance and I was being creative about keeping it that way. Doing nothing for six months gave me an experience of rethinking the notion of equilibrium and admitting to myself that I had been completely out of balance. It was valuable to just sit and think. I could also take time for the impromptu conversations with my husband and children that couldn't happen on a phone call once a day.

There was also some repair work to do at home, as my husband had been coping with a full-time job and single parenting for several years, and he was tired and depressed. I was grateful to find a family therapist who helped us to rebuild our relationship. My daughter was struggling with teenage self-esteem issues that could have taken a nasty turn, but I was home for the pivotal conversations, and was able to get professional help to enable her to reconnect to her life and have optimism for the future. My son has a quiet and introspective nature, so being around when he felt like talking was a gift to myself—the pre-teen equivalent of seeing a baby's first step. As I settled into the rhythm of my real family, it struck me that I had been spared a lot of heartache by listening to and acting on the voice in my head that knew when enough was enough.

My new life wasn't all roses. I was used to days that were chock full of busyness and I floundered looking for how I might make a living from scratch. I certainly wasn't ready to retire and knew I wasn't interested in doing more of what I had spent my previous career doing. Yet there were many highlights of this fallow time, like being a parent chaperone on my daughter's trip to France and Spain because I had the time to go. I took time to revisit my own teenage life as a student in France and meet friends I hadn't seen for over three decades. Travel gave me an opportunity to explore the inner landscape that had been a silent backdrop in my life for years.

On the train between Paris and Salzburg, I relived the thrill of being in an international community of students in the French countryside. I was an active contributor to long discussions about the meaning of life. We wrestled to find answers to intense questions about God, finding true love, and our promising futures.

I visited the cozy home of my former roommate and the fellow student she had married after graduation. I was curious about how they related to the church we grew up in, and our conversations helped me to examine my spiritual roots. I realized that my spiritual life had changed a lot since my student days. Though I no longer attended that church, I saw how my weekly workaholic recovery meetings were nourishing me deeply.

After the trip, I was invited to attend a weekend workshop with a friend who was exploring coaching, a new approach to personal development. She was considering it as a career for herself and wanted a skeptic to give her feedback about this fringe idea.

I happily volunteered for the role and fulfilled it well, not really engaging in the content, but listening for how it was flaky and a hoax.

It wasn't until the last afternoon when something shifted in me. As an afterthought, the presenters talked about their corporate coaching curriculum and how it worked to take coaching into organizations. That caught my attention. What if I had had the benefit of a coach in my former company? I wondered if I would have left or stayed and found a new way of working. Without the benefit of coaching, I could still be living miserably in a Corporate Refugee camp, mystified about what to do next.

Then I thought about all the people who hadn't left—those who were still there grappling with challenges, fighting frustration, and wishing they could leave. What if they had coaches to listen and serve as thinking partners? What if they could be fulfilled without having to leave?

Like the proverbial light bulb turning on, I got a picture of how I might provide meaningful service in an environment that I understood from the inside out. The part of me that had always wanted to save the world saw a way to throw a lifeline to at least a few people. I signed up on the spot for the coaching course they offered.

The course was pivotal in providing a name and a system for the way I had intuitively interacted with people all my life. Equally important was the introduction to a woman who became my role model, colleague, and friend. Now my new road had a sketchy map, and I liked it.

At the end of the course I hung out my shingle, so to speak. I had a name for my work and a systematic way to help others. I started telling people that I was a coach, open for business. Three of my neighbors put their hands up to become my first clients. Looking back now, I should have given them all a refund! But I learned from them, and they seemed to get value from our time together.

Through the early phase of my new business, I was drawn to conversations with other consultants who were creating companies to bring training and development services to organizations. I joined several budding consulting practices and left after months of struggling to define the business and actually sell coaching services. I felt as though I was attending endless meetings with idealists who liked to design models but lacked the practical business skills to attract clients. Part of my challenge was not being clear about what I had to offer, and this wasn't the right place to find out.

I felt a pull to stay at home in my slippers and work exclusively by phone. After years of dressing up and being on the road I was really enjoying being a homebody. The telephone-based coaching model I was taught was highly influential in my picture of what my life could be like after the corporate rat race.

Even though I had negotiated a gradually diminishing payout over three years that minimized the impact of my salary loss, I wanted to start earning money again. I started recording any new income on my calendar to begin building confidence that I could earn a living in a new way.

What emerged from this period were a few simple rules for my new life:

1. I will only do work I love.
2. I will only work with people I love spending time with.
3. I will not report to anyone again.
4. I will not have anyone reporting to me again.

After about six months working as a coach, I broke my own third rule to join my mentor in creating a new coaching services company. We had planned to write a book together but then changed our minds when she was offered the opportunity to create a company that would broker coaches for firms who wanted to hire teams of coaches. The opportunity was engaging to me, and I loved the process of defining a system for bringing groups of coaches into companies.

The glory faded when my mentor moved on to fulfill her dreams elsewhere, and I was left on my own to implement our plan. Without a thinking partner to build and plan with, the work became increasingly less attractive. I began to feel as though I was in a corporation again, breaking my third rule. I was suffocating. The time came when it felt as though I had simply traded situations rather than creating something new. I resigned my position in the coaching company and once again faced the unknown. The difference this time was that I knew I'd found the kind of work that was deeply satisfying.

Back to coaching on my own, the next milestone was to take seriously the name and nature of the company I had registered when I started coaching: Full Spectrum Coaching. It captured my desire to provide solutions through coaching for people in every aspect of life. Stepping into that mental space of business owner, I felt both excited and vulnerable at the same time. I had set myself free only a short time ago, and was facing a landscape of uncharted territory that beckoned me to explore.

The transition from my unquestioned former career path to my new road less travelled felt complete at about the three-year mark. I realized I was no longer anxious about where my income would come from. I had replaced my executive salary and begun to dream about creating more than a solo practice. I wanted to build a business that had a broader impact than I could create on my own. My transition was complete. I began to trust that my new life was real.

Wright

What aspect of your present work gives you the greatest joy and satisfaction?

Conlinn

My greatest joy comes from the moment when I'm working with a person and I can literally see the light go on in his or her eyes or hear it on the phone. I know the person has had a new idea about a troubling or challenging situation. In the moment of enlightenment, I know I am making a contribution. When it happens in a group, the air is charged with possibility, and this energy electrifies me at the cellular level. The closest experience I can relate it to is being in church. Conversations about spirituality are becoming more common in the workplace. When coaches hear them, they help people find their pathway to deeper meaning in their lives.

I wish I could bottle the formula for encouraging those enlightened moments on a consistent basis. It is a strong motivator as I create new coaching processes. There is so much good work being done to assist people to access this place of higher knowing—of exceptional willingness to do things differently—and I am a perpetual student, learning anything I think might be valuable to my clients.

I find immense satisfaction when I imagine the best approach to use in a given situation, and it works. Recently a group of senior executives were so blocked in their communication they could hardly look at each other in a meeting. My instinct was to point that out in the moment. At first, I got big push-back, so I simply asked a few more questions and waited. Gradually, they began to talk about what wasn't working and how hard it was to continue pretending there were no blocks. I could see them thaw right before my eyes. It led to some excellent work by individuals on the executive team. This has changed the culture of an entire company for the better, and had a ripple effect on the many communities the company serves.

Wright

How do you define success?

Conlinn

That's the kind of coaching question I've collected in my Great Question Game. I know when I first started my career I could have answered that in a heartbeat: achievement, title, salary—the trappings that equal progress in the world of business as I learned them. Those things drove me for a long time until one day I realized they didn't fit for me.

Today my definition of success is the experience that I have in those moments when the light goes on in another person. Another way of describing it is that I'm "in the zone"—the zone of contribution where I know that what I'm doing at that moment is the absolute right thing for the situation and the person. My intention to serve and my willingness to be totally present to people or situations have helped them to realize a profound change of perspective. So my definition of success has turned itself "outside in"—from an external to an internal definition.

Wright

Sounds like the ideas in Robert Greenleaf's book *Servant Leadership*.

Conlinn

I feel a lot of alignment with the concept of servant leadership. When I researched our family name in Ireland, our motto is "I Govern by Serving." The people who have influenced me the most are the leaders who see their job as supporting others' success.

I remember working in a hospital where the CEO spent time walking around talking to people in all kinds of jobs, looking for ways to connect them with their passion for helping others, then taking steps to make it happen. I appreciated him even more after he moved on to a bigger hospital, and was replaced by an old-fashioned authoritarian leader. I noticed how much my own and my colleagues' morale slumped. Shortly after that, I burned out on the job.

Wright

It sounds as though you are a lifelong learner. Tell me how your life experiences have impacted your current work.

Conlinn

There are many ways my life has shaped my work. As we grow and experience life, there are critical events that we can point to and say "that was it!" The first one for me was when my father died. I was fourteen. I have been conscious of the sacredness of life since that day. Without really knowing it, that life experience drove me to look for ways to contribute and instilled within me a sense that life is short.

I felt a huge relief in my own life when I passed the age he was when he died. He was forty-five, so on my forty-fifth birthday there was a place in me that seemed to relax. "Relax" isn't quite the right word, actually it was more like, "Get busy doing whatever is most important for you to do." Every year before that was preparation, and every year since has been a conscious gift and obligation to make a difference while I can.

Wright

Oddly enough, I know how that feels. My grandfather, my father, and my brother all died at fifty, and when I passed it I did the same thing you did.

Conlinn

Yes, the vantage point of a critical life event like a parent's early death is a whole new perspective from which to view the road ahead.

Wright

So who have been the greatest influences in your life?

Conlinn

The strongest influences are my intimate relationships—initially with my mother and sisters, and then with my husband and children. These are the lenses through which I see the world.

My mother is my mentor; our relationship is my rock. Her deep faith in God guides her, and I get the benefit of that in every conversation. We are confidantes in each other, and it gives me so much pleasure to see her enjoying her life at eighty-seven with the wonder of a child. Her advice always makes me think more deeply about big decisions, and I know her voice is in my head, even when she's not in the room.

My sisters are the people I can count on no matter what. They "get" me at an emotional level, which means I can't hide. They call on me to be real when I get off-track from my authentic self. They are also there to laugh and cry at life's critical moments. Their love has given me the road map for creating successful business partnerships with both women and men. I can't imagine working in isolation anymore. I've tried it, and it's difficult and lonely. With partners it feels easy, joyful, and creative. I thank them for that.

My husband is my teacher. We know we are meant to be together, and at times that's hard to remember. From him I have learned compassion for myself and others. We are very different in our fundamental make-up, so it stretches me to listen for common ground, to hear beyond my instincts, and to see the world from an entirely different perspective. After thirty-seven years together, my marriage is the accomplishment I am most proud of.

My children inspire me by the way they follow their dreams. My daughter is a jazz singer and my son a chef. Both have pursued creative interests of mine that I never believed I could make a living at. They are showing me how to do it. My daughter is still in school, yet making money in her chosen field, being both creative and energized by it. My son has come into his own through pursuing his passion as a chef, serving others by creating beautiful and healthy food.

Beyond that, my children are so much more competent at building relationships than I was at their age. Seeing how they are with their friends and partners gives me hope that their generation will be able to create a different and better world, where respect for others is strong, and clear communication is the currency.

Wright

How does your work impact the rest of your life?

Conlinn

I don't know where to begin to answer this one. My most vivid story of how coaching has infiltrated my life is the first time my son coached me. I was rushing home to a meeting, and was late. I called my son to see if he was home, and he was at his friend's. When I asked if he would bail me out by getting home first to unlock the door, his response was, "Okay, I can do it this time, Mom. What would it take for this to never happen again?" What a great coaching question! That gives you an insight into how it goes in my household. This kind of communication makes for much clearer conversations, with a new level of connection from the traditional parent/child roles I grew up with. What I notice is that as I listen to my daughter singing or enjoy a meal that my son has prepared, they are teaching me that pursuing creative interests can be fulfilling for their whole lives.

How does that relate to my work? I know from personal experience what it takes to create a fulfilling life and therefore I recognize it in others. When I'm working with my clients, they also teach me. I marvel at people who are very successful in their work and at the same time are dealing with challenging family or life issues. When I am present for them while they work through their issues, I learn from them and I can apply these lessons to my own life. I then share my learning with other clients. It's a full circle of contribution.

Wright

It's been said that at the end of life, those who look back at the rewards see them as much greater based on the hills they had to climb. What obstacles have you had to overcome?

Conlinn

One of the huge obstacles was cancer. This month, I have four people in my inner circle who are dying of cancer, and my father died of cancer. When I was diagnosed with cancer five years ago, I dismissed the first message as something that happens to other people. My subsequent journey was to completely embrace the opportunity to look my fear of dying in the face. Fortunately, the diagnosis was made very early and I sought out all the traditional and nontraditional methods I could find.

A wonderful counselor at Inspire Health, the centre for integrated healing that I attended immediately after the diagnosis, helped me immensely. I sat in the back row of the orientation meeting thinking, "This has nothing to do with me." Finally I put up my hand and asked, "What can I do about the word 'cancer'? The minute I tell people I have that diagnosis, they freeze. It's such a loaded word, can't we think of another name for it?"

He agreed with me, and shared that the only thing he could think of was to drop the "c" and call it "ancer" or "answer." As a new coach, it appealed to me, and I framed it for myself this way: "If 'c' is the answer, what's my question?" The closest question that seemed to fit was something about, "What are you waiting for?" meaning, "What are the things you really want to do and what will it take to get on with it and do more?" It was the beginning of a whole new phase of my life.

I was offered a faculty position at Royal Roads University on the day I received my cancer diagnosis. I thought, "The answer for me is to start contributing in the way that I really want to." I actually postponed my cancer surgery so I could teach my first Executive Coaching course. That decision was made during an evening walk with my dog when I came to terms with my fear of going against the medical plan.

My doctor looked at me as though I was crazy when I asked to postpone the surgery. She reminded me that most people came to her office begging for earlier treatment. Based on my research, I knew my cancer was slow-growing and not invasive, so my rational mind decided quite quickly. My self-doubt caught up with me that night on the walk with my dog. What I realized was that deciding against the advice of the medical professionals was like saying no to my dad when I was a child. As I walked, it became clear that if I had the earlier surgery I would be agreeing out of fear, and that this was a moment to trust rather than second-guess myself.

With that decision, I moved much more into the public eye through the Royal Roads position, using my Excelerator Coaching System™ as the core curriculum for the graduate level program. The System is based on the best thinking about coaching that exists at this time. I designed the learning process to engage learners through their own experiences. The outcome is that individuals, mangers, and leaders—students of the system—develop their own unique brand of coaching. They do it within a comprehensive framework that offers structure for learning and flexible interpretation to meet the needs of each person they coach.

Teaching in the program at Royal Roads has been the source of much new and deeply fulfilling work. Looking back, I can see that consciously focusing on teaching rather than cancer was the beginning of a whole new phase of creativity and contribution. Both the Excelerator Coaching System and the Great Question Coaching Game came out of that experience. I also know that making peace with my fear of dying allowed me to do what it took to be free and clear of cancer today.

Wright

What keeps your energy and enthusiasm charged today?

Conlinn

The four cornerstones for me are: spirituality, creative expression, health, and community.

My source of energy is rooted in my spiritual life, which has taken many forms since my early religious training. My most recent connection has come through a series of silent retreats that serve to help me delve deeply into my core beliefs. These are supported by a community of spiritual companions. My spiritual life has allowed me to pay attention to what really makes me happy and to follow my own rules while recognizing God's guidance.

The most important rule for my creative expression has been to do only what I love, which is still my touchstone for any work that I do or any project that I take on. A few years ago, I created a company called the Heart and Soul Millionaires with my mother and sisters. The most tangible result is the Great Question Game, which is selling all over the world. It teaches people to use coaching questions to resolve all kinds of issues at work and in their personal lives. The intangible results for my family are even stronger—we have a way to support each other in our adult lives that integrates coaching each other with our love and caring.

My creativity rule resulted in new adventures such as singing, which I hadn't done for many years. I had been too busy with work, travel, and family to fit in any recreational activities—an excuse that lasted twenty years! When a friend introduced me to the Lions Gate Chorus, I rediscovered music and a lot more. I found my "inner diva," who not only liked to perform, but also to compete. We recently ranked third in an international competition. The bonus is the feeling every week that my cells are being enlivened by the joy of singing and the rejuvenating experience of immersing myself in the sound that is created with one hundred other women.

Of course, taking care of my health is a fundamental source of energy. I have completed three mini-triathlons as part of my recovery program. Since I'm not naturally drawn to physical exertion, I had to trick myself into regular exercise by preparing for competitions. The triathlon is a great sport for me because I don't have to be exceptional at any one element and can keep myself from routine by changing activities during the week.

My early academic training was in nutrition, so I'm always adjusting my eating to keep up with my aging body. How readily it wants to behave like a hibernating bear, hanging onto extra layers in case there is no more food to be found! I'm adjusting to the idea of forming lifestyle habits that will serve me for a long time. I'm still not there, but it has begun.

Living in an intentional community is another source of energy. I love to be with people, and enjoyed numerous shared houses during my youth and early marriage. For the past twelve years, my family has lived in a cohousing community called WindSong, where we each have our own homes, but agree to create a shared living experience. We developed the $6 million structure using consensus decision-making. We still operate the business of the community using that principle. More importantly, I have learned from my neighbors how to be more courageous. I left my corporate career and started my own business after moving into WindSong.

Wright

Most successful people who open a business look around, see a need, and then try to fill it. What was the need you saw when you created your coaching program?

Conlinn

As I got into coaching, I realized the profound power of it. What I saw as missing was coaching in business that would engage the whole person. I saw plenty of coaching for specific kinds of applications like sales, or coaching for strategic planning. Alternatively, there was life coaching, which often misses the business context. What I didn't see was a blend of those two approaches that would serve people where they spend most of their waking hours, and that is at work.

To me, there is a big difference between a consultant who has the skills and knowledge to function in a business setting, and a coach who understands the playing field yet doesn't get enmeshed in it. So the effective business coaches I work with are able to get to the inner motivation, where clients can make the changes that they need to and shift their patterns of thinking and behaving. In business there are many factors we have no control over, yet the one place we have plenty of control is how we are.

All of those subtle distinctions make Excelerator executive coaches different from people who have gone to a business school, which I did, without appreciating the whole person they are working with. Executive coaching takes that understanding of the person in the business to a whole new level. It enables profound change, new perspectives, and the courage to become different.

In creating Excelerator Coaching™, I wanted to teach others to do what my partners and I do so our impact can expand beyond ourselves. We do this through licensing others to deliver our programs, and of course, by working directly inside companies that want to have far-reaching results through establishing a coaching culture.

With my partners at Essential Impact, we are expanding our scope of services to include a coach approach to leadership development. In addition to serving our clients, we support each other to fulfill our highest forms of contribution.

Wright

What is the most important message that you want others to hear?

Conlinn

I would love people to connect with their inner source of power and know that every day of their lives they are contributing. Each of us is building our legacy, whether we're aware of it or not. How much more powerful it is to live the legacy we want to leave!

Wright

What practical tips do you have for others who are on their own journey?

Conlinn

The principles that have made the biggest difference for me are the three principles of my Excelerator Coaching System™: Enlighten, Empower, and Excel. These principles reflect stages of the coaching process, so clients can experience corresponding progress through "I see," "I can," and "I will." These phases mirror my own journey. Perhaps they can be helpful to others.

The Enlighten Stage leads to clarity. Know when it's time to make a change and do it. Pay attention to the signals in your mind and body and spirit that add up to "it's time to change." For me it took several years before that moment of truth. I knew something was changing, I just didn't know initially what, when, or how.

Trust yourself. When the fragments of your truth align, trust them. The moment of truth has a clarity and an urgency to it that many people translate into immediate action. That works for some. It can be equally effective to wait for right timing for action and to be thoughtful about it. Treat yourself gently in the midst of change. Having a coach as a thinking partner can make all the difference between painful and successful transitions.

The Empower Stage takes courage. Take time to reflect and let your new direction emerge. Expect a settling period. This is the richness and possibility of transition. There's a settling that's needed to complete the letting go of the old (whatever that is). You may not even know what you need to let go until it surfaces. Ask yourself, "How can silence, stillness, and slowness be productive?" This is exactly where the kernels of the next stage are born.

Find your own rhythm. Connect with your family, friends, and community then let yourself be carried by the rhythm of those relationships. Eventually you will find your own rhythm and rediscover your definition of balance. How much activity and how much public versus private time do you need in your new life?

Discover your renewable energy resources. What kind of exercise or body movement nourishes you? What have you forgotten that you enjoy? And what is essential to your wellbeing? Once you know these answers, you are ready to move forward.

Then, ask for support from family, friends, and trusted thinking partners. If you are like me, this can be the hardest part. If you have been a loner like I was, and have bought in to the idea that in order to be successful you have to do it on your own, it is like learning something completely new. Asking can be awkward, so first discover what you need to ask for. Is it as simple as a hug when you are feeling lost? Can you be vulnerable enough to say you don't know what to do? Could you be open enough to listen to what you hear? Consider finding a coach who can hold the thread of change through your ups and downs.

The Excelling Stage fosters creativity. Be conscious of the legacy you're living. This means consciously choosing the way you make a positive difference in the world. I believe this requires a significant amount of humility, which we're not accustomed to in our culture. The notion of seeing our own brilliance and living from it seems like heresy. Yet I believe that creating a conscious legacy is both our birthright and our calling.

For some people, their legacy is crystal clear from the beginning and they retain their passion for it until the day they die. For others it is an evolving awareness based on trial and error. It is strengthened by exploring new avenues of service and noticing the power of the impact they have. Sometimes the impact is overpowering or overwhelming and it causes retreat.

I retreated from my legacy more than once thinking, "I'm not up to this, I can't do this—someone else can do it better." Fundamentally, I was asking, "Who do I think I am?" And while I know the words of Marianne Williamson in *A Return to Love*—"Who am I not to be brilliant, gorgeous, talented, fabulous?"—it is easy to say and much harder to live.

Wright

How do you see your next phase of contribution?

Conlinn

Part of my contribution includes what we're doing today, and that is becoming more public—publishing a book. Being part of this book will take me to more writing, more speaking, and wider audiences. Finding the exact vehicle to make that possible is the next inquiry for me.

Wright

You've talked about legacy. What is the legacy that you're most proud of?

Conlinn

My legacy is on two levels. The first is the very personal level: my children. They are the physical and authentic legacy I've contributed to the world, and they bring me great joy.

The second legacy is at the level of contribution with and through others. When I first published the Great Question Game™, my reaction was to retreat into a feeling of hopelessness or futility. I felt vulnerable having a product that others could evaluate. I momentarily lost the original vision of making this kind of communication accessible to everyone until I recognized the shape of vulnerability in me. As soon as I saw it, the feeling didn't have the same power. Now I am an observer of the legacy I am living in order to honor it without attaching artificial or over-inflated meaning to it. The effect of this observer in me is a deep knowing that what I do matters. From this place it's easy to support others to do the same.

I hear the word "transformation" every time I introduce people to the Excelerator System™. It used to surprise me and now it encourages me to continually evolve the system as I learn from learners. Others who teach it have added greatly to its richness as well. Not only my fellow faculty, but those who are licensed facilitators have added their own insights that embellish and enrich the curriculum far beyond what it was at the beginning.

Every graduate of the Royal Roads Executive Coaching Program embodies a part of my vision. When they make their own contribution, it's a huge source of satisfaction for me. Every time I sit in the closing circle at Royal Roads University and look around and see the brilliance, wisdom, and energy in the faces of those forty individuals, I'm happy right in that moment. I know what my legacy is because I can see it in them.

The same thing happens when I go into companies and sit with a group of leaders to teach them how a coach approach to business can enhance their contribution as leaders. When I see them grab this new way of being, then begin to make it their own, "fulfillment" is probably the word that best describes my experience. I am exhilarated in that moment, and it continues to resonate with me long afterward.

Wright

I appreciate the time you've spent with me today, Carollyne, to answer all these questions. I really appreciate your participation in this book project.

Conlinn

Thank you so much, David. What this process has allowed me to do is move my home into a new country. When I think about the refugee metaphor that I used at the beginning of this chapter, I left that familiar country of the company I'd grown up in and moved into the zone of the unknown. Where I find myself now, and what you've allowed me to express, is this new Country of Contribution. This country is borderless, filled with possibility, rich with fulfillment and connection, and ripe with the potential to leverage my life experience in service. This is the new country, this is my new home, and it's a joy to share it with you and our readers. I appreciate the opportunity to have this conversation.

Wright

It's been a pleasure sharing your unique perspective, Carollyne.

Today we've been talking with Carollyne Conlinn, an international executive coach. Facilitating her coaching are her thirty years of experience with a multinational industry-leading corporation, ten of those years at the executive level. She has devoted her professional life to helping others find what is worthwhile in their lives and guiding them to their place of positive contribution to the planet.

Carollyne, thank you so much for being with us today on *Roadmap to Success*.

Conlinn

My pleasure, David.

ABOUT THE AUTHOR

CAROLLYNE CONLINN is the 2009 recipient of the Canadian Coach of the Year Award. She is an international executive coach who integrates entrepreneurial leadership with thirty years of Fortune 500 corporate experience. She has developed programs that create profound change in individuals and organizations. Her Excelerator Coaching System™ has become the core curriculum for the Graduate Executive Coaching Program at Royal Roads University. Her Great Question Game,™ which introduces groups to coaching, has been very popular with managers and business leaders. In 2009,  Carollyne and her partners launched Essential Impact Coaching Inc. to bring systems for coaching cultures into organizations. Her commitment to her husband and her two children inspired her family to help create Canada's first co-housing community. Carollyne's infectious enthusiasm draws on a deep spiritual spring that supported her recovery from cancer and continues to bless her life today.

Carollyne Conlinn

#26 20543 96th Avenue
Langley, B.C.
604.882.9986
carollyne.conlinn@fullspectrumcoaching.com
www.exceleratorcoaching.com
www.greatquestiongame.com

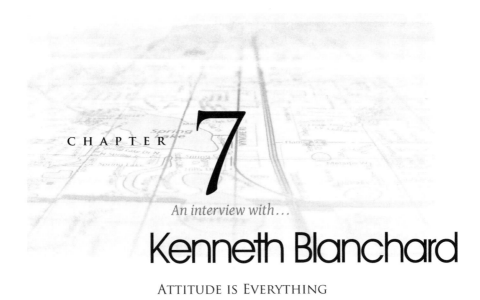

7

An interview with…

Kenneth Blanchard

ATTITUDE IS EVERYTHING

David Wright (Wright)

Few people have created a positive impact on the day-to-day management of people and companies more than Dr. Kenneth Blanchard. He is known around the world simply as Ken, a prominent, gregarious, sought-after author, speaker, and business consultant. Ken is universally characterized by friends, colleagues, and clients as one of the most insightful, powerful, and compassionate men in business today. Ken's impact as a writer is far-reaching. His phenomenal best-selling book, *The One Minute Manager*, coauthored with Spencer Johnson, has sold more than thirteen million copies worldwide and has been translated into more than twenty-five languages. Ken is Chairman and "Chief Spiritual Officer" of the Ken Blanchard Companies. The organization's focus is to energize organizations around the world with customized training in bottom-line business strategies based on the simple, yet powerful principles inspired by Ken's best-selling books.

Dr. Blanchard, welcome to *Roadmap to Success*.

Dr. Ken Blanchard (Blanchard)

Well, it's nice to talk with you, David. It's good to be here.

Wright

I must tell you that preparing for your interview took quite a bit more time than usual. The scope of your life's work and your business, the Ken Blanchard Companies, would make for a dozen fascinating interviews.

Before we dive into the specifics of some of your projects and strategies, will you give our readers a brief synopsis of your life—how you came to be the Ken Blanchard we all know and respect?

Blanchard

Well, I'll tell you, David, I think life is what you do when you are planning on doing something else. I think that was John Lennon's line. I never intended to do what I have been doing. In fact, all my professors in college told me that I couldn't write. I wanted to do college work, which I did, and they said, "You had better be an administrator." So I decided I was going to be a Dean of Students. I got provisionally accepted into my master's degree program and then provisionally accepted at Cornell because I never could take any of those standardized tests.

I took the college boards four times and finally got 502 in English. I don't have a test-taking mind. I ended up in a university in Athens, Ohio, in 1966 as an Administrative Assistant to the Dean of the Business School. When I got there he said, "Ken, I want you to teach a course. I want all my deans to teach." I had never thought about teaching because they said I couldn't write, and teachers had to publish. He put me in the manager's department.

I've taken enough bad courses in my day and I wasn't going to teach one. I really prepared and had a wonderful time with the students. I was chosen as one of the top ten teachers on the campus coming out of the chute!

I just had a marvelous time. A colleague by the name of Paul Hersey was chairman of the Management Department. He wasn't very friendly to me initially because the Dean had led me to his department, but I heard he was a great teacher. He taught Organizational Behavior and Leadership. So I said, "Can I sit in on your course next semester?"

"Nobody audits my courses," he said. "If you want to take it for credit, you're welcome."

I couldn't believe it. I had a doctoral degree and he wanted me to take his course for credit—so I signed up.

The registrar didn't know what to do with me because I already had a doctorate, but I wrote the papers and took the course, and it was great.

In June 1967, Hersey came into my office and said, "Ken, I've been teaching in this field for ten years. I think I'm better than anybody, but I can't write. I'm a nervous wreck, and I'd love to write a textbook with somebody. Would you write one with me?"

I said, "We ought to be a great team. You can't write and I'm not supposed to be able to, so let's do it!"

Thus began this great career of writing and teaching. We wrote a textbook called *Management of Organizational Behavior: Utilizing Human Resources*. It came out in its eighth edition October 3, 2000, and the ninth edition was published September 3, 2007. It has sold more than any other textbook in that area over the years. It's been over forty years since that book first came out.

I quit my administrative job, became a professor, and ended up working my way up the ranks. I got a sabbatical leave and went to California for one year twenty-five years ago. I ended up meeting Spencer Johnson at a cocktail party. He wrote children's books—a wonderful series called *Value Tales*® *for Kids*. He also wrote *The Value of Courage: The Story of Jackie Robinson* and *The Value of Believing In Yourself: The Story of Louis Pasteur*.

My wife, Margie, met him first and said, "You guys ought to write a children's book for managers because they won't read anything else." That was my introduction to Spencer. So, *The One Minute Manager* was really a kid's book for big people. That is a long way from saying that my career was well planned.

Wright

Ken, what and/or who were your early influences in the areas of business, leadership, and success? In other words, who shaped you in your early years?

Blanchard

My father had a great impact on me. He was retired as an admiral in the Navy and had a wonderful philosophy. I remember when I was elected as president of the seventh grade, and I came home all pumped up. My father said, "Son, it's great that you're the president of the seventh grade, but now that you have that leadership position, don't ever use it." He said, "Great leaders are followed because people respect them and like them, not because they have power." That was a wonderful lesson for me early on. He was just a great model for me. I got a lot from him.

Then I had this wonderful opportunity in the mid-1980s to write a book with Norman Vincent Peale. He wrote *The Power of Positive Thinking*. I met him when he was eighty-six years old; we were asked to write a book on ethics together, *The Power of Ethical Management: Integrity Pays, You Don't Have to Cheat to Win*. It didn't matter what we were writing together; I learned so much from him. He just built from the positive things I learned from my mother.

My mother said that when I was born I laughed before I cried, I danced before I walked, and I smiled before I frowned. So that, as well as Norman Vincent Peale, really impacted me as I focused on what I could do to train leaders. How do you make them positive? How do you make them realize that it's not about them, it's about who they are serving? It's not about their position—it's about what they can do to help other people win.

So, I'd say my mother and father, then Norman Vincent Peale. All had a tremendous impact on me.

Wright

I can imagine. I read a summary of your undergraduate and graduate degrees. I assumed you studied Business Administration, marketing management, and related courses. Instead, at Cornell you studied Government and Philosophy. You received your master's from Colgate in Sociology and Counseling and your PhD from Cornell in Educational Administration and Leadership. Why did you choose this course of study? How has it affected your writing and consulting?

Blanchard

Well, again, it wasn't really well planned out. I originally went to Colgate to get a master's degree in Education because I was going to be a Dean of Students over men. I had been a Government major, and I was a Government major because it was the best department at Cornell in the Liberal Arts School. It was exciting. We would study what the people were doing at the league of governments. And then, the Philosophy Department was great. I just loved the philosophical arguments. I wasn't a great student in terms of getting grades, but I'm a total learner. I would sit there and listen, and I would really soak it in.

When I went over to Colgate and got into the education courses, they were awful. They were boring. The second week, I was sitting at the bar at the Colgate Inn saying, "I can't believe I've been here two years for this." This is just the way the Lord works: Sitting next to me in the bar was a young sociology professor who had just gotten his PhD at Illinois. He was staying at the Inn. I was moaning and groaning about what I was doing, and he said, "Why don't you come and major with me in sociology? It's really exciting."

"I can do that?" I asked.

He said, "Yes."

I knew they would probably let me do whatever I wanted the first week. Suddenly, I switched out of Education and went with Warren Ramshaw. He had a tremendous impact on me. He retired some years ago as the leading professor at Colgate in the Arts and Sciences, and got me interested in leadership and organizations. That's why I got a master's in Sociology.

The reason I went into educational administration and leadership? It was a doctoral program I could get into because I knew the guy heading up the program. He said, "The greatest thing about Cornell is that you will be in the School of Education. It's not very big, so you don't have to take many education courses, and you can take stuff all over the place."

There was a marvelous man by the name of Don McCarty who eventually became the Dean of the School of Education, Wisconsin. He had an impact on my life; but I was always just searching around.

My mission statement is: to be a loving teacher and example of simple truths that help myself and others to awaken the presence of God in our lives. The reason I mention "God" is that I believe the biggest addiction in the world is the human ego; but I'm really into simple truth. I used to tell people I was trying to get the B.S. out of the behavioral sciences.

Wright

I can't help but think, when you mentioned your father, that he just bottom-lined it for you about leadership.

Blanchard

Yes.

Wright

A man named Paul Myers, in Texas, years and years ago when I went to a conference down there, said, "David, if you think you're a leader and you look around, and no one is following you, you're just out for a walk."

Blanchard

Well, you'd get a kick out of this—I'm just reaching over to pick up a picture of Paul Myers on my desk. He's a good friend, and he's a part of our Center for FaithWalk Leadership where we're trying to challenge and equip people to lead like Jesus. It's non-profit. I tell people I'm not an evangelist because we've got enough trouble with the Christians we have. We don't need any more new ones. But, this is a picture of Paul on top of a mountain. Then there's another picture below that of him under the sea with stingrays. It says, "Attitude is everything. Whether you're on the top of the mountain or the bottom of the sea, true happiness is achieved by accepting God's promises, and by having a biblically positive frame of mind. Your attitude is everything." Isn't that something?

Wright

He's a fine, fine man. He helped me tremendously. In keeping with the theme of our book, *Roadmap for Success,* I wanted to get a sense from you about your own success journey. Many people know you best from *The One Minute Manager* books you coauthored with Spencer Johnson. Would you consider these books as a high water mark for you or have you defined success for yourself in different terms?

Blanchard

Well, you know, *The One Minute Manager* was an absurdly successful book so quickly that I found I couldn't take credit for it. That was when I really got on my own spiritual journey and started to try to find out what the real meaning of life and success was.

That's been a wonderful journey for me because I think, David, the problem with most people is they think their self-worth is a function of their performance plus the opinion of others. The minute you think that is what your self-worth is, every day your self-worth is up for grabs because your performance is going to fluctuate on a day-to-day basis. People are fickle. Their opinions are going to go up and down. You need to ground your self-worth in the unconditional love that God has ready for us, and that really grew out of the unbelievable success of *The One Minute Manager*.

When I started to realize where all that came from, that's how I got involved in this ministry that I mentioned. Paul Myers is a part of it. As I started to read the Bible, I realized that everything I've ever written about, or taught, Jesus did. You know, He did it with the twelve incompetent guys He "hired." The only guy with much education was Judas, and he was His only turnover problem.

Wright

Right.

Blanchard

This is a really interesting thing. What I see in people is not only do they think their self-worth is a function of their performance plus the opinion of others, but they measure their success on the amount of accumulation of wealth, on recognition, power, and status. I think those are nice success items. There's nothing wrong with those, as long as you don't define your life by that.

What I think you need to focus on rather than success is what Bob Buford, in his book *Halftime,* calls "significance"—moving from success to significance. I think the opposite of accumulation of wealth is generosity.

I wrote a book called *The Generosity Factor* with Truett Cathy, who is the founder of Chick-fil-A. He is one of the most generous men I've ever met in my life. I thought we needed to have a model of generosity. It's not only your *treasure,* but it's your *time* and *talent.* Truett and I added *touch* as a fourth one.

The opposite of recognition is service. I think you become an adult when you realize you're here to serve rather than to be served.

Finally, the opposite of power and status is loving relationships. Take Mother Teresa as an example—she couldn't have cared less about recognition, power, and status because she was focused on generosity, service, and loving relationships; but she got all of that earthly stuff. If you focus on the earthly, such as money, recognition, and power, you're never going to get to significance. But if you focus on significance, you'll be amazed at how much success can come your way.

Wright

I spoke with Truett Cathy recently and was impressed by what a down-to-earth, good man he seems to be. When you start talking about him closing his restaurants on

Sunday, all of my friends—when they found out I had talked to him—said, "Boy, he must be a great Christian man, but he's rich." I told them, "Well, to put his faith into perspective, by closing on Sunday it costs him $500 million a year."

He lives his faith, doesn't he?

Blanchard

Absolutely, but he still outsells everybody else.

Wright

That's right.

Blanchard

According to their January 25, 2007, press release, Chick-fil-A was the nation's second-largest quick-service chicken restaurant chain in sales at that time. Its business performance marks the thirty-ninth consecutive year the chain has enjoyed a system-wide sales gain—a streak the company has sustained since opening its first chain restaurant in 1967.

Wright

The simplest market scheme, I told him, tripped me up. I walked by his first Chick-fil-A I had ever seen, and some girl came out with chicken stuck on toothpicks and handed me one; I just grabbed it and ate it; it's history from there on.

Blanchard

Yes, I think so. It's really special. It is so important that people understand generosity, service, and loving relationships because too many people are running around like a bunch of peacocks. You even see pastors who measure their success by how many are in their congregation; authors by how many books they have sold; businesspeople by what their profit margin is—how good sales are. The reality is, that's all well and good, but I think what you need to focus on is the other. I think if business did that more and we got Wall Street off our backs with all the short-term evaluation, we'd be a lot better off.

Wright

Absolutely. There seems to be a clear theme that winds through many of your books that has to do with success in business and organizations—how people are treated by management and how they feel about their value to a company. Is this an accurate observation? If so, can you elaborate on it?

Blanchard

Yes, it's a very accurate observation. See, I think the profit is the applause you get for taking care of your customers and creating a motivating environment for your people. Very often people think that business is only about the bottom line. But no, that happens to be the result of creating raving fan customers, which I've described with Sheldon Bowles in our book, *Raving Fans*. Customers want to brag about you, if you create an environment where people can be gung-ho and committed. You've got to take care of your customers and your people, and then your cash register is going to go ka-ching, and you can make some big bucks.

Wright

I noticed that your professional title with the Ken Blanchard Companies is somewhat unique—"Chairman and Chief Spiritual Officer." What does your title mean to you personally and to your company? How does it affect the books you choose to write?

Blanchard

I remember having lunch with Max DuPree one time. The legendary Chairman of Herman Miller, Max wrote a wonderful book called *Leadership Is an Art*.

"What's your job?" I asked him.

He said, "I basically work in the vision area."

"Well, what do you do?" I asked.

"I'm like a third-grade teacher," he replied. "I say our vision and values over, and over, and over again until people get it right, right, right."

I decided from that, I was going to become the Chief Spiritual Officer, which means I would be working in the vision, values, and energy part of our business. I ended up leaving a morning message every day for everybody in our company. We have twenty-eight international offices around the world.

I leave a voice mail every morning, and I do three things on that as Chief Spiritual Officer: One, people tell me who we need to pray for. Two, people tell me who we need to praise—our unsung heroes and people like that. And then three, I leave an inspirational morning message. I really am the cheerleader—the Energizer Bunny—in our company. I'm the reminder of why we're here and what we're trying to do.

We think that our business in the Ken Blanchard Companies is to help people lead at a higher level, and to help individuals and organizations. Our mission statement is to unleash the power and potential of people and organizations for the common good. So if we are going to do that, we've really got to believe in that.

I'm working on getting more Chief Spiritual Officers around the country. I think it's a great title and we should get more of them.

Wright

So those people for whom you pray, where do you get the names?

Blanchard

The people in the company tell me who needs help, whether it's a spouse who is sick or kids who are sick or if they are worried about something. We've got over five years of data about the power of prayer, which is pretty important.

One morning, my inspirational message was about my wife and five members of our company who walked sixty miles one weekend—twenty miles a day for three days—to raise money for breast cancer research.

It was amazing. I went down and waved them all in as they came. They had a ceremony; they had raised $7.6 million. There were over three thousand people walking. A lot of the walkers were dressed in pink—they were cancer victors—people who had overcome it. There were even men walking with pictures of their wives who had died from breast cancer. I thought it was incredible.

There wasn't one mention about it in the major San Diego papers. I said, "Isn't that just something." We have to be an island of positive influence because all you see in the paper today is about celebrities and their bad behavior. Here you have all these thousands of people out there walking and trying to make a difference, and nobody thinks it's news.

So every morning I pump people up about what life's about, about what's going on. That's what my Chief Spiritual Officer job is about.

Wright

I had the pleasure of reading one of your releases, *The Leadership Pill*.

Blanchard

Yes.

Wright

I must admit that my first thought was how short the book was. I wondered if I was going to get my money's worth, which by the way, I most certainly did. Many of your books are brief and based on a fictitious story. Most business books in the market today are hundreds of pages in length and are read almost like a textbook.

Will you talk a little bit about why you write these short books, and about the premise of *The Leadership Pill?*

Blanchard

I really developed my relationship with Spencer Johnson when we wrote *The One Minute Manager.* As you know, he wrote, *Who Moved My Cheese,* which was a phenomenal success. He wrote children's books and is quite a storyteller.

Jesus taught by parables, which were short stories.

My favorite books are *Jonathan Livingston Seagull* and *The Little Prince.* Og Mandino, author of seventeen books, was the greatest of them all.

I started writing parables because people can get into the story and learn the contents of the story, and they don't bring their judgmental hats into reading. You write a regular book and they'll say, "Well, where did you get the research?" They get into that judgmental side. Our books get them emotionally involved and they learn.

The Leadership Pill is a fun story about a pharmaceutical company that thinks they have discovered the secret to leadership, and they can put the ingredients in a pill. When they announce it, the country goes crazy because everybody knows we need more effective leaders. When they release it, it outsells Viagra.

The founders of the company start selling off stock and they call them Pillionaires. But along comes this guy who calls himself "the effective manager," and he challenges them to a no-pill challenge. If they identify two non-performing groups, he'll take on one and let somebody on the pill take another one, and he guarantees he will outperform that person by the end of the year. They agree, but of course they give him a drug test every week to make sure he's not sneaking pills on the side.

I wrote the book with Marc Muchnick, who is a young guy in his early thirties. We did a major study of what this interesting "Y" generation—the young people of today— want from leaders, and this is a secret blend that this effective manager uses. When you think about it, David, it is really powerful in terms of what people want from a leader.

Number one, they want integrity. A lot of people have talked about that in the past, but these young people will walk if they see people say one thing and do another. A lot of us walk to the bathroom and out into the halls to talk about it. But these people will quit. They don't want somebody to say something and not do it.

The second thing they want is a partnership relationship. They hate superior/subordinate. I mean, what awful terms those are. You know, the "head" of the department and the hired "hands"—you don't even give them a head. "What do I do? I'm in supervision. I see things a lot clearer than these stupid idiots." They want to be treated as partners; if they can get a financial partnership, great. If they can't, they really want a minimum of a psychological partnership where they can bring their brains to work and make decisions.

Then finally, they want affirmation. They not only want to be caught doing things right, but they want to be affirmed for who they are. They want to be known as individual people, not as numbers.

So those are the three ingredients that this effective manager uses. They are wonderful values when you think about them.

Rank-order values for any organization is number one, integrity. In our company we call it ethics. It is our number one value. The number two value is partnership. In our company we call it relationships. Number three is affirmation—being affirmed as a human being. I think that ties into relationships, too. They are wonderful values that can drive behavior in a great way.

Wright

I believe most people in today's business culture would agree that success in business has everything to do with successful leadership. In *The Leadership Pill*, you present a simple but profound premise; that leadership is not something you do to people; it's something you do *with* them. At face value, that seems incredibly obvious. But you must have found in your research and observations that leaders in today's culture do not get this. Would you speak to that issue?

Blanchard

Yes. I think what often happens in this is the human ego. There are too many leaders out there who are self-serving. They're not leaders who have service in mind. They think the sheep are there for the benefit of the shepherd. All the power, money, fame, and recognition move up the hierarchy. They forget that the real action in business is not up the hierarchy—it's in the one-to-one, moment-to-moment interactions that your frontline people have with your customers. It's how the phone is answered. It's how problems are dealt with and those kinds of things. If you don't think that you're doing leadership *with* them—rather, you're doing it *to* them—after a while they won't take care of your customers.

I was at a store once (not Nordstrom's, where I normally would go) and I thought of something I had to share with my wife, Margie. I asked the guy behind the counter in Men's Wear, "May I use your phone?"

He said, "No!"

"You're kidding me," I said. "I can always use the phone at Nordstrom's."

"Look, buddy," he said, "they won't let *me* use the phone here. Why should I let you use the phone?"

That is an example of leadership that's done *to* employees, not *with* them. People want a partnership. People want to be involved in a way that really makes a difference.

Wright

Dr. Blanchard, the time has flown by and there are so many more questions I'd like to ask you. In closing, would you mind sharing with our readers some thoughts on success? If you were mentoring a small group of men and women, and one of their central goals was to become successful, what kind of advice would you give them?

Blanchard

Well, I would first of all say, "What are you focused on?" If you are focused on success as being, as I said earlier, accumulation of money, recognition, power, or status, I think you've got the wrong target. What you need to really be focused on is how you can be generous in the use of your time and your talent and your treasure and touch. How can you serve people rather than be served? How can you develop caring, loving relationships with people? My sense is if you will focus on those things, success in the traditional sense will come to you. But if you go out and say, "Man, I'm going to make a fortune, and I'm going to do this," and have that kind of attitude, you might get some of those numbers. I think you become an adult, however, when you realize you are here to give rather than to get. You're here to serve, not to be served. I would just say to people, "Life is such a very special occasion. Don't miss it by aiming at a target that bypasses other people, because we're really here to serve each other."

Wright

Well, what an enlightening conversation, Dr. Blanchard. I really want you to know how much I appreciate all the time you've taken with me for this interview. I know that our readers will learn from this, and I really appreciate your being with us today.

Blanchard

Well, thank you so much, David. I really enjoyed my time with you. You've asked some great questions that made me think, and I hope my answers are helpful to other people because as I say, life is a special occasion.

Wright

Today we have been talking with Dr. Ken Blanchard. He is coauthor of the phenomenal best-selling book, *The One Minute Manager*. The fact that he's the Chief Spiritual Officer of his company should make us all think about how we are leading our companies and leading our families and leading anything, whether it is in church or civic organizations. I know I will.

Thank you so much, Dr. Blanchard, for being with us today.

Blanchard

Good to be with you, David.

ABOUT THE AUTHOR

Few people have created more of a positive impact on the day-to-day management of people and companies than Dr. Kenneth Blanchard, who is known around the world simply as "Ken."

When Ken speaks, he speaks from the heart with warmth and humor. His unique gift is to speak to an audience and communicate with each individual as if they were alone and talking one-on-one. He is a polished storyteller with a knack for making the seemingly complex easy to understand.

Ken has been a guest on a number of national television programs, including Good Morning America and The Today Show. He has been featured in Time, People, U.S. News & World Report, and a host of other popular publications.

He earned his bachelor's degree in Government and Philosophy from Cornell University, his master's degree in Sociology and Counseling from Colgate University, and his PhD in Educational Administration and Leadership from Cornell University.

Dr. Ken Blanchard

The Ken Blanchard Companies
125 State Place
Escondido, California 92029
800.728.6000
Fax: 760.489.8407
www.kenblanchard.com

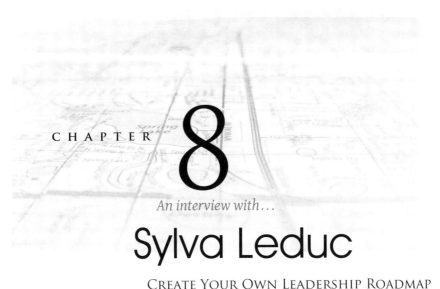

8

An interview with...

Sylva Leduc

CREATE YOUR OWN LEADERSHIP ROADMAP

David Wright (Wright)

Today, we're talking with Sylva Leduc, an executive coach, a leadership strategist, and one of the early pioneers of coaching. Sylva has been both an internal and an external coach since the early '90s. For many years she was with one of the "Big Five" Consulting Firms until the road warrior life completely lost its appeal and in 2000 she launched her own coaching and consulting company. Through her company, SageLeaders.com, Syl now coaches people around the world, from leaders in small businesses to executives in Fortune 100 companies. She also has a penchant for coaching leaders in non-profits. In 2007 she was honored with a prestigious PRISM Award from the International Coach Federation for successfully coaching the leadership team of a non-profit organization to surpass the stretch goals they had set for themselves.

Sylva, welcome to *Roadmap for Success.* Tell me, before we start, would you prefer that I call you Sylva or Syl?

Sylva Leduc (Leduc)

David, I am pleased that I was asked to be part of this series. And thanks for asking about my name, too. Either Sylva or Syl is fine, as long as you don't call me Sylvia (laughs). Sylva is a Norwegian name and there's no "i" in my name.

Wright

Thanks for clarifying. Your own path from psychology to consulting and coaching, then as the President of a software company, and now as a leadership strategist is very interesting and a little unusual. Would you tell our readers a bit about your own road map to success?

Leduc

Absolutely. Before I begin, I want to say that the road map is a powerful concept because of the visual impact it creates for people to take them from start to finish. Like many people, I have a plan; but my plan, again like most people, is not a direct route. The road map I laid out for myself had some unintended detours and, in fact, I had to create a new map when I ended up with my own company. I have an education in psychology, with a master's degree in Educational Psychology. I studied career development for adults and looked at how people make career decisions—what puts them on a path to success, how they choose their career, what makes them successful (or not), and what takes them on detours.

Here's my road map, complete with the detours I encountered: While studying at the University of Calgary in Alberta, I complemented my degrees with real world experience. While I was a full-time student, I also worked full-time.

Shortly after completing my master's degree, I co-authored a book called *Women's Work: Choice, Chance, or Socialization?* My co-writer and I investigated the impact of math and science on the career aspirations of young women. We interviewed experts in Canada and the United States. The book was written for psychologists and career development professionals, and is still used as a textbook by some colleges and universities. It was during those early years that I began honing my coaching skills when the consulting companies I worked for began to incorporate coaching as one of their service offerings.

I often say I have a "working MBA." I spent many years in the consulting field with one of the largest consulting organizations in the world, Ernst and Young. That's where I coached leaders as a change management expert, helping them to be successful in the overall implementation of programs and processes in their organizations.

Then in 2000, I said goodbye to the life of the road warrior, traded in my identity as a "Big Five Management Consultant" and became an accidental entrepreneur. While I was tired of living on the road, I didn't have a road map for this next stage of my career. After spending nearly three years on the road, I made a leap of faith and opened my own coaching and consulting company. While I work with people all over the world, the biggest difference between what I did as a road warrior and what I do now is that through using technology people do not have to travel to our location and we don't have to travel to their offices. We spend time with our clients on the phone, on webinars or videoconferencing or via the private online communities we create for them. The real beauty is that through the use of the technologies, people can work with us while being environmentally responsible. Long before being "green" was fashionable, we were environmentally conscious. We continue to promote sustainability because we know that learning can occur for leaders without their having to travel anywhere.

The next major detour that occurred was when my business partner and I bought a small software company. It was about two years after I launched my coaching and consulting company. The people we bought the company from had developed a great program for coaches to track successes with their clients. They approached us because they wanted to get out of the business. Since I've always enjoyed being a bit of a tech geek, I jumped at the chance, and we bought the company.

We hired programmers to review the software code, strip it down, and rebuild the program. Then we went through a whole rebranding process and it reemerged as Client Compass Software. I put an enormous amount of my own time, effort, and energy into the company and it became the most well-known software program in the coaching industry. A short three years later we were acquired by John Wiley & Sons, the international publishing house.

While it was, and is, a great program, what happened for me professionally was that I'd embarked on another detour. I became known as the President of a software company and not for my executive coaching expertise. I was way off course from my original plan for my coaching business. Leading the software company was also a distraction from my core business—coaching executives and their teams. It was as though I was the leader in two different companies.

What happened to me happens to many other people—they become distracted or unfocused when they have too many things going on. So that's a bit about my own circuitous road map.

Wright

I've spoken with other people about their views on coaching and consulting, and there seem to be many different opinions. You've been both an executive coach and a consultant for a long time, and I know you're also a faculty member of one of the foremost coaching schools, the College of Executive Coaching. You really are an expert in this field. What do you see as the greatest differences between coaching and consulting? Help our readers understand why it's important to know the difference between the two fields and the impact either can have on their success.

Leduc

It's true that I've been in coaching for a long time. I started in the early '90s. Here's something readers may find interesting: the first time I heard someone talk about coaching was when I lived in Canada. I met a woman named Nelly. Nelly said she had been a coach in New York and that she'd coached a lot of actors. She told me she had even been a coach to Christopher Reeve in the 1980s. When she mentioned Christopher Reeve ("Superman") naturally I was intrigued. As she told me more about how she coached people, I told her that was the kind of work I was doing with people too. Back then people called our work consulting or career counseling. After speaking with Nelly I started thinking about the differences and similarities between the two fields. Here is why it's important for the readers to know about the fields: so that they can educate themselves to ask questions to determine if a prospective coach is a good fit for them.

As I reflected about my own style, I knew it was not pure consulting, but it wasn't pure counseling, either. It was a blend. For me, coaching tapped into both psychology and business to help people recognize what was important for them, to discover where their strengths lay, how and why they were successful in business, what made them great leaders or when were they most challenged.

The easiest way to explain the difference is to think about three overlapping bell curves. In the middle is a bell curve that we'll label as coaching. On one side is another bell curve called consulting, and then on the other side is the one called counseling. Depending on whether someone is a pure counselor or a pure consultant or a pure coach will determine how much of an overlap there is between those three different bell curves.

For some people, if they are in the consulting world, they probably come from an expert model. Consultants are considered to be experts—they're subject matter experts, experts on processes, and experts how to do things.

The counseling side, which some people call therapy, is almost purely about asking questions remaining, non-judgmental and looking at the past. Coaching is a blend between the two realms. A coach asks a lot of insight-oriented questions, not from a therapeutic standpoint, but to have people look forward and to help them figure out what to do. And, sometimes a coach is also an expert who offers ideas and suggestions from his or her own experience or from the experience of other people.

According to the International Coach Federation (ICF), the largest governing body for coaches, their definition of coaching is,

"...partnering with people, to ask thought-provoking questions, and to be helpful in the creative process. To help people look at how to increase, improve, or enhance their performance to enhance the quality of their lives. Coaches are trained to listen at different levels, to observe, and to customize their approach to the individual client."

If someone has coach training through any of the many coaching schools that exist, then they are trained how to listen, how to listen for nuance, how to be aware of non-verbal communications, and impact on others. There are nearly two hundred different coach training schools with a variety of specialties. And in all the coaching schools, listening is a core competency.

The importance for readers to recognize is that if they are considering hiring a coach and the person they're interviewing says he or she is a coach, they need to ask if the "Coach" has some kind of coach training or background in coaching. What's happening in the coaching industry is that many consultants and therapists are entering the field and claiming they are coaches. If they have a background in consulting, they may revert to the expert model and not ask questions because they're so used to being in the telling mode. I'm not saying that there aren't consultants with well rounded coaching skills, there are many. Or, if they come from a therapy background and do not have coach training, then they may resort to a more therapeutic approach and delve too much into the past. What I think is most important is that the consumers of coaching know they need to educate themselves about coaching so they can make informed decisions about who they'll hire as a coach.

Wright

You've helped many people around the world to fine-tune their leadership skills. What is it about your background and experience that makes your coaching style unique and contributes to your clients' success?

Leduc

My coaching style is unique because in addition to having extensive experience as a both an internal and external coach, I also have specialized coach training and many years in consulting and education as a career counselor. I blended all my experience and education into what I call "Consultative Coaching." This allows me to wear a number of different hats when I'm working with people. For example, when I'm working with leaders I can let them know about best practices from the reading that I do or from the work that I've done with other leaders that helped those individuals be more successful. That's when I'm operating more on the consulting side of the bell curve. I also know when and how to ask the types of questions that help people dig deeper. What's also unique about my approach is the blend between coaching and consulting, coupled with my business experience as owner of a successful start-up software company. Of course, my Big Five experience consulting in large organizations is added to the mix. One more thing that makes my style unique is how I use different technologies and tools to help people get on track and reach their goals more rapidly. And, because each person's situation is unique, I custom design solutions to meet their needs.

I don't know of other coaches who have my kind of background. Most offer a more limited, single-solution approach than multiple solutions with customization. Those are the biggest differences about what I do in comparison to most other coaches and why my clients are successful.

Wright

Who are some of the authors that have influenced you as a leadership strategist and an executive coach?

Leduc

Well, there are so many. Here are a few off the top of my head. Of course, two of the most well known authors are contributors to this book, Ken Blanchard and Stephen Covey. They've both been major influences. By the way, I feel very privileged to work with the Ken Blanchard Companies as one of their executive coaches. I've been with them since 2001 and sometimes I shake my head in amazement realizing I am part of that company. One of Ken's most well known books is *Leadership and the One Minute Manager.* His concept of Situational Leadership II, regarding managers' and leaders' responsibility to change their interaction style according to the needs of their employees, is a foundation piece for my coaching. Changing or modifying one's style to match the style of the other person is a leader's responsibility. When leaders or managers learn about and practice the concept, they become much more effective.

Stephen Covey's concept of looking at what's important and what's urgent has also been instrumental for me. Again, clients really understand the concept because often they're working on things that are not important—just urgent at that moment. Sometimes it seems they are constantly putting out fires.

Daniel Goldman's work on emotional intelligence and the impact that leaders have on other individuals has influenced my coaching. He is another author whose work has influenced me. Jinny Ditzler wrote a book called *Best Year Yet,* and I use that program in a lot of the work I do. Jim Collins' book, *Good to Great,* is helpful because he looked at good companies and how to turn a good company into a great company. This, of course, goes back to leadership again.

Another influence on me is "The Leadership Challenge" model created by Jim Kouzes and Barry Posner. Their assessment, called the LPI—Leadership Practices Inventory—is very helpful. Not only do I recommend the book, *Leadership Practices Inventory,* I also use their assessment regularly with the executives I coach. What I really like about their assessment is that leaders can go online, order it, and then invite people to provide their observations. Of course, I do think it's better to have a coach or consultant set up the assessment to maintain confidentiality.

Beverly Kaye wrote a book about career development many years ago called, *Up Is Not the Only Way.* She was one of the first influences for me when she talked about managers as coaches. In 1991 a colleague and I developed a manager's coaching program for an oil company and we based it on her writings. Her recent books on employee retention are vital reading for any leader who is concerned about employee turnover.

William Bridges is another of my favorite authors. Bill has written extensively about change and transition, and how to help individuals go through change. His books have been influential because he wrote about the emotional affect that happens during change. He calls that transition. Transitions occur when people start thinking about the change. That's when their motivation and productivity increases or decreases. He outlined three stages of transition: the ending, the neutral zone, and the new beginning.

Those are the books that come to mind most readily when I think about leadership development. While there are many other books that I've read more recently, the ones I mentioned have formed my foundation and philosophy.

Of course, I can't forget about the most recent book by Marshall Goldsmith, *What Got You Here Won't Get You There*. Marshall is considered to be one of the world's foremost executive coaches. His book is great because it outlines the habits that hold leaders back.

Wright

I'm curious—as an executive coach and leadership strategist, do you work only with CEOs in companies or do you work with other people as well?

Leduc

That's a great question, David. You know, it can be confusing for individuals when they hear the words "executive coach." They may think it means we work exclusively with people in the "C suite"—the CEO, CFO, CIO, or other C level positions. In actuality, executive coaching means working with individuals in senior management or senior leadership. Executive coaching can be with a director or a manager who is being groomed for more strategic, influential levels. Executive coaching can be used in an on-boarding process for an individual new to a company.

Executive coaching also applies to the owners of small businesses. Even if there are only ten employees in their company, they are still chief executive officers because they hold the bigger picture—as they lead their employees toward their vision.

So, yes, we do work with others in addition to those at the "C" level. Actually, I prefer to call myself a leadership strategist or a leadership development specialist because I work with people who are in a leadership capacity, even if they don't hold the title of executive. Did that help to clarify?

Wright

Yes, absolutely. What are the greatest challenges organizations, their leaders, and executives face today?

Leduc

One of the biggest challenges is employee retention. Some people might think that with all the changes in the economy—after the implosion of the mortgage industry and ensuing repercussions—there would be a shift and employee retention would no longer be an issue. They think the fear of not being able to find another job will have employees stay put even if they are dissatisfied. The truth is that even in a downturn, top performers will quietly conduct job searches and look for a new place to work if they're not motivated, if they're not being recognized for their contributions, or if they don't have high levels of employee satisfaction.

Prior to the changes in the economy, many employers had trouble keeping employees, even the people who were not top performers. Employee turnover, employee retention, and employee engagement were the issues that kept leaders awake at night. And guess what? That's still the case now. Key performers—the rising stars in organizations—will quit if their needs are not met, regardless of the state of the economy. Employees want their bosses to pay attention to them and to tell them when they've done a good job. While they don't want false praise, they do want honest recognition for their contributions.

Employee retention has always been a major challenge for organizations. Whether people quit or whether they stay with the company as demotivated underperformers has a huge financial impact on the bottom line.

I have a personal example about why people want to quit their boss and how coaching facilitates leaders to get back on track. About fifteen or sixteen years ago I was asked to coach a Senior Vice President. The reason I was brought in was because the employees had threatened to quit en masse because of the way he treated them. This was a pretty dramatic example of employee dissatisfaction.

At the start of the coaching, I decided to shadow coach. So I followed this executive around for a full day. I saw how he interacted with people, how he responded, how he reacted to anyone who challenged him, and I thought, "Hmmm, here are the reasons I was brought in." He was critical, finding fault with everything and everyone. At the end of the day we returned to his office so that I could let him know what I saw as his areas of strength as well as some of the changes that would make him a better leader.

We were sitting in his office, behind closed doors, and I was telling him what I'd observed. As I was speaking, he started shaking his finger in my face, maybe five or six inches away from my nose, and I had an immediate visceral response. I told him I felt like a child being chastised for doing something wrong. That stopped him in his tracks and he asked me what I meant. I said, "Having you wag your finger in my face and speaking in that tone of voice makes me feel as though I can never do anything right, that I am being chastised." And I added, "Is this an example of what goes on with your staff?" He looked shocked and told me had never thought about it. He was completely unaware of his impact on others. That was one of the most powerful examples of Emotional Intelligence—or the lack of it—I've ever seen.

We mapped out a plan for this SVP so that he would reflect on his leadership and the impact of his behavior on his staff. Approximately six months later, after I'd been coaching him on a weekly basis, I asked him for feedback on his greatest learning lesson. He smiled and said, "Well, watch this," and he sat on his hands before continuing. "When people come into my office now and when I'm talking with them, I make sure that I sit on my hands so that I'm not intimidating anyone. And they tell me I am more approachable." That small change that led to a big difference in how he was viewed.

Wright

That's a great example.

From your experience, what are the keys to success for leaders and executives?

Leduc

While there are many keys to success for leaders, I'm going to focus on four of them.

The first key for leaders is reflection. In the previous example, this fellow was not reflective—at least not until we started coaching. It's important for leaders to set aside time to reflect on what they are doing. Too often it seems as though they are running as fast as they can, constantly putting out fires, and sometimes they are the ones starting the blazes. I recommend that leaders set aside at least one hour each week for their own personal strategic planning session.

Becoming insight-oriented is a second key. Paying attention to one's impact on others—showing high levels of emotional intelligence—is vital.

Having direction and focus—having the road map to know where one is going on his or her leadership journey—is the third key. This book, *Roadmap to Success,* has great contributors who all have their viewpoints. My viewpoint relates to the *leadership* road map because I work with leaders in organizations.

If the road map is the third key, then the fourth key is to have someone hold them accountable. Whether it's a coach, a mentor, a colleague, or a friend, it's important to have someone who will provide solid and honest feedback and help them move forward. They need to have someone continue to push them in the right direction, to ask how they are doing, where they are stuck, what type of support they need, and how they will continue to move forward if they become stuck.

Wright

If having your leadership road map is one of the most important keys, why don't more executives develop their own road map?

Leduc

Now that's the *billion*-dollar question. When I worked in career development, we had a saying that if people spent as much time planning for their careers as they did planning for their vacations, everybody would be hugely successful. I think it's the same with a leadership road map. It's not that people don't want a road map; I believe people realize that it's important. They may not know how to develop the road map or they read too many books that tell them how to be better leaders, but they don't act on anything they read. They have good intentions, yet don't follow through.

So, discovering how to create a road map is the first component, and then taking action is the second vital component. Plus, having a coach, mentor, or someone to work with you to craft that map, hold you accountable, and help you get you where you want to go is a necessity.

Wright

In your leadership coaching programs you talk about being a "SAGE leader." What does that mean and what does it take to be a SAGE leader?

Leduc

SAGE is an acronym. It stands for Set A Great Example. Like Jim Collins' book, *Good to Great,* we know great leaders lead by example. Here's what I mean: Leaders are always in the spotlight; invariably people are watching them, and they're under constant scrutiny. In large businesses they're under scrutiny by the media, shareholders, customers and employees. Even in small business, employees and customers are watching them. Leaders sometimes forget that someone is always watching—watching their every move—or taking cues from the leader about what is acceptable or required.

Let me give you an example of how leaders are scrutinized for their actions and how those actions are interpreted. When I'm working with someone I'll ask, "How late in the evening do you send out e-mail? Do you ever send them out after 10:00 at night? Do you send e-mails over the weekend?"

If they're sending e-mails outside of the hours their employees are expected to work, they are not setting a great example because they are demonstrating to employees they expect them to work late at night or on the weekend. Many companies have a values statement which indicates work-life balance is important and that people are their most important asset. Yet, do the leaders' actions align with the corporate messages? Not always.

So, the executives and leaders I coach might say they don't expect their employees to work late at night or on the weekend. If that's what they tell me, yet they continue to send late-night e-mails, I tell them they are conveying mixed messages.

That's just one specific example about being a SAGE leader. In essence, being SAGE means remaining aware of how they show up as leaders: Are they adhering to what's in their vision, mission, and values statement? Are they leading effectively or do they say one thing and do something entirely different?

Wright

Will you tell us about your leadership road map and what makes it unique?

Leduc

I'm glad that you asked that question. The "Sage Leader's Road Map" is designed to take people from where they are currently as leaders to where they want to go in the future. Each road map is customized for each individual leader to address where that person is currently in his or her career, what is to be accomplished, and how to grow as a leader.

I want to emphasize again that we are green in our leadership development programs and executive coaching. Leadership development does not have to be done on site—it's possible to coach someone via conference calls and private Web applications.

And while we don't have time to go into all of the details here, I can provide an overview of how we partner with leaders and their organizations. Our first step is to complete a review of their leadership style, their communication style, leadership history, and career path. We have them look at what's brought them to where they are in their career and in their leadership. We ask them to take a step back and look at what they've done successfully, look at their disappointments, and we address their leadership point of view. We also request feedback from others about what makes them great leaders and where they can improve. We use a variety of tools and assessments including our own proprietary instruments.

We interview the people they work with: direct reports, peers, their manager, or the Board of Directors. Sometimes I will request feedback from their customers or clients. Occasionally I've even sought feedback from a spouse.

We assemble all the information and then complete a leadership analysis where we look for themes. Sometimes the development themes are not apparent to the leader and we point out blind spots. I do think it takes a third party to be able to help a person recognize how he or she operates as a leader, and where he or she could be an even better leader by taking different actions. We are that neutral third party. That's the first step in leadership development at Sage Leaders.

Then we meet with the leader to provide the analysis and our recommendations. Sometimes we meet with leaders face-to-face, and other times we meet via video webinar or conference call to show them their private Web site. Then, together we begin to craft their road map and what their next steps will be. We develop the road map based on where they have been, where they are now, and where they want to go in the future. I might have them look out a few years. Sometimes it will be a five- or ten-year plan, sometimes longer. Depending on the individual, sometimes I'll have the person look to the end of his or her life and ask, "What do you really want to accomplish? What's the legacy you want to leave?"

Quite often people say they cannot possibly see far into the future because their careers shift or because the world changes so rapidly. In that case I'll have someone create a three-year plan. Then we start at the end and work backward. Mapping out a leadership road map is very similar to running a project; it's as though a career is a project—if you know the end goal or the end result you can track it backward to identify the milestones, activities, and tasks. At Sage Leaders we use a particular technology program to create each customized plan. It's web-based and secure, so only the "owner" of the plan and the coach see what's on the plan.

After we've created a leadership road map, the next step is to coach the leader on the goals over a period of time. And, of course, we track progress and successes.

Wright

You recently won an award for your coaching. Did you use a leadership road map with that company?

Leduc

Yes, absolutely. The award that you are referring to is called the PRISM Award. It is from the International Coach Federation (ICF) and was started a few years ago by the Toronto Chapter of the ICF. Each year, across the country and around the world, various chapters of the ICF recognize organizations, and the coaches who worked with them, for their coaching excellence and for the outcomes of the coaching.

I'm really proud of the organization I worked with in 2006 and 2007. It's a non-profit in the Seattle area which focuses on school readiness for children. I coached the CEO and six members of the leadership team and worked with them for more than a year. We created the road map for the team when we spent two days at a strategic planning retreat. We developed a very in-depth road map about what they, as an organization, wanted to achieve and where they wanted to go as an organization. Then each month we met either in person or via a conference call and tracked their progress with that program.

When I first started coaching the leadership team in 2006, I was still living in the Seattle area. Then I made a lifestyle choice and moved to Phoenix, Arizona. Through the use of our technology we continued the program and would "meet" via Web conferencing and teleconferencing. We were each able to log in to the private site and see the same information at the same point in time.

The overall result was an increase in revenues through grants, and their annual luncheon. They increased their total revenues by 53 percent within one year. I know that sounds absolutely fantastic and it was. Of course, while it was not all attributed to coaching, coaching was a component. One of the coaching keys for their success was that they were able to focus on what was most important and not become distracted.

We all have projects and activities that compete for our attention at the same time. Differentiating between what's important or just urgent helps us stay on track with our goals and to sidestep distractions. That's what the leadership team of the non-profit was able to do. The organization is growing, they're helping more families, and it's because they were able to say "no," when needed.

Wright

Sylva, do you have any final words to help our readers develop their leadership skills?

Leduc

Yes, there are two main ways to develop your leadership and your leadership skills. You can either develop them by accident or you can develop them by design. Many people fall onto the accidental side. I used to call myself an "accidental entrepreneur" because I ended up with my own business even though I had not planned to become an entrepreneur. My situation was not unique. Like me, many leaders do not plan their long term career.

While I am comfortable with ambiguity and have a relatively high tolerance for risk, not everyone shares those same characteristics. I coach many new leaders who do not thrive in ambiguity, who may feel that they are leadership imposters and are waiting to be found out. Maybe they've not received any leadership training; maybe they don't have a plan, yet continue to be promoted. As they are promoted to higher levels in their organizations and find themselves in more influential positions, they're just not sure if they're on the right track or doing the right things. Some people are comfortable living in ambiguity and they learn as they go. If it works for them, that's fine. However, many people want to have a road map; they want to be able to know if they are still on the right road or have ended up on a detour—or worse, a dead end.

Having a design, a grand plan, a road map, or whatever you want to call it is essential. My words of wisdom? Create a plan. Be proactive and in control of your career as a leader. Read this chapter again, read all the other chapters, and then look for the nuggets. Look for what's going to be most relevant for you.

You won't be able to act on all the great advice you read. Choose the one, two, or possibly three nuggets you can do something about. Don't just read this book, put it aside, and go on to the next book. Think about what's important and what you are going to act upon. It's too easy to say, "What's next?" and buy another book. Read all of the chapters in this book more than once and *then do something.* One thing you can do is to get a coach to help you move forward.

At Sage Leaders, we'd love to work with everybody who requests our services to develop their leadership road map, yet we know that's not even remotely possible because there aren't enough hours in the day. What we do offer, though, is an online self-help workshop which people can access at our site. There's no charge to complete it. If any of the readers of this book want to design their own road map, then the first step is to go to www.SAGELeaders.com and look for the link to the free leadership road map.

Again, don't just read this book and put it aside—take some steps; create your road map by design, not by accident.

Wright

Well, what a great conversation. I've learned a lot about coaching that I didn't know. I really appreciate the time you've taken to answer all these questions for me; it's really been enlightening.

Leduc

Thank you, David. I know that everyone has the *potential* to be a great leader; people just need to discover *how* to develop those skills. My mission is to show people the "how."

I'm really glad that I was part of this project, so thank you very much, David.

Wright

Today we've been talking with Sylva Leduc. She is an executive coach, leadership strategist, and was one of the early pioneers of coaching. She coaches people all around the world, from leaders in small businesses to executives in Fortune 100 companies. She also coaches leaders in non-profit organizations.

Sylva, thank you so much for being with us today on *Roadmap to Success*.

Leduc

David, it was my pleasure.

About the Author

Sylva (Syl) Leduc, MEd, MPEC, is the Managing Partner of Sage Leaders Inc., www.SAGELeaders.com, a Phoenix-based coaching and consulting firm that delivers proven approaches for leadership development, performance improvement, and employee retention.

She has partnered with executives in the development of their leadership skills for nearly twenty years. Her practical and pragmatic approach is a blend of graduate level psychology, advanced education in executive coaching and leadership development, together with real-world experience as a consultant with a major consulting firm and as an executive in a start-up software company.

In 2007, Sylva and her company were honored with a PRISM Award for consulting/coaching the executive team of a non-profit organization. The leaders in the organization increased their effectiveness by focusing on and executing their Leadership Roadmap, which lead to greater results. To read more about the award and the results obtained, visit the Sage Leaders website.

Sylva invites you to visit www.SageLeaders.com and create your own *Roadmap for Success*. The only cost to complete the road map is your time and commitment.

Sylva (Syl) Leduc, MEd, MPEC

Leadership Strategist
Toll Free: 800-509-6823
info@sageleaders.com
www.SageLeaders.com

An interview with…

Derrick Chevalier

THE POWER OF INFLUENCE IN NEGOTIATION

David Wright (Wright)

Today we're talking with Derrick Chevalier and the subject is the power of influence in negotiation. Derrick is Executive Vice President of Harrison-Chevalier, Inc., a training and consulting firm located in Los Angeles. He has conducted hundreds of seminars, workshops, and presentations worldwide for numerous industries and organizations and has served as a consulting broker and a negotiation consultant/strategist for dozens of clients and organizations. He is author of two books, *Beyond Negotiating: From Fear to Fearless* and *Influence-Rapport-Results,* and he has written numerous articles on sales, management, negotiation, and a broad array of other topics. A Phi Beta Kappa, Derrick holds two BA degrees and a master's degree. He is also a broker licensed by the California Department of Real Estate.

Derrick, welcome to *Roadmap to Success.*

Derrick Chevalier (Chevalier)

Thank you, I appreciate it. I'm looking forward to the opportunity of talking about the power of influence in negotiation with you.

Wright

So how exactly do you define "influence"?

Chevalier

David, influence is the ability of someone to have an impact on the character, beliefs, or thoughts of another person or another entity. In other words, if person A acts or thinks in a specific way because of the actions or words of person B then Person B has exerted their influence and expanded their impact

Wright

Expanding your impact—that is powerful!

Chevalier

Yes. If you can change the way someone's thinking or the way the person acts or what the person believes, that's enormous.

Wright

So is that the power of influence?

Chevalier

Absolutely! If we think about it, the world itself has been shaped by the influence of great military officers, politicians, inventors, writers, and the clergy.

Think about how people are influenced by their parents or their siblings long after they've left home. How many of us grow up and find that what we think and how we act is precisely as our parents did because of their influence on our thoughts and actions, even though as teens we may have thought, "I'd never do what my mom and dad did or say the things they said to me when I have children."

People have all been influenced by their upbringing, their socioeconomic status, their education, or their lack of education. Influence plays a pivotal role in the way each of us thinks and the way each of us acts.

Wright

In your view, what is the power of influence in negotiation?

Chevalier

Well that's a great question. If a negotiator can successfully influence what an opponent chooses to focus on, the negotiator can essentially dictate the outcome of the negotiation as well as how the other party feels about the negotiation after the fact.

By contrast, if we don't influence the thoughts and actions of our opponents and if we don't have their attention we are less likely to influence what they focus on. If we don't control or influence what our opponents focus on we stand little hope of actually achieving our desired outcome or resolution. So the power of influence in negotiation, again, is enormous because we're influencing where a person or organization places its focus.

Wright

What is a negotiation consultant or a negotiation strategist?

Chevalier

Well, a negotiation consultant or strategist works with clients to develop, implement, and monitor a negotiation strategy based on the client's specific goals and objectives. We'll help a client ask the right questions and avoid critical mistakes that otherwise might be made.

Without our input many people and organizations make critical mistakes long before the negotiation actually begins. Because every client is unique, the process and the way we'll work with each client is a bit different, but essentially we want to help them avoid the three fundamental reasons negotiators fail and thereby increase their potential for maximizing their desired results.

If you keep in mind that negotiation is a very specific skill and that not many people are trained specifically as negotiators, having a negotiation consultant/strategist vastly enhances the opportunities for an optimal result.

For example, many people assume that lawyers, because of their training, are great negotiators and yet lawyers are primarily trained to make connections between existing precedent in the law and the facts of the case or the issue they're representing. The best lawyer in the world is going to be one who's able to find an exception to an existing precedent, and that's very different from competency in negotiation. There are professionals in the realm of finance, medicine, engineering, business administration, information technology, and Real Estate. All of these professions involve many facets of negotiation, but not one of these professions requires a measured competency in negotiation as a requirement for licensing or entry into its particular field.

An experienced negotiation consultant/strategist is someone who has a highly developed expertise, specifically in the process or realm of negotiation.

Wright

So how does that differ from being a negotiation trainer or coach?

Chevalier

That's a great question too. A negotiation trainer is like a professor in college or high school. He or she is someone who presents a curriculum or what I refer to as a *framework* consisting of various information, strategies, or tactics to participants or students. The trainer isn't usually responsible for determining whether or not a person actually achieves real world competency outside of perhaps giving a test or administering some other particular measurement. But results from tests or measurements don't mean that a student or participant actually has mastery of the information that can immediately produce a desired result in complex real world situations. So a trainer is someone who teaches and presents information and strategy.

A coach, by contrast, is specifically focused on helping someone—a client—memorize and learn the ABCs of the framework or the curriculum that is taught. A coach is focused on helping a person raise the information that was presented in the classroom to a level of knowledge where the student/client can recall and prioritize what he or she has learned *under fire.* When students achieve a level of knowledge, they can go beyond what they were taught to finding solutions that were never identified in the material that was presented to them during the course they attended. The analogy is simple—when you know how to swim you don't have to read a book on it before you jump in the water. Although, it is important to remember that many of the best and most competent business professionals and athletes in the world still work with coaches and consultants in order to achieve or extend or enhance their performance and results.

Wright

How do negotiation and influence differ from one another?

Chevalier

Negotiation involves specific tactics, techniques, strategies, and rules. Influence, on the other hand, involves the identification and assessment of the underlying psychological and physiological elements that cause the negotiator to use a specific tactic, technique, or approach. In other words, negotiation is the nail and influence is actually the hammer.

Wright

Several years ago you wrote an article titled "Three Fundamental Reasons Negotiators Fail." Was influence one of those three?

Chevalier

No, not specifically. I wrote a book called *Influence-Rapport-Results.* The first chapter of that book is titled "Three Fundamental Reasons People Fail." The first of those reasons is a failure to take the *information* that's presented in a class or seminar and raise it to a level of *knowledge.* In other words, if I ask somebody what two plus two is, he or she knows that the answer is four; but if I ask somebody what negotiating or sales framework he or she uses, I am likely to get a blank stare because the person has never even thought about it.

Imagine having a physician operating on your heart with the same level of competency in medicine that most people have as negotiators; would you be comfortable with that physician? Yet, every day of the week business professionals worldwide negotiate multimillion-dollar deals with little more than an elementary foundation in negotiation. They walk away thoroughly convinced that they have achieved the best possible outcome when in fact all they've done is successfully negotiate against their own expectations and perceptions.

The second reason is that people so often focus on what they already know rather than trying to find out what they don't yet know or developing a process for finding out what they don't know. That approach (focusing on what you already know) automatically limits the possibilities for the best outcome.

Now, because of fundamental reasons one and two, the third fundamental reason is that people are often hampered by fear—all types of fear—but often at the core of the fear are fundamental reasons number one and two.

Wright

Will you explain what you mean by physiology, focus, and neuro-association?

Chevalier

Well, yes. Physiology involves the way people breathe, how quickly they speak, how fast their heart is beating, and where their attention is placed. Physiology also involves the tone of a person's voice so that someone speaking in higher registers will have a very different affect on people than someone who speaks in a lower bass or baritone register. Together these elements define our physiology.

Focus has to do with what is presently influencing our belief or behavior—where is our attention? For example, people who have been bitten by a mosquito or spider or stung by a bee without realizing it until much later probably didn't realize they had been bitten because they were engaged in a sport or some other physically or mentally demanding activity. Because their focus was totally committed to the activities they were engaged in, they never even registered that the bite or sting had occurred until their focus was shifted away from the activity that previously consumed them. Then their focus shifted to the bee sting or spider bite or whatever it was and they realized that *"ouch!"* it hurt. So focus has to do with where our energy and attention are placed and thus, what we do and do not pay attention to at a given moment.

Neuro-association refers to beliefs, thoughts, and reactions that are already indelible parts of our behavior and thought processes. For instance, if someone is walking out in the woods and stumbles upon a stick lying on the ground, most people will jump back in case it's a snake. Then the person will see that the stick is a stick and not a snake and feel a little embarrassed about jumping backward because of a mere stick. Somebody who is a trained herpetologist, however, is likely to grab the stick immediately in hopes that it is a snake, because that is the person's neuro-associative or predisposed reaction to that specific set of circumstances or events.

Wright

Who are your greatest influences, professionally speaking?

Chevalier

Certainly the first person who comes to mind is Dr. Chester Karrass. In my view he is the quintessential authority of contemporary negotiation training and theory, particularly with regard to corporate or transactional negotiation. After thirty years, his books and his work have had a profound affect on billions and billions of dollars of commerce worldwide and on thousands of professionals in countless industries and professions. Like Drucker in management theory, it's difficult to look at a book on negotiation (particularly contemporary negotiation) and not be able to identify his footprint or influence. So I would definitely say that Dr. Karrass has influenced me a great deal.

Then I'd include people such as Dr. Stephen Covey whom I've written about previously. Dr. Covey and people like Ken Blanchard have had such a profound affect on our contemporary beliefs. They have taken material from various resources and synthesized it in a way that allows us to maximize the results that we get and the way we live our lives.

So those are certainly people who have influenced me professionally.

Then there are people who include Dr. Nightingale, who has influenced so many of us, from Zig Ziglar to Tony Robbins, and so many others. Dr. Nightingale certainly laid a fundamental foundation that's had an influence on me professionally.

Finally, there are people like Peter Drucker, John Nash, Stephen Hawking, and classical figures like Aristotle, Sun Tzu, Attila the Hun, Alexander the Great, and Jesus Christ, to name a few.

Wright

Those are some great names.

Chevalier

I'm sure I've forgotten some others who are important as well.

Wright

What is a negotiation framework?

Chevalier

When I speak of a framework I'm really talking about the specific rudiments of a persuasive sales procurement or negotiating approach. For instance, you have Dr. Karrass's Effective Negotiating Seminar that contains a specific set of rules and tactics and strategies that differ from those you would find in the Harvard Negotiation Project, which is headed by Roger Fisher and taught in Harvard School of Law.

Dr. Karrass's framework was developed in the corporate realm, so you'll find that his framework or approaches are framed differently than those from the Harvard and other programs.

So a framework is the *bone structure—the specific* strategies, tactics, techniques, and approaches—associated with a particular body of knowledge.

Wright

Will you give our readers some examples of pertinent negotiation frameworks?

Chevalier

Sure. As I mentioned, I would certainly say Dr. Karrass's Effective Negotiating Seminar, because that framework has had such an enormous affect on domestic and international commerce. His programs are conducted all over the world and are attended by thousands every year from virtually every industry and profession. I would also include The Harvard Negotiating Project, the Co-Opetition framework developed by Adam Brandenburger of Harvard and Barry Nalebuff of the Yale School of Management. There are also significant elements of a negotiation framework contained in the work of people like Dr. John Nash who refined the Theory of Equilibrium and Game Theory.

These would be examples of different *frameworks.*

Wright

So what's in the future for Derrick Chevalier?

Chevalier

I'm excited; over the last couple of years we've been working to transition Harrison-Chevalier, Inc. from a training company that does consulting into a consulting company that does training. We believe that while people will continue to need top quality training and training services in many areas, the twenty-first century will also need to provide professionals and their companies with significant support for the integration of the training that is provided to them.

We think that the demands on professionals will continue to grow just as the world shrinks as the result of the proliferation of technology. This is going to mean that professionals and their organizations are going to require specific strategies and insights from skilled consultants/strategists who specialize in areas like negotiation.

We want to be the world leader in negotiation consulting and I am working to see that vision come to fruition. Rather than just teach people how to negotiate, we want to guide, nurture, advise, and collaborate with our clients to get the results they are pursuing and help them be able to measure those results by comparing and analyzing the outcomes that we help them achieve.

I am also excited about the *Roadmap to Success* project and have a fourth book coming out in 2009, which is titled: *All Assumptions Are Wrong!*

Wright

I can't wait for that one.

So what is the most significant thing you've learned about the power of influence in negotiation?

Chevalier

Two things: that *all* assumptions are wrong and that in the twenty-first century perception not only *is reality,* perception *trumps reality,* as I discussed in my second book, *Influence-Rapport-Results.*

These are the two things that I've brought to the table that nobody else has really laid out in the same way. These are concepts that will revolutionize the way we look at business and the way we look at human interaction forever.

For instance, the idea that there is no such thing as an accurate estimate is a simple realization, but think of the enormity of its impact on engineering, architecture, and business in general.

I'll give you an example of what I mean by asking a simple question: what is the definition of the phrase *"accurate estimate"?* The answer of course is: *oxymoron.* If an estimate were accurate, it would by definition not be an estimate, and yet the entire world is built on the principle that an estimate could be or can be accurate. Engineers look at an estimate or a hypothesis as though it is right and then work to prove that it's right when, in point of fact, all estimates and all hypotheses are wrong by definition.

The questions we should really be asking are: How wrong are our estimates? How wrong are our hypotheses? I feel strongly that this fourth book and that the "all assumptions are wrong" concept should have a significant affect on the way our children think and on the way we study, pursue, and expand the body of knowledge going forward.

Wright

I'm working on a twelve-million-dollar building project right now. Is it okay if I tell the designer and general contractor what you said about estimates?

Chevalier

Absolutely! Think about it David: if your designer or general contractor could give you an estimate that was precise to the penny, it would mean that so much fat would be built in that his or her profits would be many times over what the profits should be or the "accurate estimates" would mean that the designer or general contractor had underestimated the project and met estimates only by lowering profit expectations in order to meet estimates. If an estimate is a statement of fact then it isn't an estimate at all but an accurate financial picture of the project *before* it breaks ground. You and I both know that if that could be done, the person who did it would be a genius with a skill beyond that of anyone else in the world.

The fact is that five minutes after your project breaks ground the designer or the general contractor will see things differently than he or she did when estimating the project.

Imagine if a designer/contractor was able to say that your project was going to cost $12,679,431.67 and not a penny more. Well, that would certainly make it better for you because you would know what the project is going to cost to the exact penny, and your designer/contractor would know exactly what it was going to cost to design and build the project. But your designer/contractor cannot honestly or accurately tell you down to the penny what it's going to cost at the end of the project *before* the project begins. All that is possible is to guess and hope the guess isn't too far off the mark.

Imagine it—if GM or Ford could have had accurate estimates of the number of SUVs they needed to build, the entire U.S. automotive industry would not find itself under siege.

The same is true of the financial markets. What if anyone could have accurately estimated when the housing bubble was going to burst or how long the war in Iraq was going to take or what it would cost? Would that change things significantly?

So it's not a question of *if* an estimate is wrong, it's a question of *how wrong* the estimate is. If it's not very wrong and fits within a margin of error that is tolerable and/or acceptable, then we make slight adjustments and move forward; but if an estimate is really wrong or outside of an acceptable margin of error or tolerance, then that may be something you'd certainly want to be aware of, because your twelve-million-dollar building could end up costing twenty million! Just as GM and Ford built too many SUVs, no one accurately estimated the timing, the cost, or extent of the housing crisis. And no one has yet accurately determined how long we're going to be in Iraq or how much it's going to cost or how many lives will be sacrificed in the process. All we know is that every estimate associated with all of these issues is wrong!

Wright

In your opinion, why are skill in negotiation and knowledge about the power of influence important parts of achieving success in business and in our readers' personal lives?

Chevalier

Because the fact is that negotiation skill and the significance of the power of influence literally affects everything that we do in life both personally and professionally.

For instance, on a personal level I often start a program or keynote by giving people an example of how I needed a roof for my home and the top estimate was

$30,000. I ended up getting several different estimates—one for $30,000, one for $18,000, and one person gave me an estimate for $11,000. The $11,000 estimate only included one-third of my roof. He said that $11,000 would repair the *really* damaged part, but to get the entire roof done would cost $30,000.

I then ask people, "What do you think I wrote the check for to get the entire roof done?" Nobody comes close to answering that question accurately. If someone says, "You probably did it for $15,000," that person thinks it's a big step to say $15,000 because the estimate was for $30,000. Well, I then explain to the audience that I wrote a check for $3,995 and not only did I get the $30,000 roof, but I got three years extended on the warranty and other elements that made the roof a great deal. Not only was it a great deal for me, but it was also a great deal for the contractor who did the job.

Then, over the course of a program or keynote, I'll explain to the audience how I did it. I explain that the same skill I used for the roof is the same power of influence that can and has been used to negotiate the cost of shoes and suits. That same skill and knowledge has been used to help doctors double their salary and to help people who are designing everything from weapon systems down to businesses that sell widgets, to people who have been unfairly fired, and almost everything in between.

As I see it, every negotiation is like a game of chess and every personal or professional situation represents a different style board with pieces of varying sizes, shapes, colors, and textures. Yet, while the board itself and the pieces themselves may vary, the game of chess hasn't changed significantly in hundreds of years. The skill is really the ability to determine who in the negotiation represents the role of the king, where the queen is, and who and how the bishops, castles, and pawns are moved before we get involved. Once we understand the board and who the players are, we begin the process of gaining the knowledge and making the choices that we have to make to best achieve the stated goals and objectives.

Negotiation is the process of being able to navigate the different ways that the "board" is going to be set up in a particular organization or in a particular personal or professional situation. Influence involves the affect of and the anticipation of how and when a particular piece is going to move or what it's going to take to get the piece to move.

So negotiation and influence are parallel, not synonymous entities. They actually involve two very different bodies of knowledge and skill but, used skillfully or not, they affect every stage of an interaction and define the very essence and quality of our lives in so many ways that are simultaneously apparent and virtually invisible because *perception* does indeed *trump reality.*

Wright

So you're going to make me come to a seminar or program to find out about the roof?

Chevalier

Well of course, of course.

Wright

We have published a book on negotiation. I tell you, I learned more about selling in those negotiation conversations than I have in the last five decades of working in sales and professional development.

Chevalier

Isn't it amazing? I often tell people that it is amazing to me how often salespeople actually begin negotiating before they've made the sale (and how often other negotiators begin negotiating before they know or understand what the real issues separating the parties are). See, the selling process is the process of getting somebody to make a decision to do business with you. Negotiation is the process of defining the limitations of that relationship—not whether or not you're going to do it with me, but what's going to govern how we do business. Once the sale is done you understand that the process of negotiation defines and monitors the relationship after the sale has been made.

Influence involves identifying and affecting what, why, how, and when the underlying choices are made. But so often there are people who think they're negotiating and influencing a sale or their counterpart's choices when all they're really doing is moving the price up and down or adding or subtracting concessions. That's not skilled negotiation or taking advantage of the power of influence at all.

Wright

I'm glad you said that assumptions are always wrong; I have lost more money assuming that people didn't have money.

Chevalier

Just to be clear on this, an assumption is merely what we *say* we believe about something, but assumptions are often not a basis for our actions. If we assume something is wrong, then our perception is that it is wrong. While no one can argue with our *perception* about something (because presumption trumps reality), if our assumption turns out to be a truth or a fact, it was *always* a truth or a fact and we just didn't realize it. Truths and facts do not change themselves just because we do not realize they *are* truths or facts.

I often give people the example of how one of the smartest men in the world *presumed* or *hypothesized* that black holes were portals through which we were going to go into new dimensions of the universe (I am referring to Stephen Hawking). Literally millions, if not billions of dollars were spent pursuing insight into black holes as portals, only to determine some time later that in fact, Stephen Hawking was 180 degrees wrong! Despite his mathematical computations, the primary thing those many millions of dollars of research proved was that black holes are not portals at all—they are *repositories*. Nothing goes through them, so you're certainly not going through a black hole into another dimension in the universe.

Now, for a period of time, many really smart people believed (*presumed* or *assumed*) that because Hawking is a genius and because he used mathematical computation, that his presumptions or hypothesis about black holes was correct; but the fact of the matter is that Stephen Hawking was absolutely *wrong* about black holes being portals. Black holes didn't change just to make Stephen Hawking wrong. Facts don't care how you feel about them, and a truth is a truth no matter what you or I hypothesize about it.

The other example I share with people is that when I was in school I remember being told by a teacher that there were nine planets in our solar system. I remember asking, "Well, how do you know that there are only nine planets?" I was ultimately sent to the office and given an opportunity to adjust my attitude, so to speak. When I came back the teacher asked, "Well, what do you think now?"

I replied with a simple question, "Do we have bigger telescopes today than we had fifty years ago?"

"Yes," she answered.

"Well, are we likely to have bigger telescopes fifty years from now?"

"Yes."

"Then how do we know that there aren't more planets?" At which point I was sent back to the office.

We now know (Because we have bigger telescopes), that Pluto is not the ninth planet in our solar system—it's not even a planet! We also know that new planets have been discovered and many others will presumably be discovered as we get even better access to the secrets of the universe. Now, the fact is that Pluto wasn't a planet on the day I was disciplined for being disrespectful. The truth doesn't change because somebody doesn't know it. The truth is or it isn't and the fact that we assume something has no affect on a fact or a truth. So if an assumption is right, it was always right and we just didn't know it. In point of fact: "All Assumptions Are Wrong!"

Because of this we need to completely re-evaluate the way we look at and react to all of our interactions, both in business and in our personal interactions. And some of the crucial tools for that re-evaluation are found within the context of the relationship between the power of influence and negotiation.

Wright

What a great conversation. I really have enjoyed this, Derrick, and I have learned a lot. You have given me a lot to think about.

Chevalier

My privilege—it's been great for me as well. I've enjoyed the opportunity to be a small part of the *Roadmap to Success* project with great people like Ken Blanchard, Dr. Covey, and yourself. I really appreciate it and look forward to more conversations in the future.

Wright

Today we've been talking with Derrick Chevalier, and the subject has been the power of influence in negotiation.

ABOUT THE AUTHOR

"Passionate" and "inspirational" are the two words most often used by clients and by those who have attended the seminars, workshops, and keynotes facilitated by Derrick Chevalier. "Results-oriented," "effective," and "highly satisfied" are the comments most frequently associated with Derrick's consulting work, whether from top tier multi-nationals, small businesses, professionals, or simply from individuals seeking the highest and best outcomes in the face of their challenges. Derrick possesses a unique combination of practical hands-on experience, superior academic preparation, and mentoring from some of the world's most  prestigious and influential minds. "Circumstances do not dictate outcomes," is a driving force and core belief of Derrick's along with an intense dedication and a consistent expectation of excellence.

Derrick Chevalier

Harrison-Chevalier, Inc.
1800 Century Park East, Suite 600
Los Angeles, CA 90067
310.229.5950
818.242.8005
info@h-c.com
www.h-c.com

CHAPTER **10**

An interview with...

Joseph Price

INTENTIONAL SUCCESS

David Wright (Wright)

Today we're talking with Joseph M. Price. Joe is Founder and President of Intentional Achievements™, LLC and Customized Training Solutions, Inc. He has over twenty-five years of experience in the training and development field with expertise in areas such as organizational development, design and implementation of performance-based training programs, strategic visioning and planning, motivation and coaching at all levels. Prior to founding CTS and Intentional Achievements, Joe was General Manager, Senior Instructor, and Corporate Solutions Director for Dale Carnegie Training of Southeastern Pennsylvania. By demonstrating a rare combination of skills, Joe became one of the few instructors to become certified for all nine Dale Carnegie Training Programs and attained the distinction of being the twelfth highest producer of Dale Carnegie enrollments in the world, a feat he maintained for over five consecutive years.

Joe, welcome to *Roadmap to Success.* We're glad to have you here.

Tell me, what exactly is an "intentional life"?

Joseph M. Price (Price)

Thank you David for giving me this opportunity to share these intentional life principles. To answer that we first have to take a step backward and define what the word "intentional" means. Definitions are important to start with because our actions

137

are based on our definitions. So if we understand what a word or concept's definition is, we will better understand how it influences our behavior, and therefore be more conscious and in control of our actions. Many times, when we change our definitions, we change our actions and when we change our actions we change our life.

So what does "intentional" mean? Being intentional means that you clearly see an outcome you desire to have happen, design and plan a course of action and then deliberately follow it. So an intentional life is defining, designing, and planning out the kind of life you want to have, working that plan, and doing everything with a purpose and on purpose—including the decisions you make every day in order to live the life you truly desire.

You and I make hundreds of decisions every day. Some of them are small like should I get my car washed today or what am I going to have for lunch? Some are pretty significant like should I take this new job or should I show someone I care about them. We make each decision in one of four ways: by 1) *default,* which means either we don't make it and therefore we make it or someone else makes it for us, by 2) *accident,* 3) *reaction,* or 4) *intention.* So, one part of intentional living is to make each of these decisions with a clear purpose in mind and deliberately on purpose, not by accident, reacting, or by giving control over to somebody else.

On a grander scale, living an intentional life means that you've discovered your overall purpose in life, the reason you're here, and are living it to the fullest every day. Each of the actions you take and choices you make is intentionally designed to help you fulfill that purpose and enjoy an empowered, fulfilled, joyful, and successful life.

Wright

Let's go back to decision-making for a minute. How do we make decisions with a purpose and on purpose?

Price

With a very simple yet very effective tool we call the "Double Triangle." It's a process of asking yourself three questions—twice. Picture an equilateral triangle. The right side of the triangle is labeled with the question "what." The bottom is labeled "why" and the left side "how." Now, picture that triangle in the middle of a larger equilateral triangle with the same three questions labeled in the same way.

Now think of a situation in which you need to make a decision. Not a trivial decision like "which way should I go to work today," but a fairly important decision that you should take some time and employ some thought to make. Now picture the right side of the smaller inside triangle and ask yourself the "what" question like this: "*What* action do I want to take?" or "*What* do I want to do?" Then answer the question.

I recommend that a person write the answers down the first couple of times he or she does this. It's a good way to practice, and when you put something on paper it looks and sounds a lot different from what was just in your head. Then ask yourself the "why" question like this, "*Why* do I want to do that?" This is the most important question in the whole process and you shouldn't continue to the next step until this question is fully answered. It is the answer to this question that will make your final decision "with a purpose."

Now ask yourself, "how?" "*How* am I going to take that action?" or "*How* am I going to do that?" Be very specific with this answer. The more specific the answer here, the easier the second triangle questions are to answer.

So now you know what you want to do, why you want to do it, and how you are going to do it. Now let's look at the second, outer triangle. Ask yourself and answer these questions: "*What* could happen if I do that?" or "*What* could be the result?" "*Why* would that happen" and "*How* am I going to deal with that if and when it does happen?" Again, be as specific as you can in answering these questions.

You might be saying to yourself, "There could be several ways it might go after I take the original action" and you'd be right. The key to making this decision "on purpose" is to answer the questions of the second triangle for each potential outcome. Now, no matter what happens, you are prepared for it—you are being intentional and you are ensuring as best you can that the outcome of that decision is as much within your control as you can make it. You are no longer making decisions by default, reaction, or accident because you have thought it through, you understand why you are doing it, you have planned for each possible contingency, and you have deliberately acted. That decision was made "with a purpose and on purpose."

Wright

So, tell us why you think an intentional life is a better life.

Price

Well, an intentional life is a more rewarding, fulfilling, and fun life. Everything you do has more significance and joy. An intentional life is a more peaceful life because you know who you are, where you're going, and what you're supposed to do with your life so it's a less stressful life as well. It's a more challenging and exciting life because you have more confidence to step outside your comfort zone and do things you never thought you could do. It's a life in which you know that when you make a decision you are making the right decision, at the right time, and for the right reasons. By living an intentional life you reach higher and attain more, and you do it with more balance and control.

Wright

Is there a process or a road map to follow to live an intentional life?

Price

Absolutely. We have a system of nine keys that when followed systematically will enable you to live your life more intentionally, achieve the goals you've set for yourself, and experience all the benefits of living an intentional life. The nine-key Intentional Living Model™ is broken down into three modules that we call "Know it," "Plan It," and "Be It."

First you have to know something such as where you want to be or what you want to do, then you plan how to accomplish it; then you need to be and do what you've seen and planned. The three modules themselves are then broken down further into three keys each. Let me explain.

Know It

The first module deals with knowing ourselves and what we want. It deals with Purpose, Values, and Vision.

The first key to the system is called *"Constancy to Purpose."* This means that first, every decision you make is made with a purpose and on purpose, and second, it means that you discover and find what your life's purpose is, live it to the fullest every day, and experience the benefits of living a life in which you not only know where you're going, but most importantly, what it looks like when you get there.

The second key deals with our (Core) *Values.* You and I make decisions every day based on our value system. The problem is that most people haven't taken the time to consciously identify their values, so they don't realize that's what's really happening. With this second key you can discover your own unique value system and, if you have one, your core value.

One of our members was once asked, "Have you ever quit a job because of your values?" After some thought, she said, "yes, two." At that moment she realized what it really meant to make decisions based on values. It helped her further clarify what they were and gave her greater peace and confidence when making future decisions.

Another of our members was struggling in her job. She was being pressured by her supervisors to increase her production, but as much as she tried she wasn't able to do it. She began to doubt herself and question her skills and abilities. Her confidence was waning. She was constantly frustrated and stressed. After identifying her values and being coached to analyze her performance and the expectations of her bosses against those values, she discovered that it wasn't her lack of skill that was causing the problem. The problem was that they were demanding her to take actions that were in violation of her values. Internally she struggled with their requirements but never knew that was the issue. As soon as she realized this, she quit, found another job that was in alignment with her value system and is doing extremely well there.

Identify your values, live in alignment with them, and you will be happier, more peaceful, and you will succeed where others fail.

Once you've found your purpose and are living your life in alignment with your values, your life is much more fulfilled—you are doing what you love and loving what you do.

The third key is to understand accurately what a (Clear) *Vision* is and how to create one for your life. The analogy that I like to use when teaching this concept is that of a jigsaw puzzle. Most of us, at some time in our life, have put jigsaw puzzles together and we have a process that we go through. We take the box top off and put it aside, we dump out all the pieces, turn them over, and then maybe we start putting pieces together by color or borders. Everybody has a different strategy they use, but the question is what do most people do with the box top?

Wright

Well, I've done a few puzzles in my day. I would constantly check the picture on the box top because I wasn't very good at putting it together without that picture there. I'd get lost.

Price

It's true. Most of us put the box top where we can always see the picture because that helps us to know which way to put the puzzle pieces together in order to get the end result. We understand from the very clear picture on the box where we're heading and it motivates and inspires us to put all of those tiny pieces together so that we can actually make and see the picture on the box and feel the accomplishment of completing it.

The same is true of your life's vision. You need to create a very clear vision for your life and (like the picture on the puzzle box) keep it in front of you all the time as you're putting the pieces of your intentional life together. By doing this, you know exactly where you're going. You know exactly what it looks like when you get there, and you are inspired and motivated to do what you need to do in order to attain it, feel the accomplishment, and enjoy the benefits of completing it.

Now, there are many who are teaching about purpose, values, and vision. I believe we do many things differently here to help people get these concepts faster and better, but if we stopped there we would also leave folks still asking the question, "Well what now? How do I live my daily life in order to actually achieve those things?" That's where the second module comes in.

Plan It

The second module in our system is called "Plan It," which has three more keys to help create a firm foundation on which you can build your intentional life.

The first of these keys is called *"A Well-Defined Plan."* Planning is essential to accomplishing the goals you truly want, and you need clearly defined steps along the way in order to ensure that you're getting there. Planning is the most efficient and effective way to make sure you get from where you are to where you want to be. Planning helps you avoid wasting time, anticipate the factors that could influence whether the task gets done, done right, and done on time, and helps you prepare for inevitable detours that will surely come along the way. Planning is essential for an intentional life.

The Intentional Planning Process is both simple and comprehensive. It consists of four steps:

1. *Clearly define* where you want to go and where you are right now. Without this step it would be like trying to map out a trip from somewhere on the West Coast to somewhere on the East Coast without knowing exactly where you are or where you want to wind up. Without the two end points, how could you put a good map together?

2. *Analyze the gap.* Ask yourself two questions in this step to help you identify what would either hinder or stop you from getting to the desired outcome or what resources would be crucial to ensure success. These questions are: "What is missing" and "what is needed" to get from here to there.

3. *Establish milestones.* A milestone, or goal, is a measurable checkpoint along the way to indicate you are going in the right direction. Think of milestones as your interim destinations and mile markers on that road trip from the West to the East Coast. Let's say you're heading to New York City from Phoenix, Arizona. Your first milestone might be lunch in Albuquerque. Your second could be a stretch break in Tulsa, and so on. Remember, when you set these milestones make sure you test them using the SMART formula. Unless your checkpoints are Specific, Measurable, Attainable, Realistic, and Time-phased they won't be as effective in helping you get where you want to go.

4. *Back Plan.* Once you have your starting and ending points, you've analyzed the gap and established milestones, now it's time to lay out the steps you will take to get where you want to go or accomplish that task. This step is called *Back Plan* because you plan backwards from where you want to be (the future) to where you are now (the present).

   It's easy to understand this process by thinking of something we all have done and do so naturally we don't even think about it—catching a flight at the airport. How do you decide what time to leave your house? Probably like this. The flight leaves at 5:15. It takes me forty-five minutes to drive and park. That means I have to be on the road at 4:30. I have to stop at the bank and get some cash, and of course my Starbuck latte is a must, that takes me about thirty minutes so I have to be out of my house by 4:00. Most of us even keep going backward to determine what time to wake up.

Do you plan your projects this way? Do you plan your life this way? Why is it so natural planning to get to the airport this way and not anything else?

Many people object to planning, thinking they either don't have time to plan or the plan never works out the way they wanted so why bother? These concerns are addressed with the second key in this module, *"Well-Organized Structure."*

The "Structure" key helps you understand that all of the areas of your life, such as your career, finances, family, etc., are connected to each other and what you do in one affects each of the others in some way. Peter Senge calls this "Systems Thinking."

You also learn that there is no such thing as "time management." You can't manage time—you can only manage yourself in relation to time. So, develop and enhance the management skills of planning, organizing, directing, coordinating, and controlling to restructure your life. Use your time more effectively and stop the vicious cycle of fire-fighting most of us find ourselves in today. One hint here regarding using your time more effectively and efficiently: You can't coach yourself or have others coach you in your use of time unless you know where it is going. A financial advisor couldn't advise you on better allocation of your money until he or she knew exactly where you are spending it right now. The same is true with time. Get to know exactly how you spend (and waste) time in order to know how to make the most of it.

The third key in this second module is *"Right People in the Right Place."* We say here that "We can't and shouldn't do it alone." Many of us need more people in the different areas of our lives to help us get where we want to be; to motivate us, challenge us, and encourage us. We also have people in our lives who probably shouldn't be there, who are hindering us or holding us back from where we want to go. Take the time to identify the people who should and shouldn't be in your life. Identify your goals in each area of your life and then determine who you might need to help you achieve them.

Be It

The final module, Be It, also has three keys to help you be and do what you've seen and planned for, through the first two modules.

The first key is to develop internal and external *Leadership* through what we call the "Three 'ations'"—inspire-ation, human rel-ations, and communic-ations. You need to take charge of your life and inspire yourself and others to help you stay true to your purpose and vision and carry out the plans you have made. Since you can't and shouldn't take this journey alone, an intentional life requires you to develop and constantly hone your people and communication skills. Whether people are in your life for a reason, season, or a lifetime, your human relations skills will help you develop and maintain the best possible relationships throughout your intentional journey. And, since communications is the vehicle through which all of this takes place, your dedication toward improving your sender and receiver skills should never end.

An intentional life will be a major lifestyle change for some and a more subtle one for others. No matter the degree, there will be challenges, distractions, setbacks, and emotional hurdles to overcome. The person living an intentional life has the *Emotional Intelligence* to handle it all, which is the second key in this last module. Highly emotionally intelligent individuals have taken the time and energy to discover their true nature with all its strengths and restraints, and have developed a level of personal mastery and the strength to handle what life throws at them.

How well do you know yourself? If you completed an inventory of your skills, talents, and abilities and were asked whether you use your emotions intentionally and intelligently when making decisions and dealing with other people, how well would you rate yourself? Would others rate you the same way? Do you know? Have you ever asked? Emotional Intelligence, and therefore personal mastery, is being aware of your strengths and restraints, accepting what they are, making a commitment to change the ones that need changing, and then taking the action to internalize and execute the changes.

The last key that ties this whole system together is called *"Courage and Fortitude."* Absorb the following phrase into the depths of your being, "Where there is no fear— there is no courage." Courage is not the absence of fear; it is action in the face of fear." I define courage as "the strength to take the first step" and fortitude as "the strength to continue and finish." Many times the first step is the hardest, so you need the courage to charge into your intentional journey—or whatever that scary situation is. And since many of us start something and don't finish, we need the fortitude to overcome the barriers and challenges we know are going to occur along the way in order to fully enjoy the intentional life we want. You might be asking, "How do I develop or strengthen my courage and fortitude?"

Do you realize and admit you talk to yourself? If you just said to yourself, "I don't talk to myself"—you just did. Do you talk to yourself more positively or negatively? Take this little challenge to find out. Put a three-inch by five-inch card in your pocket or purse on which you wrote the word *positive* on one side and *negative* on the other. Throughout your day when you catch yourself saying something positive to yourself, put a checkmark on that side of the card. Do the same with the negative. At the end of the day, tally up the checkmarks on each side. Mark down even the slightest little positive or negative thought to get a real picture of your self-talk habits. I believe you will be surprised at what you find. To develop and strengthen your courage and fortitude you have to gain control over those voices in your head, which are really you, telling you to be scared or quit. Change your self-talk, change your life.

So that, in a nutshell is the entire system which, of course, we explore much more in depth in our programs and coaching sessions. The great thing is we know it works, so we are able to guarantee that if you start at the beginning of the system and go around to the end, you will live a more intentional life and achieve any goal you set for yourself.

Wright

Can anyone learn to live an intentional life?

Price

The answer is very simple—yes. Anyone can learn the system and principles to live a more intentional life. It's a systematic process, and since a predictable process produces predictable results, if you start at the beginning and complete it, you intentionally will get where you want to go, get what you want to get, and do what you want to do.

Wright

So what does it take for a person like me to learn to live a more intentional life?

Price

The first step is to: 1) *decide* what you want to do. A lot of people are walking around today almost robotic—sleepwalking through life, not realizing they can take control. You need to decide what you want and have the confidence to know you can get it. So, the first thing is to make a decision to say, "Yes, I want to change my life, I want to live it more intentionally, and now I want to find out how to do that."

The next step is: 2) *gain the knowledge* necessary to make the changes you want. You can do this by reading books, listening to tapes and CDs, and going to motivational and educational seminars or a good training program. However, that is not enough.

The next steps are: 3) *practice the principles* and actually 4) *apply the knowledge* you're learning. Since we know that "knowledge doesn't change performance," it takes a systematic process to break old habits and create new ones. That doesn't happen overnight. It takes time, commitment, dedication, and a willingness to be coached along the way.

I don't know of any winning athlete who doesn't have a coach helping him or her practice the right things right. And then it takes lots of: 5) *repetition*. Keep doing it. Keep relearning and reapplying the intentional principles until they become second nature.

Wright

So what would the obstacles or challenges be along the way? I mean, what would hinder a person from being able to live an intentional life?

Price

There are three major obstacles or challenges you will face on your intentional journey. These obstacles are tied together and affect each other. The first are *old habits*. The second are *reactions caused by triggers*. The third is your *comfort zone*. What would hinder you from living your intentional life is allowing your old habits, reactions, and comfort zone to keep you from following the foundational formula necessary to overcome these obstacles and live the kind of life you truly want. Here's what I mean. The formula I'm talking about is A+A+C+A=C. Awareness + Acceptance + Commitment + Action = Change.

Abraham Maslow said, "What is necessary to change a person is to change his awareness of himself." We can't change what we don't see or know is wrong. You must be open and alert enough to become *aware* of what you need to change in order to live more intentionally.

Second, if you are aware that there might be a problem but don't *accept* you really have a problem and need to fix it, nothing will happen and your life won't change. You could become aware and accept that you need to do something differently but not make the *commitment* to do it. You will then stay the same and so does your life. How many of us make commitments but don't follow them up with *action*? So, without following the formula of Awareness + Acceptance + Commitment + Action, you will continue to live your life of insanity—continuing to do the same thing over and over and expecting things to change.

The change formula, if diligently adhered to, will help you overcome your old habits and create new ones. How do you handle your reactions? Typically, something happens to you—some sort of trigger—and instead of stepping back, being intentional, and thinking through what you want to do or say, you react. Without even being aware until sometime later, you have reverted back to old habits of how you deal with certain situations. Had you thought first, you probably wouldn't have reacted the way you did and would not have to kick yourself later for the way you handled it.

So, instead, start to identify "triggers"—those things that someone says or does that get inside you and cause you to react. As you sensitize yourself to those triggers, the time it takes you to realize what happened shortens. You start to gain more control in those situations and eventually learn how to respond instead of react. Once that happens, you become more intentional and avoid the situation all together.

The third obstacle is tied together with the other two. Everyone has a comfort zone with things that are inside, on the edge, and outside it. Let's say you want to do something but it is outside your comfort zone. You react to your fear, follow old habits, and revert back into your existing comfort zone. Because you didn't have a positive experience outside your comfort zone, it will be more difficult and frightening for you to take steps outside it the next time.

Your comfort zone (CZ) is very powerful. It has more control and hold over you than you think. "How do I overcome the stronghold my comfort zone has on me?" The answer is to enlarge it by doing something every day to step outside it. It doesn't even have to be in the area of your concern or fear. When you enlarge your CZ in one area, it automatically grows in others. Go to work taking a different route. Meet a new person and say hi. Eat something you have never eaten before. There are hundreds of things you can do. When you do, your confidence grows with your CZ and you begin to realize you can do more than you ever thought possible.

Wright

Is intentional living just for certain areas of one's life?

Price

You can't live an intentional life without being intentional in every area. It's that concept of systems thinking again. If you try to live intentionally in one without anticipating the affect on the others, you will inevitably cause conflicts and problems in all areas of your life. Then, to reduce the conflict and tension, you revert back to old habits of how you typically deal with problems, tension, and the "insanity" life continues—and you're stuck.

Wright

Sounds like a lot of discipline to me. How disciplined do you need to be to live an intentional life?

Price

I really like this question. A lot of people think that going through this system and learning to implement all the tools and processes means they need to be really disciplined to do it. That's really not the case. However, there's a hard way of living the intentional life and there's an easy way. If you're going to pick the hard way you do need a lot of discipline. Here's what I mean. If you take the hard way, you do it like this: You think of an area you want to change. You think of what you need to do differently and then you try to force yourself to do it in order to get the change you want—like exercising or dieting.

Now, because you're *forcing* yourself to do it, you need a whole lot of discipline. Discipline actually means "to bring yourself under control of a system or to create a habit of obedience to the things that you want to do." So if you're going to do it the hard way, you will need a lot of discipline to force yourself to follow the routine and not revert back to your old ways. This is why most people can't stick to it.

So, what's different about the easy way that doesn't require much discipline? The easy way is 1) to discover and internalize your *purpose* for the change and 2) to see a very clear and well defined *picture* of what that future looks like when you attain it. Then you 3) incorporate a *passion*, 4) attach a very deep internal *meaning* for making the change, and 5) use the clarity of that purpose, vision, passion, and meaning to help *inspire* and pull you to do it. There's very little, if any, discipline needed when you have the power of those ingredients working for you.

Wright

You know, there are hundreds, if not thousands of programs out there teaching us how to succeed, how to be better, how to be more productive, and so on. Why is the Intentional Achievements Program different from all those other programs?

Price

You are right. Over nine billion dollars a year is spent on motivation, education, and training for personal and professional development. That's a lot of money and a lot of books, DVDs, CDs, seminars, and training programs. Can one more program be that different and make any significant difference in a person's life more than the others? The answer is Yes and the difference is found in a definition—the definition of "training."

What I have found over my twenty-five years in this industry is that there's a lack of understanding of what I call "true training." I separate what is done in our industry into three categories: Motivation, Education, and Training. How many times have you and I attended a motivational seminar or event where great motivational speakers inspire us and pump us up to go out and take charge of our lives. Inspiring movies give us the encouragement that we can accomplish anything we set our minds to. But what happens when we leave the event or finish watching the movie and real life starts smacking us in the face again? We face a challenge or problem, and without the knowledge or skill to handle the situation we have difficulty overcoming it, we become discouraged, and we lose our motivation. We get frustrated with ourselves and our circumstances so we look for another event to go to, another movie to watch, another CD to listen to, or another book to read hoping that this one will work for us this time. This creates the "yo-yo" effect that so many of us experience in our lives. Motivation affects the way we "feel" and feelings don't change behavior. They are an important first ingredient, but without the other two, no lasting change takes place.

The next category is Education. If motivation affects what we "feel," education affects what we "know" and *knowledge doesn't change performance.* Just because you know something different doesn't mean you're going to do something different. I like to kill axioms that we have grown up with and are so attached to. One of them is "knowledge is power." Let me give you an analogy to demonstrate why I don't believe that's true.

Let's say you and I both want to learn how to fly a plane. We each spend three months getting ready for our first solo flight. I spend all of my time in the library. I read everything there is on flying and aerodynamics. I gain so much knowledge that I ace every test I take. By comparison, I know twice or three times as much as you do about the subject. On the other hand, you spend your three months up in the plane flying with an instructor. You are actually doing it all and learning as you go. Now it's time for our first solo flight. Let's assume that we are allowed to take someone up with us. Who do you think the person would rather go with—you or me?

Wright

Me.

Price

Why?

Wright

Because I have the experience of doing it.

Price

Right! But the axiom so many believe is that "knowledge is power." I certainly have much more knowledge than you do so why would people go up with you instead of me? Because knowledge isn't power. The *"application of knowledge is power."* What good is knowledge to us if we don't know how to use it or don't do something with it?

Now, motivation affects "how you feel," education affects "what you know," and training affects "what you do." You need the motivation and education to change your behavior, but alone they won't do it. This is where "true training" comes in. True training incorporates and utilizes motivation and education as the foundation on which to build skills, but adds three more ingredients you need to break the old habits that have taken ten, fifteen, twenty, or twenty-five years to develop.

Substitution of new skills for the old habits is the only solution. New skills and habits are only built through training and coaching, utilizing a concept called time-spaced repetition. Over a period of time, you follow a systematic process to develop new habits and skills, which involves working in an instructor-led program as well as practicing and applying what you have learned out in the real world in real-life situations. It can be supplemented with more education from other sources such as books, videos, multimedia, or online applications. Remember, though, these are only supplements to help you further learn how to practice and apply.

However, an integral part of true training and time-spaced repetition is the coaching you receive when you come back into class and tell us how you are practicing what you have learned. It's not just the practice by itself that works.

Here is another axiom I like to kill: "Practice makes perfect." Let's say I want to learn how to play golf. I buy some clubs and go out to the first tee. I set up, swing, and slice the ball. If I believe the axiom, all I have to do is keep on practicing and someday I will be a perfect golfer. If you play golf at all you probably know that isn't the case. *"Practice makes Permanent."* If I keep swinging and slicing the ball, all that is going to happen is that I get really good at slicing the ball. Only "Perfect Practice makes Perfect."

And the only way to get close to perfect practice is to have a coach. A coach teaches and shows you how to practice the right things right so you are developing the right skills and habits from the very beginning. So, a true training program incorporates motivation, education, time-spaced repetition, and coaching to ensure the development of your new skills and habits. This process also gives you the confidence in yourself and your abilities to step outside your comfort zone and reach higher and further than you ever have before.

That's a long answer to your question about why the Intentional Achievements programs are different, but I hope it helps you understand the depth of the issues involved. We want people to go through the process and walk out the other end, not just hoping that they're going to lead an intentional life, but knowing that when they follow the processes, they will be seeing and living that life of purpose and intention they have really wanted.

And, since I believe so strongly and confidently about our system, we're the only company and the only program in the industry that gives a special promise and 100 percent guarantee. If you go through the Intentional Achievements Intentional Living System™, you follow the processes, you show us that you've been applying and trying to demonstrate the principles in your life, and you don't get the intentional life that you were looking for or don't achieve the goals that you've set for yourself, we will either give you your full investment back or we'll continue your training and coaching at no cost to you until you do. We are that dedicated to each individual's growth and success, and are not simply selling another product.

Wright

Joe, thank you; what a great conversation. I've actually learned a great deal here and you've given me a lot to think about.

Price

Thanks. We sincerely want the concepts and principles of intentional living out there. We'd like to see as many people as possible come to understand what the necessary ingredients are to creating the life they envision so they can get that picture on the box—their very own intentional life.

Wright

Today we've been talking with Joseph M. Price, an industry leader who has taken over twenty-five years of experience, research, and training, and fused them into the development of a complete and comprehensive system of life-changing personal and business improvement processes. Each one is designed to help people be able to cultivate the necessary attitudes, knowledge, and habits to take control of all aspects of their life and achieve more than they ever thought possible. By employing both time-tested and innovative training methodologies, Intentional Achievements utilizes all aspects of an individual's learning style, making the training and coaching not only appealing but motivating, enlightening, enriching, and enduring, as I think we've seen a glimpse of today in this conversation.

Joe, thank you so much for being with us today on *Roadmap to Success.*

Price

Thank you so much for having me here and allowing me share our Intentional principles with your audience.

ABOUT THE AUTHOR

JOSEPH PRICE is the founder of Intentional Achievements, LLC, which provides professional and personal training and coaching to help individuals achieve greater success and happiness through a comprehensive system of Nine Key Principles for Intentional Living™.

Joe's practical, proven, and powerful processes train and coach participants to live and work "With and On Purpose"™ in order to gain control of their professional and personal lives. Whether it is business success, quality relationships, improved communication skills, financial independence, balance of priorities, or personal fulfillment and peace, Intentional Achievements™ (IA™) is dedicated to helping individuals intentionally achieve it.

IA also provides proven solutions for small, medium, and large businesses to help train executives, managers, sales professionals, and all employees to better attain company goals through Intentional Decision-Making.

Watch for Joe's new book, *9 Keys to an Intentional Life,* due out in December 2009.

Joseph M. Price

9506 W Mariposa St
Phoenix, AZ 85037
Phone: 623.680.1776
joe@intentionalachievements.com
www.intentionalachievements.com

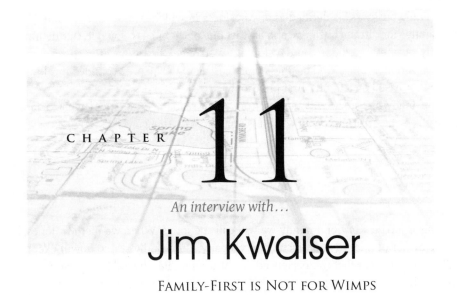

CHAPTER 11

An interview with...

Jim Kwaiser

FAMILY-FIRST IS NOT FOR WIMPS

David Wright (Wright)

Today we are talking with Jim Kwaiser, a certified management consultant and a recognized expert with over thirty-five years of experience working exclusively with families in business. Jim has successfully assisted hundreds of national and international family businesses in identifying and implementing the right road map that is the right fit for their families and their businesses. Jim and his wife, Ann Marie, specialize in the areas of communication, succession planning, operational/organizational development, and strategic implementation. Theirs is a family business assisting families in business.

Jim has stated that his family, religion, and friendships, blended with his passion for assisting family businesses, are the drivers that keep his vision focused and his path straight. Over the years Jim has shared his belief that in order to achieve true success, love of the family must be the basis by which a family in business is guided. It is this understanding that Jim fosters in his business and his daily example.

Jim, welcome to *Roadmap to Success*.

Jim Kwaiser (Kwaiser)

Thank you, David. I'm honored to be part of this project.

Wright

My first question has to be, how do you define "family business"?

Kwaiser

"Family business" is defined as any business in which two or more people of the same family work in the business, and at least one of them has to own it. Our definition of family business includes the developing of stronger family relationships through shared traditions, values, and business practices, all of which are grounded in a love for one another based on a family-first philosophy.

The following story will help you and our readers understand what a family business is by illustrating to you what it is not. May I do that?

Wright

Certainly.

Kwaiser

This is a true story of a family we will call the Jones. When we met Mr. Jones, he was the owner of a large manufacturing company. He proudly stated how he kept his family from the conflicts experienced by other families by taking great pains to separate the family interaction from their involvement in the business. We wanted to hear more from Mr. Jones because we have grown to realize the separation of the personal and the business, with all the family businesses we have worked with, leads to one (or both) of two unhappy endings. The first is poor family relationships and the second is an underperforming family business.

We asked Mr. Jones, "How did you successfully accomplish the family separation, and is it really working for you?" Mr. Jones proudly answered, "I hired a consultant who came in and helped me set up separate divisions for each of my children so they could each work in the business without crossing paths or stepping on each other's toes."

Mr. Jones went on to tell us that in order to insure business conflicts never crossed with family, his family only came together as a group on Thanksgiving, Christmas, weddings, funerals, and sometimes christenings. He proudly stated, "Our business has achieved double-digit increases in net profit every year for the last twenty years."

Mr. Jones retained all authority over coordinating the corporate structure and he dealt with each one of his children one-on-one in order to maintain the separation of business life and personal life. No one else could do it better than Mr. Jones.

Unfortunately, he did not realize that he was setting up his family and his business for failure, as the day will come when the family will have to deal with the very real personal and business issues he kept them away from.

To this day, Mr. Jones still does not realize his separating of personal from business has resulted in a family with no opportunity to learn respect and trust for one another. They don't know how to make decisions together and there is no trust for the decisions of their siblings! Mr. Jones does not realize that while he and his children have all the money they need, he has fostered a family of strangers. Mr. Jones doesn't even know his grandchildren in an authentic and personal way. His focus is first the success of the business, unfortunately at the failure of family relationships.

Is this what having a family business is all about? We don't think so. Just making money and using family members as tools to make it is not our definition of a family business.

Wright

When it comes to the "road map to success," just how successful are families in business?

Kwaiser

Well, David, the statistics on families in business survival are not very encouraging. First, only three out of ten family businesses survive into the second generation, only one out of three into the third generation, and literally less than 5 percent into the fourth generation.

A reason for family business failures is demonstrated in a recent study where almost one-half of the family businesses in the United States admitted to not having a chosen successor. The same survey states that 71 percent of family businesses surveyed indicated they really had no formal succession plan. Believe it or not, the average life of a family business is only twenty-four years!

Looking at these statistics, a conclusion can be reached that the road map most family businesses are obviously using doesn't lead to success.

Wright

What are the biggest causes for family business failures?

Kwaiser

About 10 percent of all failures are due to bankruptcy, and much of that happens in the first twenty-four years! Most people have the misconception that family businesses fail because the "next" generation has squandered the money or they were just bad managers. The real reasons for the failures usually lie in the family's inability or lack of willingness to address the personal issues that revolve around family relationships, business ownership, and business management.

While it hasn't happened yet, there is a real probability in our first story of Mr. Jones that his family and his company will eventually be added to those bleak family business statistics.

Wright

What are some of the other roadblocks that families in business face?

Kwaiser

Let me illustrate a major roadblock to family business success by telling you another true story about a family we will call the Smith Corporation.

The company is a successful design firm founded by Jason Smith. Mr. Smith has two daughters and a son. After they graduated from college, all of them worked for a few years in a related market. After a minimum of three years with other companies, Mr. Smith brought them into the company and placed them in executive positions. Each is paid a market-based salary and receives additional company perks.

Let's set the stage. Picture in your mind a large boardroom. You know the kind. It *smells* like money. There is a long, rich mahogany table with fourteen high-backed, red leather chairs and floors dressed in plush burgundy carpeting. Over one of the chairs is draped a full-length mink coat. Sitting nearby is Mom. She's decked out in her designer dress and shoes, with diamond rings on her fingers and a large diamond heart-shaped necklace around her neck. Her hair is elegantly set and her nails are professionally done, but there is something out of place as tears begin to streak her perfect makeup.

You begin to hear loud voices arguing as you enter further into the room. You can now see the father and his children arguing and yelling at each other. The children are arguing about who should be in charge and who should make the most money. They are even trying to convince Dad why he should fire the other two and increase the salary of the remaining one with the money saved! Dad isn't sure how to handle it because he had stated (as many other parents do) for years, "We don't have to worry about the kids getting along in the business, and they will work it out for themselves." But they never will and there is no hope for a resolution. Finally, Mom, filled with emotion, literally jumps up and screams, "Sell the business! This is tearing up my family. I won't allow it to continue. We were happier and more of a family when we made seventy-five dollars a week!"

David, this is a true story and it illustrates how roadblocks made up of perceptions and personal issues can tear into the very fabric of family. It destroys relationships, pulls families apart, and, as it actually did in this case, caused the business to be sold. It also demonstrates major roadblocks families in business face that revolve around a lack of communication, lack of trust, and the lack of respect for one another. Failure is destined to happen when the family environment is void of love and void of a family-first commitment.

As was demonstrated with the Jones family, it's important to restate that many times it is those in the senior generation who are reluctant to address the emotional, personal, and business issues in their hope of avoiding the conflicts we heard about with the Smith family.

Wright

How can these families in business turn these roadblocks into road maps for success?

Kwaiser

It begins with the commitment of the entire family to communicate with one another as equals. This seems like it should be a "slam dunk" for most families, but the opposite is usually the norm. "Communicate as equals" is a lot easier to say then to practice for most families. Most families continue to deal with one another as siblings to siblings or parent to child or child to parent well into adulthood. They drag the old "emotional" baggage with them into the business as well. Perceptions such as, "Nobody listens to me" or "If I bring it up it is just going to cause a fight" as well as the inability to let go of past "hurts" are what continue to build roadblocks to the family and business success.

The road map to success strategy can become a lot clearer when family members begin with a commitment to communicate as equals as adults, and to let go of the perceptions they had as children or when their children were much younger. This part of the road map has to include realistic expectations of one another. It begins by getting to know one another from a different point of view—as "adults." Communication must be on-going with the establishment of understood and agreed-upon roles, rules, and expectations that will guide the family in how they interact with one another and how they will interact with others inside and outside of the company.

It is the lack of rules that usually leads to conflict in many family businesses. The need for realistic expectations of one another, including defined duties, authority, compensation, and accountability for each person is another area often neglected. Because of the lack of rules, roadblocks increase because of the lack of communication and lack of trust as well as other emotional setbacks that would never have happened if the family had spent more time being open and honest with one another.

Wright

Would you give us an example of how open communication is a key sign along the way on the road map to success?

Kwaiser

Let me illustrate by introducing you to another real family that I will call the Harry family. Their business is a third-generation antique dealership. Tom Harry knew it was time to do future planning for his family. His son and daughter have been active in the business off and on since they were kids. His son, Ted, had gained experience and was successful with another company. Working outside the family business was a requirement Tom had for all of his children.

After five years, Ted agreed to come back and enter into the family business. He assumed the duties of general manager. Tom's daughter, Cindy, had successful outside business experience as well. She also entered the family business and was in charge of promotions. A "roadblock" in this family was that Ted and Cindy had a very strained relationship. They did not communicate with one another and appeared not to trust one another. No one knew why their communication stopped or what caused the strained relationship. What they both shared though, was a true love of family and a strong defined passion for the business.

After some interviews, we discovered that Dad had given the two of them his forty-foot Chris-Craft Roamer boat. Ted and Cindy were delighted! Tom had given it to them two years earlier and that seemed to be when the communication between Ted and Cindy stopped. They were to share the operations of the boat and to work out a schedule of when to use it.

The stress in their relationship began over storage and dock fees that Ted did not pay. Cindy had paid the fees and expected Ted to reimburse her. The problem was that no one had told Ted about the outstanding fees! Ted couldn't figure out why Cindy was so stressed. Because of her refusing to communicate with him, he in turn shut communication off with her. After the problem was discovered, Ted immediately apologized to his sister and wrote out a check for his share of the fees (plus the interest). He and Cindy instituted a process to openly deal with issues out of love for one another. Love of the family came back.

This story stresses the need for family members to continually work on their interpersonal communication by making it a priority of the family and the business. Many of us spend more time on our golf game, our exercise routine, or whatever our hobbies are than we do on our family relationships. And we wonder why we have communication roadblocks!

Wright

You had stated that families in business together have great difficulty in addressing their personal issues. With that in mind, how do these families even begin to lay out their road map to success?

Kwaiser

The problem is that most do not. Most families usually decide to try something about the way they currently interact because they are in a crisis situation. They just can't stand the family fighting or the family business conflicts anymore. Common sense and reason lose out. Emotion takes over and nothing is ever resolved. It is only at that time do many families make a decision to get the help they need.

It begins when family members forget to realize that each member of the family grows and matures in different ways. Family members each pass through stages in their lives that literally make them different people. They are not the same people they were in grade school or high school or later in life. Today they may not even like the people they once were! Family members must each take the time to get to know other family members as they go through their "stages" of life. If family members don't do this, they will never really know one another. They won't grow with one another. They will never have a respect and appreciation for the person their family member has become. Strong relationships are worth the effort but they do take time and commitment—time and commitment that are freely given to other things while family relationships suffer!

Families in business should seek help in planning their road map to success by first securing the right "guide." Many families turn to current advisors to fill the role of the relationship and succession consultant. Unfortunately, many of these advisors have a past history of siding with one family member over another. They are not perceived as working for the best interest of the entire family. These advisors do not have the experience for this type of guidance and many times they make the road map to success more confusing and much more difficult to follow.

What is needed is a "family business travel guide" so to speak—someone whom all the family members can agree upon. This person would help keep the family together as the primary goal and would assist in plotting an agreed-upon road map for the success of the family and business. Deciding to use a "guide" can be a roadblock to many families in business—difficult because many families hate to "hang out their dirty laundry" to "strangers." Because of this image based belief, very few family businesses secure guidance and assistance from the right advisors—and statistics prove it!

Select the right advisor with the experience needed for your concerns. Professional advisors maintain confidentiality and hold the trust of the family very close. Just make sure the "travel guide" you select has the tools to deal with both family and business issues. The family will be the guide's first consideration. "Family first" is a must philosophy of any family business advisor you choose.

Wright

What is your "Family-First" philosophy and how does it work when it comes to developing a successful road map for a business and the family who owns it?

Kwaiser

Primarily, the Family-First philosophy is not for wimps! It is a philosophy that requires a conscious commitment by each member of the family business to place other family members before themselves in the business's decision-making process. What this means is that before every decision made, each family member must ask themselves two basic questions. The first is: "How will this situation affect other members of my family and business?" The second is: "Will this situation be in the best interest of the family and the business as a whole?"

Family-First is a philosophy of caring enough for other family members so you will not make decisions that would be hurtful to another family member. The family defines what is hurtful with the assistance of the travel "guide." When "hurtful" is clearly the case, the decision in question is presented to the working family members who consider all sides of the issue and then decide on the solution they deem is in the

159

best interest of the entire family. This keeps one or two family members from "dumping" additional work on others. It is a safety net to keep family members from complaining about the decision just to avoid work (oh yeah, it happens!).

Decisions about how to handle business must include how the business affects the lives of the family members.

Let me illustrate how decisions involving both "hurtful" to the family and Family-First issues can be blended together to make decisions in the best interest of the family. This cannot be demonstrated better than by a family we will call the Steele family.

The Steeles' largest customer was 50 percent of their business. This customer had a buyer who was foulmouthed and enjoyed throwing his weight around to vendors who called upon him. Mr. Steele's daughter, Sue, had been calling on this customer for five years. The verbal abuse and disrespect began to escalate and Sue just could not take it anymore. She went to her dad and explained the situation. Mr. Steele was actually shocked; he hadn't realized what had been going on. He called the buyer and expressed his concern. The buyer pretty much told him that was the way he worked and to tell Sue to quit being such a "girl." Mr. Steele then contacted the general manager of the company and expressed his concern again and even though the manager listened, nothing was done to correct the issue.

After six months of trying, the Steeles made a decision. They were going to officially withdraw as a supplier to this company. Now remember, this is 50 percent of their business. They also decided they would not, under any condition, lay off any employees because of this decision. The Steeles informed all of their employees of their decision.

Mr. Steele and his daughter then visited the buyer. They explained to him that they were no longer going to supply a company that had so little respect for them. The Steeles explained their values, which included respect for all people, and that their values were no longer going to be compromised by this customer. This was also the reason they would not assign another person to this account. The buyer couldn't believe his ears. This was his company's largest supplier. He apologized and stated he needed them as a supplier and would they reconsider. Mr. Steele stated that it was too late because they had tried to correct the situation for the past six months and enough was enough. The Steeles left! The general manager called Mr. Steele asking him to reconsider but the family stood firm.

To the Steeles, the Family-First is more than just words or a concept in their value system. Family-First includes family members standing up for one another, even when it may seem like a bad business decision. Family-First means holding themselves accountable to a higher standard in the way they work, how they treat others, and how they expect others to treat them. So they did it.

After their inventories were gone, the Steeles dropped the company as a client. The Steeles lost half of their business and profits in one day, yet they knew they were doing the right thing.

Wright

Family-First sounds like it is a hard philosophy to follow and could even be expensive to implement. Is that true?

Kwaiser

The Family-First philosophy is not easy. It is placing the honor, respect, and love of the family before the business and before money. "Expensive" depends on how you measure it. To the Steeles it was not expensive. For them, the loss of a customer's business, that may be replaceable through hard work, was less expensive than the stress Sue was under for dealing with an abusive buyer.

Family-First can get harder when it moves beyond just dealing with "outsiders." It includes dealing with family members who don't want to show honor and respect for one another. It makes Family-First harder because the central goal is the "good of the family" and yet the process can actually remove individual members from the family business! Family-First is not for wimps. Love of the family is the top priority of Family-First and it must be given in a non-selfish way. When anyone, even family members, don't align with that philosophy (after real attempts to get them to do so), it is time to have them "move on" in the best interest of the majority of the family. A very difficult decision, when not made, can destroy the whole family and the business. If this happens, everyone will pay the price for the one family member who will not agree to honor and respect other family members!

On a happier note, let me tell you what has happened to the Steele family. Within three years of their decision, they had increased their business four times above their previous high and are extremely profitable! They expanded their facility and continued to take on customers of high caliber who wanted to do business with them. There is a company calling the Steeles asking them to be their supplier, but it hasn't happened yet—I'll bet you can guess who that company is.

Wright

I bet I can too!

What other personal issues must consciously be plotted on the road map to success?

Kwaiser

There are literally thousands of them, David, and they can be very different for each family. Families have to begin their road map to success by working together and truly identifying their potential roadblocks *before* they lay out the road map. The major difference from family to family in their roadblocks is the degree to which emotion is involved.

A good example of this is the issue of compensation. While compensation might not always seem like an emotional issue, family businesses have a real knack for making it one. Believe it or not, there are still families in business who establish wages based upon *need* instead of contribution to the success of the business. This is what makes it really emotional. A family member, married with children, may end up getting paid more than a sibling who is president of the company but is single. Unfortunately, this type of thinking catches up with the family when the senior generation is gone and the next generation has to deal with it. This is exactly what the Jones—our first family example—have yet to face.

Getting the right travel guide upfront will help the family. The right guide, as we stated earlier, becomes a must in helping families discover the best direction for the good of the family. Personal issues—roadblocks to success, if you will—pop up all over the place and the right guide can help the family avoid being stalled at roadblocks for too long. The right guide can also assist the family to obtain respect for the people they have become, not just for who they are remembered as.

Personal issues can turn very ugly when individuals allow their emotions to take over. Let me give you a few more examples of personal issues that have torn families and their businesses apart. They are great examples of just some of the issues that get in the way of family relationships. The following examples were taken from articles I've read in *Family in Business* and *FORTUNE* magazines.

The founders of Adidas (the shoe people), Adolph and Rudolph Dessler, had a violent falling out when they were younger. When Adolph died, the brothers hadn't spoken in twenty-nine years. The surviving brother couldn't remember what they fought about.

The Dart Group was one of the largest discount retailers in the world. Founder Herbert Haft fired his son, Robert, because he perceived that Robert was trying to displace him as CEO. The family split up. The Hafts lost control of the company and the company ended up in Chapter Eleven. I wonder where "love of the family" figured into all of this?

Unresolved issues have plagued a lot of well-known families. One that has always bothered me is the von Trapp family. (The von Trapps were the family whose story was told in the musical *The Sound of Music.*) They sued each other over ownership of their family resort in Vermont. I can't believe Maria would sue anybody! But it actually happened.

Some emotional questions that families should openly address include:
- What would happen today if the current "owner generation" were together in a plane crash?
- Who in the family gets ownership of what?

- Who reports to whom and how is it decided in the business?
- Who gets what "perks" in the family business and how is it decided?
- Who makes the final business decisions and how is that person selected (after Dad or the family member who has controlling ownership)?
- How much does each get paid and how is that decided?
- Are in-laws allowed in the business? Who do they report to?
- Does the business have a board of directors and who makes the decision about who will serve on the board?
- How are working family members evaluated?
- What are the rules for relatives entering and leaving the business?
- How is conflict between family members handled?
- How will compensation of working family members be determined?

And there are as many additional questions as there are families in business!

Some emotional family issues revolve around preconceived notions and statements that assume each family member really knows one another. Statement like:

"I know who you are. I know what you're going to say, so, I have no need to speak to you about it."

"You were a bum as a kid you will be a bum now!"

And yes, the one statement that we still hear from time to time, "The reason you get so much is because Mom and Dad always loved you best." This is the statement that causes the most heartache to the parents. Most parents tell us, "We just want our family to get along!"

Wright

You identified succession planning as key to the family business road map to success. What are some of the additional succession issues that need to be addressed?

Kwaiser

Succession planning is a major factor in the road map to success. Without it there is no legacy and no real plan to have the business survive beyond the founding generation. Let's first identify what succession planning is. Succession planning is a structured ongoing process of securing competent family ownership who understand and support the Family-First concept. It includes the securing of qualified, knowledgeable leadership for all positions in the company. Often the leadership succession never is completed because of family conflict over ownership succession. For succession planning to be effective, management succession has to be considered as a part of the family business succession plan. Without it, there will be conflict and stress as the "next generation" tries to figure out where each family member's responsibilities fit in to the decision-making process of the company. This lack of management succession can also create interpersonal conflict between family members when not properly addressed.

Other succession planning issues include:

- The senior generation's reluctance to allow the next generation to take on more responsibility when they are prepared!
- The senior generation's inability to let go.
- The strict adherence to the family's natural "pecking order" instead of the best person for the right job.
- The next generation's demand to take on higher levels of responsibility when they are not prepared.
- The lack of joint generation planning.
- The lack of open communication between generations of working family members.

David, additional succession concerns revolve around other interesting statistics such as:

- 45 percent of family business owners plan to retire in the next five years.
- Less than 32 percent have any type of estate plan beyond a will.
- 30 percent of people said, "Ahh, I'm not going to retire. You're going to have to carry me out of here boots first!"
- And many more!

There are a large number of issues concerning succession planning that must be addressed if a family in business is going to properly plot out their road map to success. With love of the family as the compass, and the right guide, the road map is much easier to navigate!

Wright

If there was just one message you could give to all the families in business—a message that could give them the right starting point on the road map to success—what would that be?

Kwaiser

Our first answer to this question usually surprises most people because it comes in a form of a question. We begin by asking every family member in a family-owned business that is considering working with us what we consider the most important question we can ask, "Do you love one another—not in just unspoken ways, but in ways that your family members experience and experience often?" When love is not present, it is *not* a family business, it is a partnership and usually a partnership with hostile partners!

I cannot overemphasize the importance of this question. Successful family businesses take a lot of time and commitment. A family whose members really love one another is much better armed to deal with long hours and tough decisions when they realize they have people who love them in it with them! That type of support is the prime motivator to getting around roadblocks and proceeding steadily along the road to success. A true family business is when it is the love of the family that holds the family together, not the financial aspects of the business.

Wright

Over the last thirty-five years you have been a successful internal and external consultant. You have held leadership positions in family businesses as well as Fortune 500 companies that worked with families in business, and you and your wife, Ann Marie, founded your successful consulting family business over fifteen years ago. Will you sum up for our readers what has been your personal road map to success?

Kwaiser

First, who we are as a family business is solidly based on our Family-First philosophy. We live what we preach and we do follow that road map. There are a few lessons we have learned along our journey:

- *Passion:* We have all heard this one before, but for us it goes a little deeper. Passion for what you do must identify with who you are, what you believe in, how you act, and how others see you—always! It is more than just your enthusiasm; it is who you are and how you treat others in every aspect of your life. Passion is a love for what you are doing—whatever that is—when you are doing it, and other people really seeing it in you!

- *People:* Surround yourself with others who can teach you and "stretch" you mentally and with those you can find ways to help in return! Place your family first and help them to grow just as you need them to help you grow every day of your life! No longer mix with "users." You know who they are. Stay away from them because they are a waste of time. Network with the people who do business with the people you want to do business with. It is easier to get to the decision-maker when you have his or her banker, attorney, or other trusted advisor introduce you!

- *Process:* For your business or your life, plan out your next thirty days. Know who you are and where you are going. For your business, have a sales process or a consulting process that always leads you through the first thirty days of assisting the client. Also, include a monthly retainer in your process plan. No matter what business you are in, there is a way to set up a process for a monthly fee. Examples include: retainers for services to service contracts for product deliveries or maintenance contracts. Clients don't mind paying for people who can demonstrate on-going process thinking that assists in finding solutions to their challenges!

- *Persistence:* Know when to keep going and know when to change direction, but don't quit! Don't be afraid to take some risk, especially if you are depending upon your skills or those of people you trust. "So stick with the fight when you are hardest hit—it's when things go wrong that you mustn't quit!"—author unknown. That is what divides the successful people from the ones who never quite make it.

- *Patience:* Patience is not waiting and doing nothing. It is doing everything you know how to do, getting the help you need, and still having the patience to realize that even the results of hard work may take a little more time than you expect. Patience is realizing that some failures are just a few of the roadblocks to success. Patience goes hand-in-hand with persistence, yet it is the patience to keep doing what needs to be done, even with minimal results at first, that usually separates those who are personally successful from those who are not. And finally:

- *Pray:* No matter how good you think you are, you cannot do anything without the right help. Prayer before meetings, before decisions, with our families, at home, and in business, with employees, when times are bad or good—anytime, all the time—will always bring you the right help.

Wright

What a great conversation! We have been talking with Jim Kwaiser, a certified management consultant. Now I understand what his mission is—to stop the generational erosion of family businesses through a process based on strong family relationships and strategies developed to fit the uniqueness of the family and the business. Since I am in a family business, what he said here has really meant a lot to me. I am sure our readers will gain a lot of insight from this chapter also.

Jim, thank you so much for being with us today on *Roadmap to Success.*

Kwaiser

Thank you, David, for your kind remarks. I too hope that our readers will find this information helpful to their families and businesses.

ABOUT THE AUTHOR

JIM KWAISER, CMC, and his wife, Ann Marie, RN, founded their family business C.H.A.L.L.E.N.G.E.S. inc. in 1993. They specialize in working with families in business in the areas of communication, succession planning, and operational development. Jim has over thirty-five years of experience working in, with, and for a variety of family businesses on a regional, national, and international level. He has written many articles on family business issues, he is a featured author of *The Communication Coach,* and was quoted by Dr. Alan Weiss in his book, *The Ultimate Consultant.*

To discover if Jim and Ann Marie's services are a "fit" for you and your family, feel free to contact them.

Jim Kwaiser, CMC

C.H.A.L.L.E.N.G.E.S.° inc.
P.O. Box 6
Mercer, PA 16137
888.273.8307
jim@challengesinc.com
ann@challengesinc.com
www.challengesinc.com

CHAPTER 12

An interview with...

Bea Fields

MANAGING AND LEADING THE
GENERATION Y WORKFORCE

David Wright (Wright)

Today, we're talking to Bea Fields; she is an executive coach and the President of Bea Fields Companies Inc. She is the Founder of FiveStarLeader.com, a leadership consulting firm currently serving over 800 clients worldwide. She is the co-author of *Millennial Leaders Success Stories from Today's Most Brilliant Generation Y Leaders*, and *Edge: A Leadership Story*. She holds a Bachelor of Science Degree from the University of Alabama, and a Certificate Degree in Leadership Coaching from Georgetown University. She is a Professional Certified Coach (PCC) with the International Coach Federation and is a member of the American Society of Training and Development. Ms. Fields welcome to *Roadmap to Success*.

Bea Fields (Fields)

Thank you so much David. It's great to be here.

Wright

So, who is generation Y and why do our readers need to know about this generation?

Fields

When people discuss generations, there is a natural tendency to assign each generation an age category. While this is certainly a part of defining Generation Y, there is a much bigger picture to consider, which includes taking into account the world events which have helped shape their world view and the values they hold dear in life. Generation Y includes approximately 72 million men and women who were born between the ages of 1977, and 1992. You will hear demographers and generational consultants debate these birth years, but these dates are in the ballpark. Gen Y was born into a high tech, digital, plug and play world with quick access to massive amounts of information and the ability to connect to a global community in a matter of seconds. They will soon outnumber the Baby Boomers, born between 1945-1964 and are approximately 70% larger than Generation X, which is the generation born between 1965 and 1976.

Wright

And you said there were 72 million of them?

Fields

Yes, 72 million at least.

Wright

So, how does Generation Y define success?

Fields

I have worked with thousands of people over the last 20 years, and there is one thing I can say with confidence. Each person I have met defines success differently. If you talk to a variety of Gen Y's, each will most likely tell you something different because they're unique individuals with their own cultural values and ideas of what it means to be successful in life. However, more often than not, Generation Y considers success to be defined by the amount of joy they feel from doing meaningful work, having a great personal life, building strong relationships with friends, peers and romantic partners and being able to have the freedom and flexibility to change careers, travel the world and continue their education. While earning income and having a great career are certainly motivators for everyone, including Generation Y, these young men and women are much more vocal about not just having a great career, but having a great life where their skills and talents are working to create something meaningful to help improve our world. Organizations like the Peace Corps and Teach for America are very popular with this generation, because they allow Gen Y to exercise their commitment to volunteerism, community and civic pride and this drive to do work which positively impacts a social concern. With these two companies,

Gen Y can quickly see that their work is not in vain. They can see in a matter of days that their work is meaningful and is changing lives of the people they serve.

Wright

I know you have discussed some world events which have shaped Gen Y's perspective, so could you share with our readers what some of those events were?

Fields

David, answering this question is critical for older generations and generations to come to be able to truly understand who Generation Y is, how to best communicate with them and to grasp the full context of what they are doing to change the world and create a strong future for our children and grandchildren. Generation Y's perspective and values are actually defined by some very significant global events which took place during their formative years. This generation was born with a laptop and cell phone in their cribs. They have watched the unfortunate events of September 11 and have stood by as members of their generation were killed during the massacres at Columbine and Virginia Tech. They have observed their parents being downsized or fired from corporations around the world. They have become connected to thousands of new faces and names worldwide through online social networks like Facebook, My Space, Twitter and Second Life, and many of these interactions have taken place with people who have violated their safety and security including child predators, stalkers and online bullies. To compound this, Generation Y was born into an era where over-involved parents have planned and managed each and every decision their children have made and have coddled them along the way, preventing this generation from making mistakes which can teach them valuable life lessons. When you consider not just one of these but all of these events combined, I think it is safe to say that Gen Y is coming into adulthood and our workforce with a brand new skill set, a unique belief system and a huge bucket of concerns that older generations did not have when they were young adults.

Wright

So how have these world events shaped Gen Y's worldview?

Fields

As a result of these events, Gen Y is coming into adulthood and the working world with a unique belief system and set of skills and talents which are changing the way we work and live. They are the most technologically savvy, entrepreneurial generation in history and their easy access to information is creating a thirst for more knowledge and a need for a variety of stimuli. The majority of Gen Yers not only work full time for companies. Many run a small business on the side and a large percentage either work for or own their own non-profit organization. Gen Yers are saying they want to change the world and live a balanced life while they are doing it. They see the world as a wealth of opportunity, knowledge and community. They have been raised by parents who have taught them to believe that they can do anything and be anything, and they really believe this. Many senior leaders are commenting that Generation Y is coming into the working world with some very high expectations and "wanting it all" and that they are often experiencing a let-down effect when they don't get what they want. This makes perfect sense considering the messages they have been sent by their parents, teachers and the media.

Wright

What does Generation Y most value in their life and work?

Fields

Each time I hear this question, I think about a colleague of mine, Rebecca Ryan, who is the Founder of Next Generation Consulting. She says that Gen Y really wants to "live first and work second", and she actually has a book by the same name, *Live First, Work Second,* which I highly recommend to anyone who wants to know more about what Gen Y values. Generation Y learned from their older siblings, Generation X, that flexibility and living first are critical to being able to do meaningful work and to achieve life balance. They value their leisure time and time with friends. They have often watched their Baby Boomer parents work 60-70 hours a week only to get downsized or fired, and they don't want this same lifestyle. They place a high value on the ability to learn and develop and gain quick access to information at the touch of a button. Because Generation Y has been born into a melting pot society, they also value diversity, acceptance and open, divergent thinking.

Wright

So what are some of the most common challenges that arise in the workplace regarding more senior leaders and Generation Y?

Fields

I think one thing we have to understand is that right now in our workforce we have an aging population that is transitioning out of the workforce. Some of these workers are of the Traditionalist age, which are men and women that were born in the 1930's and 40's. Then we have the Baby Boomers that were born in the years 1946 to 1964, and of course Generation X and then Generation Y followed the Boomers. Each of these generations were born and raised during different times and as a result have formed very distinct world views. Whenever you have four generations that are trying to work together, live together and make political decisions together, you're going to have four different perspectives playing a role in decision making. So each generation's perspective being unique and different creates a dynamic which creates a clashing of ideas and opinions.

With Generation Y, the biggest gaps that we see right now are in the way they communicate and their views around how work should be done. Generation Y wants to communicate using technology. They are quite comfortable with text messaging and online social networks such as Facebook, and many senior leaders are much more comfortable with face to face conversations and telephone conversations. The communication gap seems to be widening because of the advancement in technology and the shift from face to face interactions to communication by text, instant message and online networks.

When it comes to the topic of work ethic, Generation Y is looking for balance, and this does not include wanting to work 50 or 60 hours a week, sometimes not even wanting to work 40 hours per week. Many senior leaders will tell you that they are not accustomed to this view of work. They believe if you are asked to work more than 40 hours per week, you should be dedicated enough to your employer and company to do it without question.

In my opinion, these gaps are offering us the opportunity to implement a reverse mentoring program in our companies and organizations. With this approach, Generation Y would be teaching and mentoring more senior leaders on the use of technology to expedite communication and to perform work in a more efficient manner so that we get the free time that we all crave. I have actually watched first-hand a Generation Y worker do the same task in half the time of a Baby Boomer, simply because she knew how to use technology to speed up the process. On the flip side of this mentoring relationship, senior leaders have the opportunity to teach and mentor Generation Y on how to engage in professional, face-to-face conversations and presentations with poise and to educate them on how working overtime occasionally (occasionally is the operative word here) is necessary to complete a project on time and under budget so that the customer and the greater organization are served.

Wright

So what do companies need to do to be more successful in addressing these challenges?

Fields

I believe that companies can start to address these challenges by asking four very important questions of Generation Y:

1. What do you most value? Sit down with your Gen Y employees and spend time listening to what they most value in work and life, and by all means, challenge your assumptions about what may have worked in the past with older generations. New times call for new values and new approaches to

inspiring young talent. Once they have shared their values with you, talk with them about both your values and the organization's values and how their values align with yours.

2. What do you most want to achieve in your career? Generation Y wants to develop a great career, and they do have leadership aspirations. This question can provide you with the opportunity to discuss the vision for your company and how he/she can play a significant role in helping your organization reach this vision.

3. What do you most need to know about working with our company so that you achieve success? As more senior leaders, it is important that we not make assumptions about what Gen Y knows or does not know about the company culture or the way work is done in an organization. They may not know your dress code, what you expect during projects or how to interact with customers and other employees. Use this question as an opportunity to let your young worker know about your culture and also to listen for ideas about what you can do to make your company more efficient and effective.

4. What do you most need from me as a leader? Many leaders never ask this question of their younger workers. If you ask Gen Y, listen with both your heart and your head, and be open to what they have to say. Many Gen Yers will tell you "I just want to be heard" or "I want to know that I have a voice and that you respect my opinion". If they say "I don't know", engage with them in a dialogue which offers them examples of what you wanted from your boss when you were in your twenties. Through building rapport, a Gen Y employee will eventually feel psychologically safe enough to talk with you openly about what they are looking for in a leader.

Wright

What is Gen Y saying they most want from a career?

Fields

I think that many leaders are assuming that Gen Yers just want a big salary and a list of great perks and while I agree that this does often get Gen Y in the door, I am not convinced that this keeps them in your company. Many senior leaders are saying that Gen Yers job-hop frequently, often leaving a job for something better every two to three years. From what I am hearing, Generation Y is saying that they are leave a company when they feel they have no other choice...that usually leave a boss who makes life difficult or a culture that is stagnant or when they feel they are no longer heard and or receiving the training they need to grow their career. Generation Y is saying that what they really want is ongoing learning and development and this doesn't necessarily mean classroom training. They want on the spot, in the moment, coaching, learning and development. They want constant feedback about their job performance and the opportunity to engage in work that they know is going to change the world.

Generation Y is a very civic minded generation, so they want to know that their employer is actually contributing back to their local and greater community and they want to be a part of that process. The companies who have a culture based on a true learning organizations and who are addressing incentives like reimbursement for ongoing education, or days off to do volunteer work in the local community and opportunities to build a strong network locally, are finding much more success in getting Gen Y to stick around than companies who are not addressing these issues.

Wright

What changes do senior leaders need to make in the way they think in order to work successfully with Gen Y.

Fields

I think that the first step is for a senior leader is to sit down and challenge their assumptions about what they think Gen Y most values, needs and wants from an employer. From there, I think you have to ask yourself a very tough question which is "Does your recruitment package address what Gen Y most values, needs and wants, and can you compete with other companies who are succeeding with attracting young talent"? If your company is not in a position to offer a competitive employment package, then it's time for you and your team to go back to the drawing board and start getting really creative about what you are going to offer Gen Y that is attractive enough to have them want to work for your company and stick around for a few years. Taking a few calculated risks such as developing a sharp reverse mentoring/coaching program, a career rotational program or a future leaders development program that is first class may be in order. Rather than giving money back to the community, look at contributing manpower to the community so that Gen Y can be a part of that process. I believe a great week-end brainstorming on paper can serve a company well in beginning to look at some of these and other highly creative options to start attracting the young worker.

Wright

So how can managers, leaders, and coaches support Generation Y in becoming successful leaders for our future?

Fields

I think the first step in that direction is for senior leaders to become role models for what they want to see in Gen Y, and that first step involves looking at your own life as a leader and performing a transparency and integrity check. Ask yourself these questions:

- "Is my brand to the public lining up with my brand on the inside of my company?"

- "Am I doing what I said I would do?"

- "Am I leading with an authentic leadership style?"

- "Am I making quick, smart decisions which are moving this company forward, or am I stuck?"

- "On a scale of 1-10, how much am I modeling loyalty, a strong work ethic and dedication to high quality and ongoing learning and development?"

By answering these questions first, you will find some valuable answers which can get you started moving in the right direction of being a great role model for your young employees.

Wright

So how can Gen Y employees be successful team players?

Fields

To start with, I want to state that I believe Gen Y is going to be a very powerful contributing force to teams in the future, because they have been born and raised in teams. As with all teams and all ages, it is not uncommon to find what I call the "lone wolf" who works better alone than with teams, yet Generation Y is the first generation to have teamwork ingrained in them from a very young age, as young as age three or four. Playing and working on teams is a part of their DNA.

As Gen Y's move into teams, there are four main steps leaders can take to make sure they are successful team players:

1. Define the team design. The first step to making sure that Gen Y is a successful team player is to explain the team design to your Gen Y's and make sure that they really understand and know what kind of team they're playing with. Is your team leader-directed, self-directed or does leadership rotate from team member to team member?

2. Ask powerful questions. Generation Y is a generation that will tell you that they have grown weary by hearing gobs of unsolicited advice from their parents (who are now becoming known as "helicopter parents"...parents who hover over their child's every move) and authority figures. As their boss, you now fall into the category of being an authority figure. By asking great questions, Gen Y will usually come up with some great answers, and these answers are often in the same vein as the advice you had intended to give them in the first place. People play better on teams when they feel they have had a voice during decision making and problem solving rather than being told what to do every step of the way.

3. Give them a voice. In order for a Gen Y to be a great team player, they have to know that their voice is being heard, taken to heart and acted on. While you are never going to act on 100% of the ideas Gen Y brings to the team, it is important for their own self validation that you implement a few ideas now and then to let them know that their voice has been heard and that you took them seriously enough to do something about it. If you are not acting on their ideas and suggestions on occasion, they will think you are not listening.

4. Communicate clearly. As we move into the next 5-7 years and into the future, our teams are going to become less visible and more virtual. It is important for teams of the future to be using every communication tool they can get their hands on, including text messaging, instant messaging, online social networks and services like Twitter to be able to communicate quickly and in real time. Don't leave any question unanswered or stone unturned.

Wright

Could you tell our readers what type of feedback Gen Y is seeking so they can be successful as they can be in both work and life?

Fields

I love talking about this topic because I'm really big on performing 360 feedback reviews. Many Baby Boomers are accustomed to having an annual review, either a 360 degree feedback review or some kind of personnel review, and I don't think that's going to go away. But Gen Y wants a much different approach with feedback. They want it every day, sometimes multiple times a day. Gen Y wants to constantly know "How am I doing" and "Am I stacking up to your expectations"? Remember: Gen Y has been raised by parents who have doted over them and have told them how great they are, and simply because they are now in the working world does not mean that this need for validation magically disappears. I believe that managers and senior leaders can add a great deal of value to their organizations by developing an ongoing feedback cycle, where they provide Gen Y with feedback, coaching, and then of course instruction on how they can improve a certain skill set. If you've got that feedback loop built into your daily interactions company-wide, then your Gen Y employees will know that this is a part of your culture, and they then learn how to accept and respond to both positive and constructive feedback. The key to success with this process is to explain in detail upfront that the feedback is a part of your culture and that both the positive and constructive feedback are being offered on an ongoing basis to help them to strengthen their career and leadership skills and so they won't have any surprises come up during the end of the year annual review. There is nothing more disheartening to a Gen Yer than to hear a piece of constructive feedback for the first time at the end of the year, especially when the feedback or review may have an impact on a bonus, salary increase or promotion.

Wright

Well what a great conversation, I have learned a lot about Generation Y here this morning. I've got a lot of them working for me, and you basically taught me a lot in how to treat them.

Fields

Does it sound familiar?

Wright

Oh, yes, it sure does. I really appreciate you taking so much time with me this morning to answer all these questions, and as I've said I have really, really learned a lot.

Fields

You are welcome; thank you.

Wright

Today we have been talking to Bea Fields, she is an executive coach, and President of Bea Fields Companies Inc., she is also the Founder of Fivestarleader.com, a leadership consulting firm currently serving over 800 clients worldwide. She's a Professional Certified Coach, with the International Coach Federation, and a member of the American Society of Training and Development. Bea thank you so much for being with us today on Roadmap to Success.

Fields

Thank you David.

ABOUT THE AUTHOR

BEA FIELDS IS AN EXECUTIVE Coach and the President of Bea Fields Companies, Inc. She is the Founder of Five Star Leader.com, a leadership consulting firm currently serving over 800 clients world-wide. She is the author of *Millennial Leaders: Success Stories From Today's Most Brilliant Generation Y Leaders* and *Edge: A Leadership Story*. Fields holds a Bachelor of Science Degree from the University of Alabama and a Certificate Degree in Leadership Coaching from Georgetown University. She is a Professional Certified Coach (PCC) with the International Coach Federation and is a member of the American Society of Training and Development.

Bea Fields

P.O. Box 117
Southern Pines, NC 28387
(910) 692-6118
beafields@beafields.com
www.BeaFields.com
www.MillennialLeaders.com

CHAPTER 13

An interview with...

David Alexander

NETWORKING LIKE A PRO

David Wright (Wright)

Today is yet again another good day and we are going to talk about something that I know is at the heart of every business owner—how to get more referrals. This is something I know everybody wants to do.

Let me tell you a little bit about David Alexander. David's vision is to build a thriving community of professionals who believe that investing in each other's success is the path to prosperity. David creates this vision through being the CNO (Chief Networking Officer) of Referrals4Life, LLC. Referrals4Life manages BNI (Business Network International) in several states. David and his teams have won numerous awards with BNI that include: BNI Hall of Fame, Top Ten Region, Excellence in Goal Setting, Analyses and Planning, Top Directors Performance Reviews, and Most New Members during Member Extravaganza. David is also a member of BNI Founders' Circle and Platinum Club.

David and his company also provide customized corporate training through the Referral Institute and Intensity Business Leadership. David's latest project is CNOWorks. He has identified a huge need in corporate America to put chief networking officers in place to manage social capital. David will be providing this resource to companies. He's been featured in numerous articles and is currently working on three books: *Networking Like a Pro, Referrals for Life,* and *Intensity Business Leadership.*

One thing that is also very important and very clear about David is he's a very big family guy as well. This will be revealed very clearly in the information you're going to read about in this chapter because ultimately he has his goals in the right place. He is married to the love of his life, Kimberly, and they have two children, Christian and Peyton. David has a fantastic life. I know you're wondering why I'm telling you this, but we're going to bring this all back around because he is going to explain to you why all of this is important. Let's go ahead and jump back to why you really want to apply as much of this information as you can.

David has taught thousands of businesspeople and companies to network like a pro which has helped them dramatically increase their business referrals. This, of course, adds to their bottom line. David is going to show you how to increase your sales by 30, 50 or even 100 percent by enhancing the relationships you already have and learning how to create new ones. David is a firm believer in "Givers Gain" and he's driven to help others achieve success. I'm very honored and blessed to have David provide this chapter for our book.

I only have a few questions for you, David, but they are loaded. I know you're going to provide a lot of value.

The first question that I have for you is what exactly is a referral? Everyone wants them, but there is a lot of misunderstanding about what a referral is.

David Alexander (Alexander)

That's a great question, and I agree with you—I think many people tend to have trouble wrapping their hands around it. We go into sales, we come out of school, or college, and work for a company and everybody tells us what a great thing referrals are—let's go get them and go make them happen, but we don't really understand what the term means. I'm going to challenge the commonly understood concept of what a referral is. Many times people will consider a referral as simply a connection with somebody else—someone with whom they can call upon to do business. Let's use, for example, a Real Estate agent and an insurance guy. The Real Estate agent needs insurance and knows someone who sells insurance. They get together and the insurance guy makes the sale. That's the traditional definition of a referral.

I look at referrals a little differently in that I tend to look at referrals as very high level relationship-building opportunities. For example, I do corporate training and consulting on personal referral marketing. When I get a referral to do that kind of work, the minimum expectation that I have for people in my network (and I know this is going to shock a few people when I say this) is that you know the person you are referring so well that you can set up a meeting.

Now, if you think about it, when I get a referral to do some work for somebody and the meeting has been set, what do you think my chances are of closing that deal? *They are very good.*

Now, let's go a little bit lower down the scale, and say that the referral came in and all I knew was just the name and some contact information. Maybe I was authorized to use somebody's name when I made the phone call. What do you think the chances are of even getting the appointment? Probably not as good.

So basically I take relationships that I already have in place and leverage those, so that when I'm interacting with a new client, it's a slam dunk—it's a lay-up.

Here is another way to look at it. I know that there are probably a lot of folks out there who are as fortunate as I am to have a wonderful wife. There have been times when my wife, Kimberly, would call me in the afternoon (oh, and by the way, it is five o'clock in the afternoon, I've been working since six o'clock that morning, networking and doing my thing). "Hey honey," she says, "would you pick up a gallon of milk on the way home?" You know, the natural inclination is to say, "You've got to be kidding! I've been working all day, you go get the milk!" If I say that, I've just damaged the relationship. My opportunity or my thought is that when this happens, I take the lay-up—I say, "Yes dear, what type, what size, skim or whole milk?" and I make it happen.

How this illustration relates to the referral process is this: often we don't take "lay-ups" when we're looking for referrals. We take the three-point shot versus taking the lay-up. I like to teach people how to take the lay-ups. I teach you to take the relationships you have in place and teach them how to refer you to people they know at a very high level.

Wright

I'm hearing a lot of parallels between good networking and getting solid referrals. I like what you said about the fact that after the conversation they ought to be able to set up a meeting for you. When you have a clear focus, that enables the end result to happen. If you're thinking, "I'll go to this networking function and hand out all seventy-five business cards in my pocket," well, that doesn't have anything to do with referrals or setting up a meeting or meeting anybody new or generating any business—your end result will be an empty pocket.

Alexander

Absolutely. I think we go to networking events and we often do exactly what you said—we want to cast our net as far and wide as we possibly can. We get that stack of twenty-five business cards we collected, we come back to our office, we put it underneath the piece of clay artwork our cousin gave us fifteen years ago, and we probably don't do anything about them. Networking events are great, I don't want to lead people down the road of thinking these aren't great opportunities, but you have to be very strategic about it. When you go to a networking event, what is your goal for that networking event?

I'll give you an example. I went to a networking event two nights ago. When I went to that event, I had one goal—to meet one business contact through referral with whom I could potentially follow up and do business. That happened. Notice I said "through referral." You might wonder how I was able to meet somebody through referral at a networking event. I took people with me. I don't go to these events alone—I take my "posse." So when you go into an event, take people you know—people you have connections with. They will know people there they can connect you with.

With the connections I made at this event, I am 95 percent sure that the connection I received will be a done deal, and the connection is with somebody I didn't know before I walked into the room. I maximized the effectiveness of that networking event. By the way, I also knew the speaker, Brian Hilliard. (You can learn about him at his Web site: www.agitoconsulting.com.)

Wright

That's very good. I've never heard anybody recommend taking "a posse."

Alexander

Yes, absolutely—don't network alone.

Wright

So is there a particular type of person you are looking for when you're at a networking event? And is there a type of person you always want to make sure that you bring to a networking event? Those are my first two questions. I also want to know, what if I don't want to bring a bunch of people or go talk to a bunch of people? Maybe that is just not my personality. What can I do about that?

Alexander

Well, the latter question is pretty easy, just don't go. But the first part of the question is that you know you want to soar with the eagles, you know if you're going to go to a networking event and have an opportunity to bring people with you, then you will be better connected than if you didn't.

I like to play tennis with people who are better than I am, which is not hard. Why? I want to improve my game, and I look at networking as the same kind of opportunity. But the basic advice is to take people with whom you have a relationship—people you know and trust. Invite them to bring a couple of people they know and trust so you can go in as a community. You will all go with the purpose of helping each other make introductions.

Believe it or not, I'm a shy person, which is why networking referrals, strategic networking, and strategic referrals are so important to me—I want those high level introductions. For me, personally, it's because I'm shy, and that's good, but the hidden benefit of that is, when I get those personal high level introductions it leads to business almost all the time.

Wright

Okay, we're going to this high level event and we have promised that we're going to introduce each other to ten people with the goal of getting at least one engagement or some type of business. What does that conversation look like?

Alexander

Great question. It starts like this and I want to throw the question back to you. What type of person do you want to meet?

Wright

Let's say I want to meet a meeting planner who has the ability to book fifty conferences this year.

Alexander

So, we are going to this event. I will look at my database in advance and I know you need to meet a meeting planner, so I invite one to come along with us. Whether I introduce you to somebody I've invited or I introduce you to somebody I know at the event, the conversation usually goes like this:

"Hi, Suzy Meeting Planner, it's good to see you. It's been quite some time since we've connected. Let me take a second to introduce you to David Wright, a really good friend of mine. He has a number of programs that I think would be fantastic for you to work with when you are planning your meetings, conventions, and events. I'd love for you to take a few minutes and discuss that, if you're open to that possibility."

So, stated in that fashion, what is she going to say?

"Absolutely, let's talk."

Then you can both discuss those opportunities.

The way you would end this conversation is, "Well, Suzy, I really enjoyed meeting you. Let's get together next Tuesday for a cup of coffee."

Now you have a set appointment.

Wouldn't it be nice if we walked away with set appointments? You might not walk away with business that day, but you can certainly walk away with set appointments.

Wright

That's good. So it changes one's focus then. If I start off saying I want to get one piece of business from this event, it makes my approach very different from just wanting to hand out all seventy-five of my business cards. I could stand on the corner and do that. So what you're saying is a lot more strategic and obviously a lot more effective.

Alexander

Yes, and here's my opinion about it. I'm sure I could be challenged on this, and that's okay. If I cannot go to an event and be strategic about it, I'm not going to go because my time is better spent developing relationships in other areas and doing other things. That's how strongly I feel about being strategic when going to these types of events. It's incredibly important, and most people miss that.

Wright

Let's say you're there by yourself. You didn't happen to bring anyone—maybe it is a private party. Do you have a standard approach? Do you have something specific you say or a pattern of how you zigzag the room? I really want to pick your brain so I can find out what you're doing that is making you so incredibly effective.

Alexander

That's a good question. I'll start by saying that I'm probably not going to be there if I'm going solo. The exception to that is if it's a private party or if I've received a personal invitation to go. What I'm going to tell you is actually advice from a book called, *The World's Best Known Marketing Secret,* by Dr. Ivan Misner. If you don't have a copy of it, get one. The advice is to act like a host, not a guest.

The first thing I would do is go to the host say, "Hey, my name is David Alexander and I really appreciate you inviting me. What can I do to help out? Would you like me to greet people as they come in the door? Would you like me to hang their coats up or help carry around trays of food—what can I do to assist you at this event?" First of all, that deepens your relationship with your host because he or she might be thinking, "I wish someone would help out," which is a good thing. Secondly, it gives a reason to interact with everybody there.

Wright

That is so smart; I never, ever would have thought about that.

Alexander

I think we all have some reluctance to meet people. Some of us don't like to admit it but we all have that little uncomfortable feeling when we meet somebody out of the blue.

Wright

Sure. I think about it when I have been in more of an official capacity, when people have come to me, and the conversation has been very different versus when I go up to them and I'm looking shy, they're looking shy and we're all wondering, "Okay what do you want from me?"

I will be doing what you suggest at every event I attend.

Let's talk about this. We talked about being in service toward people and obviously I know that is one of your core values. You said in some of your materials that people who like, care, and respect you will refer business to you. Talk about that for a little bit.

Alexander

Oh, that is a great one. I think that is a common misconception that we all have. We think that if people like, know, and care about us, they will refer us business. My question about that is how many of you have gotten a referral from Mom? Think about that—you know your Mom likes you, Mom cares about you, Mom trusts you, but Mom probably doesn't give you a whole lot of business. (Now, I'm different in that, my Mom actually does give me a whole lot of business because I've taken the time to teach her what I do. She has many good connections, so it works out.) Generally speaking, however, people think that all they have to do is be likeable and they'll get referrals. It's not about how much people like you, it's not about how familiar they are with you, it's about how well you know them, and how much time you've taken to inspire them to refer you.

If people who like, know, care, and trust you aren't referring business to you, it's probably because they have no idea how. You haven't made it easy for them. Have you taken the time to sit down with them and do a one-to-one so they develop an understanding of how to refer business to you? Have you taken the time to call Mom and say, "Hey Mom, I need an introduction to Joe Smith who owns an insurance company. I know you and Joe went to high school together and I've heard you talk about him before." What do you think the answer is going to be?

The moral of that story is that we have to take responsibility to make that happen. Often we put the responsibility for people referring business to us on them; I don't think that's a good move. I think it's our responsibility to inspire them and to make referrals easy by being very, very specific.

I'm involved in an organization called BNI and in that organization members attend a weekly meeting. In that meeting, we have the opportunity to ask for specific referrals. If I am vague, I won't create any connections. If I'm very specific, I get connections.

I'll give you an example that just happened recently. In this case, I needed to meet the Governor of the State of Georgia because I want the state of Georgia to proclaim the first week of February every year as International Networking Week. My specific request was met that week. The only thing I did was ask for this specific introduction from a group of people who like, know, and trust me.

Wright

So what you are saying is that we need to be specific about the person we need to meet, and we need to be specific about the reason why we'd like to meet that person because then that gives people a little bit more substance so they know how to approach this.

Alexander

I think both are good; however, if you're networking with somebody or you're meeting with somebody who likes, knows, cares, and trusts you, they probably don't need to know why you want to meet the person. They just need to know the person you want to meet so they can make the connection for you. If the person has the connection, then I would say, "If you could, go ahead and set a meeting. That would be great and you are welcome to join us." As soon as I find that someone has a connection, I literally take it to the next level—I get others to set up a meeting if possible.

Wright

Wonderful. And that's almost like creating a teamwork environment when you go to a networking event. It's the same principle, is that correct?

Alexander

Absolutely—it's a very similar principle.

Wright

I like how you think. This goes right back to something that I heard you refer to. You talk about the concept of keeping score and how keeping score improves the score. You have a referral plan right?

Alexander

Absolutely. We have a program or process called the "Networking Score Card." We have different versions of it. We have versions for managers, for salespeople, and a version for entrepreneurs. The purpose is to keep score of your networking activities because networking can be a little bit nebulous in nature—it's a little bit hard to define.

I think one of the reasons many people do lots of cold-calls and then get frustrated and burned out is they don't have a way to keep track of the process. When you look at cold-calling, that's pretty easy to track, right? You make a hundred calls, you get ten appointments, and one of those turn into a sale. Of course, different people have different numbers. Anybody can figure that out, but it gets a little tougher when you're talking about relationships.

In our system, we assign points to various activities involving networking. For example, when you're filling out the "Networking Score Card" on a week-to-week basis. You also earn points when you send somebody a thank-you card because that's important from a follow-up perspective (and many other perspectives). You can get as many as sixteen points for passing somebody a great referral. Now, see the difference there? You send somebody a card, which is nice, and you get your point, but you actually help others by referring business. You get a lot of points there because they will want to refer business back to you, right? They're going to want to help you.

So the whole system is really designed on giving—what you're contributing. We know that if you score a one hundred or better in this system, you're going to get most of your business by referral (actually you should be getting all your business by referral at that point). I really get a kick out of teaching this to companies. We can take sales from being a scary, intimidating process to a fun relationship-building process.

Another analogy is sports—golf, for example. Do you know what the average difference between scores of a professional in golf, and the club pro or amateur? The difference is two strokes. Do you know what the difference in salary between the pro and an amateur is? It is about ten million dollars! The difference in score is two strokes. Keeping score improves the score.

When you go to that activity with no way of tracking success, you're shooting in the dark; if you're tracking your success, you can build upon that success and get better. I love helping people improve the score. Visit my website referrals4life.com/roadmap for a free demonstration of a database that will track your networking scorecard.

Wright

Wow, that is actually extremely useful and very profound. I'm just thinking about how many opportunities I might have let slip away. I'm thinking about the names and the opportunities and the events I've attended. If I had I just gone there with somebody else and had a plan and had one of those score sheets to record what I did with these people afterward, who knows how much business could have come my way?

Alexander

I have not made a cold-call in fifteen years and I have built multiple companies completely though networking. This really shows how successful you can be when you understand the referral process.

People will often come up to me with this great question, "David, how are things going?" My natural response is, "Oh, things are great!" That's everyone's natural response to a question like that, right? I usually like to say, "It's great, but it can always be better." That answer leads people to say, "Well, okay, if things are going great, how can it be better?" Now you have something to talk about.

Here is another question I am often asked, "So is there anything I can do to help you?" Have you ever been asked that before? What is our natural response? It is usually something like, "Yep, I'm good. I'm fine—don't worry about me." I always have questions and thoughts in my mind prepared for that question. If I'm at an event somewhere and maybe I need an introduction to someone in that town, my response to that question is, "Absolutely, you can help me and here's how." I lay it out there for them. Then they have the choice of actually honoring that question they asked me or not. Either way it's okay, but it puts them in a position of being engaged in helping me out because they asked.

Wright

That's a great question because, again, what I like about your style is that you talk about the things we all go through. It's not as though you're saying that this is some kind of new system or that you have to change. What I hear you saying is to take what I've got and just start making something of it. This is a question that everybody is asked, maybe several times a week.

Alexander

Absolutely, and our response is usually not beneficial for anybody.

Wright

Right. Thank you very much for this information.

My next question to you, David, is what about the flip side of it? What if I'm new in business, I don't know very many people, and I don't know how to get referrals. What do I do then?

Alexander

That's a common challenge that people have. They graduate college and generally there's not a whole lot taught in college about networking. Some schools are starting to teach some courses in it, but people graduate, get a job, and somebody at that job—their manager or mentor—tells them to pick up the phone, start making calls, hit the streets, and good luck. They wear off a few layers of rubber from the soles of their shoes and they don't achieve much success.

What we can teach people is to sit down and take a look at their networks and to take a look at the people they do know. We have a couple of ways that we can stratify that. If they have just graduated from school and are new to business, they can look at people who would be in what I would call a "support network." They probably have some people in this network, be it family or friends. They may have mentors who are in a second network—the "information network." These are people from whom you can just garner information, maybe information about your business or your industry or connections and contacts.

We also have a third network called a "referral network." Those are people who have the ability, for whatever reason, to send you referrals. Maybe they're in sales as well and talking to the same clients you are. Maybe they're friends who are in businesses that are talking to clients you could be talking to.

So the first step is to look at all the people you have in your rolodex, Outlook, Act, or whatever database program you use, including your friends. This is where a lot of people miss the boat. They think they don't know anybody. Well, that's not true, you know all kinds of people, you just don't know how to teach those people to refer business to you.

So, at Referrals4Life, we look at the people our clients do know and then we start creating some communication with those people so they understand what our clients are now doing and can send referrals our clients' way. I have just condensed two days worth of training into two minutes, but that is the basic process.

In addition to that you've got to get involved. If you don't know a lot of people, go to the Internet, look up networking events in your town. Get involved in some organizations—join the Chamber of Commerce. Don't just join, be a part of it—be an ambassador—get involved. Go find your local BNI chapter. BNI chapters are all over the world. Find your local BNI chapter and join that chapter. Get involved in some sort of civic or social organization like the Jaycees, Rotary, or Kiwanis. Check out other local networking events and bring one or two people you know to those events. Go out there and get some introductions. Then you leverage the connections and the relationships that you already have.

Dr. Ivan Misner, founder of BNI, says that it is easy to become a "cave dweller." Think about it, we get up in the morning in a "cave" that has a bed in it; we call that our bedroom. We get into another cave that has four wheels. We go into a great big cave that has computer screens all over the place. We come home and we go into another big cave that has a big screen television in the middle of it; we call that a den. You have to get out of the cave. Networking is a contact sport.

Wright

It's a "contact sport"—I like that. Obviously this is just the tip of the iceberg. You say that this is just a summary in a couple of minutes of a two-day training. You actually do training on this topic, correct?

Alexander

Yes, we do. We have a number of programs that we teach. One of our cornerstone programs is called the Certified Networker Program, which is actually a twenty-four-hour program that teaches people pretty much everything they need to know about building a solid relationship-based marketing plan. It's really exciting; many of our clients have booked hundreds of thousands of dollars of new business prior to graduating.

We have many other referral training programs available through our affiliation with the Referral Institute.

Speaking of training, here is another example of how to begin identifying if a new contact would be beneficial for you. When I have my training and consulting hat on, I will often ask people I'm interacting with a "funneling question." This is a question that will help me identify if this contact would be a good candidate for a training program.

One of the questions that I ask people is, "Do you read books?" It's a simple question. If the answer is yes, I say, "Well, how many business books did you read last year?" If the answer is four, five, or six business books, I know that they will probably want to read more and they will probably invest in training programs. They're also probably very successful in their field. If the answer is, "I don't really read that much," I think to myself, "Best of luck." I certainly don't say that out loud, but that is what I'm thinking. To be successful in anything, be it networking or anything else, you have to be willing to invest in yourself. We can all create a few questions that can help us determine if we can indeed help a new contact.

Wright

Great advice, this has been one of the more action-packed and value filled interviews that I've done for this series.

Alexander

May I touch on that also?

Wright

Sure.

Alexander

"Value filled" is an important concept in networking. I appreciate you putting that out there. I know you were leading me right down that road. Whenever you interact with people, here's a simple question you can just ask yourself, "What can I do to add value to this person?" When I do programs for people—when I do work like this book—my goal is to give as much information as I possibly can because I know it will help other people. It's a giver's game and I think we can all take that point home.

I'm glad you brought that up because that's a big concept when you think about networking.

Wright

Well, I believe that great networkers are givers and not takers. Everybody knows how to take and we all know how we feel once we've "been taken." This is a philosophy to live and abide by—giving allows you to win. You'll find that people who are givers are always going to come out on top.

I really appreciate the transparency that you've also given us—not only information, but also your values.

I just have a couple more questions I want to ask you, but I am pretty sure that these may provide some very valuable information.

In some of your materials, David, you talk about the VCP Process™. This stands for Visibility, Credibility, and Profitability. Of course, this is something that's in the forefront of every small business owner's mind. How can I increase my VCP?

Alexander

That's actually a great question. It goes back to the discussion we were having a few minutes ago about our tendency to cast our nets really wide. We know a lot of people and just because we know them does not mean that they're going to refer business to us or they're going to help us out in any way. People we have visibility with may just be acquaintances. Perhaps these people include those you know at the grocery store or at PTA meetings, for example. You might or might not know their names but you've seen them a couple of times. Visability is the first step of the VCP process.

How you get credibility, the second step, is to use a filtering process. Look at all the people you know and decide which ones you want to take into a credible relationship with you. How do you do that? You honor your commitments—you do what you say you're going to do. If you say you're going to be there at 6:00, you're there at 5:45. That's honoring commitments and it's the way you move from visibility to credibility.

To put it in a different perspective, visibility is when you have met someone, and credibility is when you know the person and you respect them. Some people call that resonance or harmony, but whatever you call it, you start building that connection.

The third step of the process, after you get into a credible relationship with people, is to move them into profitability with you. They will really start thinking about how they can help you. We actually filter people's networks by this process. We look at how many people our clients have a visible relationship with and which of those people they want to move into a credible relationship with. We then determine which of those we can move into a profitable relationship.

When you are in a profitable relationship with people, it simply means that they implicitly trust you—they trust you so much that they're willing to refer their top client to you. Here's another little nugget: the reason they're willing to refer their top client to you is because they know you'll do such a good job that their top client is going to come back to them and say, "Wow, thank you so much for referring me to David Alexander. He came into our company and our sales have increased by 60 percent since he's been working with us. I cannot thank you enough for making that connection!" As someone you've referred your top client to, I have just deepened your relationship with your top client. I've just made your relationship better, and, oh, by the way, I picked up some business in the process, as part of the process.

Let me give you another way to look at it. Let's say you are a Real Estate agent. This scene plays out at a private party. The following is an example of how a conversation might play out with someone you have a visible relationship with. A guest at the party mentions to your contact that he needs to sell a house. He talks about where the house is located and what it's worth and the fact that he really, really needs to sell it as soon as possible because he is moving out of state but he doesn't have a Real Estate agent. Maybe then he (your visible contact) might think to actually mention you. Now, if you had a credible relationship with him, the moment the other person says, "Hey I'm getting ready to move," the person who has a credible relationship with you would say, "Oh, I know somebody who is a Real Estate agent and I recommend that you go talk to him."

Do you see the difference between visible and credible? It is huge. If that relationship were a profitable relationship, he would be saying something like, "Hey, is anybody in the room planning on moving?" He would be out there finding business for you, which is a whole different level of relationship.

Wright

I really like that. I don't know if anybody else has drawn the distinction between being visible and being credible. As a matter of fact, I know of a lot of a people who talk of increasing visibility in terms of more people knowing you, but it's a whole different level of texture and substance when you say, "I don't want you to just know who I am, I want you to believe in me."

Alexander

Absolutely. And you know that successful networkers are going to have a pretty deep network. You do have to cast that net because you have to think of it as a funnel. People who are in visibility with you are certainly at the top of the funnel. You might have hundreds, and in some cases thousands, of people in visibility with you. Then you're going to have just a handful—a hundred, fifty, twenty—in credibility. This will depend upon how many people you have in your network and the relationships you have with them. The people out there making that happen for you—maybe eight or ten—are in profitability with you.

Wright

Right. One thing I really like that you brought out as well is the fact that you have to give them a reason to want to refer you.

Alexander

You have to make it easy for them.

Wright

Right. You have to make it easy and there has to be a reason—either they're going to get some type of gratification or they're going to get some type of benefit from it.

Sometimes people will give you a referral fee. What are your thoughts on referral fees, by the way?

Alexander

I don't like them. I know that goes against what a lot of people say, but I don't like them because I don't think it's relationship-oriented. Have you ever given someone a referral and he or she gave you twenty or a hundred dollars? Now, have you ever given someone a referral and that person gave you something really unique—a special gift, a special trip, or whatever? Which of those two people do you remember?

Wright

I guess I would remember the gift a lot more.

Alexander

Absolutely. You would remember the person who gave you the gift because money is transparent. If someone gives you a hundred dollars for a referral, you go buy groceries or something else forgettable and you're done; you've forgotten about it. I'm in favor of referral incentive programs which are unique. They are creative and they encourage relationship-building. I'm not really in favor of referral fees from a dollar standpoint.

Wright

Okay, is there ever a time where you've seen that a monetarily based referral system worked out better? Some people say it's great to have a pretty vase but I want the money.

Alexander

I'm sure they're out there, but you know, if a business has a cash referral system, it's better than nothing. Don't get me wrong, if you're not doing anything, do something, but if you create something unique as a referral thank you, that would be even better. This takes us to the next level. Are you ready?

Wright

Yes, let's go.

Alexander

With a referral thank you or a referral incentive program or whatever you want to call it, what if you designed that referral program around people you are in a relationship with? This is something I do—I keep a personal inventory of people in my network. I keep up with what they like; I keep up with the magazines they read; I keep up with the things they do.

I'm going to ask you a question here, David, what's one of the favorite things that you like to do? Maybe it's going to the movies or playing golf—what is one of the favorite things you like to do?

Wright

I'll go with tennis. I haven't played tennis in a while, but I do like the game.

Alexander

Okay, so let's say that you give me a great referral. If tennis is one of your passions, what would you appreciate more: my sending you a ten- or fifty-dollar check or my sending you ten tennis lessons?

Wright

Right, I understand.

Alexander

My point being that instead of treating referral sources as we want to treat them, treat them as they want to be treated. See how powerful your program could become at that point. Maybe there is somebody out there who would prefer the check, but I think we can have a much deeper impact on most people with a more creative thank you.

I went to a party about a year ago in Los Angeles. At this party people were showing up with all different kinds of gifts. I arrived with an unwrapped bag of pistachios. I guess, with hindsight, maybe I could have wrapped them. This party was at Dr. Ivan Misner's house. He is a networking guru. I received more gratitude and thanks for that bag of pistachios than anything else I could have brought, and it was just a ten-dollar bag of pistachios from the grocery store. Why did that work? It worked because I know Dr. Misner absolutely loves pistachios. You treat people the way they want to be treated, not how you want to treat them, that's the moral of the story.

Another example we mentioned earlier is Brian Hilliard with Agito. I referred a client to Brian recently. His company got the deal and it was very profitable. He gave me a gift certificate to a great—not a good—a great Italian restaurant here in town. Now most people would think that's the same as giving money, right? Not for me, because I love Italian food, specifically great Italian food, and this is a place I had never been. I had mentioned that I wanted to go there and he picked that up along the way, and he nailed it. I'm looking for more business for him right now because I want another reward. That's how the process works.

Wright

The last I question I have for you is about action steps. A lot of people might think this is all well and good and they're going to be able to do great things, but what are five things that a businessperson can do right now that can help increase referrals?

Alexander

Another great question and I'm glad we're wrapping up with it. A general answer is to do something—just do something. If you've read something that resonates with you, go out there and make that happen. Get involved, get connected, get out of your "cave," go out there and meet people.

Specifically, step one is to join some organizations. If you're not in a close contact network organization whose sole purpose is for members to pass referrals to one another, join one of those. A great one is BNI. Join a chamber, get involved in a civic organization, or join a community group.

Here's a little advice on that though: don't over-stimulate yourself. Sometimes we over-network—we tend to get involved in too many things and we dilute our efforts. Here's a basic recommendation: if you want to be really successful in networking, join three groups. Join BNI, the Chamber of Commerce, a Rotary or Kiwanis or Lions, or something civic. Join three different groups that have three different focuses and that will get you connected pretty quickly.

Step two is to invest in yourself by participating in training programs. We talked a good bit about this earlier. If you want to be successful at whatever you're doing, invest in yourself to make that happen.

Step three is reading. I probably read anywhere from eight to ten books a year about business and all kinds of different things. I go to anywhere from six to ten seminars, training programs, or training presentations a year. I keep the sword sharp. I listen to many CDs. You have to be willing to take the time to invest in yourself. Go out tomorrow and buy a book about networking. Most of the material in this chapter has come from a book I am writing called *Networking Like a Pro*. (If you would like to pre-order the book, send me an e-mail and I will add you to the list.)

I have three more recommendations for reading. One is *Truth or Delusion* co-authored by Ivan Misner, Mike Macedonio, and Mike Garrison. This is a great book about dispelling the myths surrounding networking. Two others are, *Masters of Networking* and *The World's Best Known Marketing Secret,* both by Ivan Misner. Read about this topic of networking. I invite you to connect with my company and we will guide you in the right direction as well.

So, taking training programs and reading are steps two and three. Step four: go to some events, look at the local event calendars in your town, and most importantly, when you go to an event take your posse with you. Make sure you take people with you who can connect you with other people in the community.

Step five is last, but not least, follow up with everyone you meet. If you make a connection with someone, make sure you have a system in place so that you can follow up with that person.

So, those are some steps you can take right now to start creating some success with personal referral marketing.

I also suggest analyzing your network. Figure out who is in your information network and support network—who you have a visible relationship with, who you have a credible relationship with, and who you have a profitable relationship with. What activities do you have on your calendar next week to start building your business through referrals? You'll add a lot of value in doing just that and taking what we've talked about today and turning it into action steps.

Wright

This is amazing information. I can see the dollar signs beginning to mount up as I think about how all of this can be put into play. I appreciate you contributing so much information. You are preaching what you practice.

We've been talking with David Alexander. David has taught thousands of businesspeople and companies to network like a pro, which has helped them dramatically increase their business referrals.

David, thank you for being with us in *Roadmap to Success*.

About the Author

DAVID ALEXANDER'S VISION is to build thriving communities of professionals who believe that investing in others' success is the path to prosperity. David creates this vision through being the CNO (Chief Networking Officer) of Referrals4life, LLC. David and his company are one of the largest franchises of BNI in the world. David also provides corporate training and individual coaching using programs from the Referral Institute and Intensity Business Leadership. He is currently working on three books, *Networking Like a Pro*, *Referrals for Life*, and *Intensity Leadership: From Solopreneur to Entrepreneur*. David's latest project is CNOWorks. Please visit referrals4life.com/roadmap for resources to help you Network Like A Pro.

David currently resides with the love of his life, Kimberly, and their two children, Christian and Peyton, in Marietta, Georgia. David is a firm believer in "Givers Gain" and is driven to help others achieve success.

David Alexander

Referrals4life, LLC
4994 Lower Roswell Road, Suite 11
Marietta, GA 30068
678.888.0200
david@referrals4life.com
www.referrals4life.com

CHAPTER

14

An interview with…

Gabriella Contreras

David Wright (Wright)

We're talking today with Gabriella Contreras. At the age of nine, Gabriella founded a youth service club called Be Alert, Don't Do Drugs (BADDD), where participants learn to take the time to care for themselves and others. Gabriella continues to discover and develop her skills and talents as she shares them with those around her to create a positive impact in homes, neighborhoods, and communities. She enjoys getting involved and making a positive difference in her community. When the Tucson, Arizona, resident was just a third-grader, Gabriella and her friends found themselves observing gang-related happenings at the high school across the street. They wished they could find a way to make them stop. Luckily, Gabriella didn't just wish—she started the club, BADDD. From going on peace marches around the school to participating in a variety of fundraisers, the club founded by Gabriella has made a real difference in the community. Along the way, she learned how to tap into resources and work with others to cause change instead of just looking across the street and feeling helpless.

Gabriella, welcome to *Roadmap to Success.*

Gabriella (Contreras)

Well, thank you very much. I'm very excited about talking with you today.

Wright

So you began volunteering in your community at the age of six. Elaborate about what happened to stir your interest and your action to get involved with such enthusiasm.

Contreras

Well, ever since I was very young—as you said at age six—I continued to see my mom's involvement with the elderly care home center. I also collected canned food from my neighbors for the food bank—I wanted to get involved with helping people also. I began helping at the food bank during holidays and then, as I grew older, I wanted to volunteer at other organizations like the American Lung Association. What really got me involved was seeing that other people needed help, which just really touched my heart.

I realized that having a better community starts with one person at a time. Regardless of age, one is never too young or too old to contribute toward making positive changes. I knew at age six how important and close family is and I just knew that things needed to change—I knew people should help each other and I knew that even being only six years old, I could make some kind of difference for at least one other person. So that's really what got me involved. Ever since then I've continued keeping that focus in mind.

My dad began joining in to help Club BADDD. Even though my parents were divorced, Dad put aside their differences to help the Club. My Grampa Ben Montaño also donated his time and money to help the Club.

Wright

Tell more about the club you founded, BADDD.

Contreras

Sure. I started the club when I was a third-grader. I was trying to think of something that a lot of other kids would like to say they were involved with. It was started because of what I saw across the street at the high school—the riots that they had one day really disturbed my friends and me. It happened during our lunch hour and we could see across the street through our playground gates. I remember my friend telling me that she wished someone would go over there and do something or let them know that we can see them.

An idea just popped up in my mind and I thought, "Well, why don't we do something instead of waiting for someone else?" That was the motivation behind my creating the club.

The club involved kids from kindergarten through eighth grade. Throughout the entire year these elementary and middle school students become motivated and empowered knowing that they could make a difference in their community and that there was something else other than drugs and gang violence. They became aware that they could be a positive influence. I created the club motto, which was: *even as youths, we can make a positive difference in our homes, neighborhood, school, and community.* Where this starts is at home with family members and then it goes to the next level, which is helping in the neighborhoods where we play. Then, as youths, we go to school and learn about our community. We can then learn about youth boards and mentorship programs so that we can learn to become connected and be part of the solution to our community youth issues.

Wright

Tell me about the March for Peace in Tucson, Arizona. Will you share with our readers how you did it?

Contreras

Sure. That was something that came about a little later on, while the club developed. At the time, there was a lot of "copycat" violence throughout the nation at schools and I just felt that something needed to be done at school that would involve the community also. So the March for Peace was actually a peace march that was completely citywide in Tucson. The march started at Roskruge Elementary and Middle School. We invited the entire community to march from that school to the downtown area of Tucson. The idea was to get everybody involved. Youths and adults made a positive connection and demonstrated unity for our city.

We had a lot of different organizations donate water bottles and snacks for people. Over a thousand people participated and it was really amazing. I think that the whole reason why it turned out so well is because of the idea of just everyone—regardless of age, gender, or ethnicity—could come together to show the rest of the nation and our state that we wanted something different instead of these violent situations. We wanted to show that youth and adults working together can make a positive difference. With mentorship and guidance, youth can make a huge impact on the community. So that's how the idea came about. The Peace March motto I created was: "Si *se puete por la paz*"—"Yes, we can have peace. Yes, we can."

Wright

I read in one article where even the mayor showed up.

Contreras

Yes he did. We had many different speakers speak at the end of the peace march. The mayor came and gave a speech and made a Proclamation. Many other political and community leaders, such as Raul Grijalva attended and gave speeches. The whole idea was to get different levels of the community involved. Other youth leaders of all ages also participated. We had family members speak as well and teachers from other schools, including some of the university professors. It was important to have the huge variety of people there—it was evident that there were many elements of the community involved. I guess you could say that the pieces of the puzzle that made up the whole community fit together at that moment.

Wright

You were an invited guest and you made quite an impact in meeting with Colin Powell. In fact, other concerned celebrities such as Michael Bolton and Andrew Shue also attended. Will you tell our readers what the meeting was about and what happened?

Contreras

The meeting was the "Presidents' Summit for America's Future" held in late April 1997 in Philadelphia, by the Alliance for Youth. Attending were former Presidents Bill Clinton, George Bush, Jimmy Carter, and Gerald Ford and First Lady Nancy Reagan, representing President Ronald Reagan. Also present were thirty governors, one hundred mayors, one hundred and forty-five community delegations, dozens of prominent business leaders, and several thousand citizens. At the Conference, the Presidents asked the nation to make youth a top priority. Colin Powell was chairman of the Conference and subsequently became chairman of the organization.

The point of the event was to get everybody from all of the states to come together and share ideas about how to involve their communities in making positive differences for the better.

It was really amazing talking to General Colin Powell and addressing our nation as the youth speaker. I learned later that this broadcast aired in two thousand cities. Meeting various people and having the opportunity to give a speech with Colin Powell right there sitting beside me was almost like a dream. I was very grateful to learn that what I said as a youth mattered to these important adults.

My whole focus was just trying to get the word out—youth working with adults as their mentors, coaches, and leaders can really make a huge impact. They can get other youth involved and motivated to want to do the same. That's what my whole focus was. Bringing that back was what really helped spearhead a lot of the other things that have happened in my life.

I created a youth summit. It was a citywide outreach and was the start of giving youth citywide awareness and opportunities to be involved with various community organizations.

Wright

Most people in the United States have never seen a president in person and you saw four of them in one day; that's pretty good. So what other celebrities have you met and who would you like to meet in the future and why?

Contreras

I have met Hilary Clinton when I spoke at the Raising Resourceful Youth Conference in 2000. I shared some ideas about how to get youth motivated. I've also met Danny Devito and a couple of other famous actors.

The one person I would really like to meet is Oprah. She's a very powerful woman and does many different things here in our country as well as globally. She helps families reunite and become stronger and more powerful. She empowers people. An example is the school she started in Africa for young girls. I just feel I can really connect to that because I have strong feelings for women and children's issues as well. I believe Oprah is the one person I'd really like to meet. I would like to follow in her footsteps helping people.

I have a dream to complete my university education and create documentary films educating our global viewers of the many issues that still need to be changed. The purpose is to promote global awareness and ignite global connections to make positive changes.

Wright

As a young adult now, what is your new mission?

Contreras

Now, as a college student and having these experiences in my background, I feel that it is my mission and goal in life to spread the word that even as youth—no matter what our ages are—we can unite to make a positive difference now! It's really important to have some kind of leadership and mentorship.

My mom helped me in starting out as a young leader. I had these great ideas but I didn't quite know how to go about it. Having Mom in my life was very helpful. It was my mom who helped me get those ideas and goals out there. As a young adult, I want to share how important it really is to help other people implement their ideas. I want to help better other people's lives and I feel my new mission is to just go out and share that story and to help motivate others to do the same. Club BADDD was very strong in membership for ages kindergarten through eighth grade.

I moved to South Carolina, so I also learned that my life would change. My focus has grown during my college years and I became involved in my university's student government. I learned to express myself in the arts through the university dance company, and in my journal writing.

Wright

Being such a young leader and activist, what helps you stay grounded and centered?

Contreras

I feel that it's really important for me to stay grounded with my belief in God. Without my Christian beliefs, I wouldn't be able to stay as strong throughout the trials I've been experiencing in my life, especially in college. Going into my third year was really impressive and my faith has been very helpful. I made many mistakes in college.

I've learned that whenever difficult times happen, it's important to pray and ask for guidance. It's also important to be able to depend on family and to be able to find strength through people who know me. They know about my good choices and the bad ones. They know the things that have helped motivate me in the past, so they can help motivate me again. I learned that seeking counseling and life coaching is important.

I just feel that those are two huge important grounding elements for me. Together both of those really help me stay grounded. When I feel that things are becoming more difficult, my faith and my family help motivate me. I have made efforts to reach out to my parents and to my grandparents for strength.

I feel that my personal mentor would be my mom. I feel that she has helped me to stay focused and to stay centered. Prayer has helped me also.

So I feel that those things have been the most important influences in my life. I am also learning to have balance in my life and to limit my commitments, which will avoid my giving so much of my time that I could experience burnout. I have learned to say no at times to ensure self-care and to achieve a balanced life.

Wright

I've met your mom and I can see that she's proud of you. Gabriella, thank you so much for being with us today. I've really enjoyed our conversation; I've learned a lot. I had no idea that someone so young could do so much while some of us sit back on the sidelines and don't get involved as much. You've just really done a great job. I appreciate all this time you've taken with me today to answer these questions. I'm sure that our readers are really going to learn a lot from the experiences you've shared here.

Contreras

Thank you. I really appreciate our time here together and being able to share just a little bit of my goals and my motivations.

The lessons I have learned thus far are that I cannot accomplish my goals on my own. I learned that I can ask for help; I can make networking connections to create a larger circle of Arizona alliances and this creates diversity. This created diversity is creating unity of vision for the mission of positive volunteerism to make a positive difference.

During my second year of attending a public high school (Tucson High School) in the Tuscon Unified School District (TUSD), my mom and I moved to South Carolina, creating a new environment for us. I was sixteen and realized it would be a good opportunity to spend time with my dad because his father, my grandfather, was ill with cancer. During my high school years, I also received help from my Grandfather Ben Monteño and grandmother, Della Monteño, which made a big difference in my realizing that family is very important.

In my junior and senior year I relocated to Tucson, Arizona, and remained very involved in my local Tucson community volunteering at the American Lung Association Youth President, continued volunteering overseeing the Kindergarten through Junior High Club BADDD and other activities. I graduated high school in 2004 and relocated to South Carolina to join my mom, as she discovered she was in need of a serious surgery.

I remained in South Carolina and enrolled in Lander University located in Greenwood, South Carolina. While I became involved in my local non-denomination Christian-based church, I achieved great personal success in building my spiritual path along with my educational path as a university student. I have learned from watching my mom's strong motivation, actions, and intuition what personal success is for our family. Her actions have continued to motivate me to also dream big and take action in my personal life. I have also learned from my dad the importance of applying creative God-given gifts to assist others and myself.

While in South Carolina, Greenwood, I ran for Lander University student government during my freshman year, and the student body elected me as Freshman Senator of Lander University. During my sophomore year, I ran for Vice President of Student Academic Affairs, developing my talent to serve others. I was elected once again by the student body for this office. I auditioned for the Lander Dance Company and made the Dance Company. I also worked very hard and earned a GPA to obtain a South Carolina Life Scholarship during my sophomore year. I applied for the Lander Ambassadorship and the interview was a success—I was elected to this University position also.

I lived on the University Campus in Centennial Hall for a semester and then during my junior year, I was able to travel abroad to Northampton University in England, studying abroad through the Larder University honors program. I traveled abroad for short summer terms during my junior high and high school years with the People To People Student Ambassador Program where we met with other International Youth Ambassadors and their European Official Dignitaries for global youth summits and youth forums.

These experiences motivated me to set a goal to attend a university and to study abroad for a real life cultural experience. I completed this dream of mine in 2008. *Wow!* I was able to visit many museums and historical sites. I met many diverse multicultural people and embraced the many differences of the various European lifestyles.

My mom has always coached me to embrace the concept of what life is about—life is about change. During my four-month study abroad, I learned that I wanted to change my direction. I changed my major from journalism to media and graphic design. Studying in England allowed me to really tap into my passion for the arts.

The steps I have made in my personal choices did not come without struggles and mistakes. I have worked hard and at times, I slacked off and had to backtrack and redo courses. My University experiences as a young adult made me realize that I will make mistakes but not to spend a lot of time beating myself with guilt. Instead, my mom encourages me to stop, reflect, and ask myself what I learned about myself in making the mistake, and make a choice to do something different. I learned to make choices, to have personal accountability, and own up to my mistakes. I also learned what I want to change in my personal choices to create results that will support me in my greatness and move me forward. I learned stepping forward into the reflecting stage to the creating a new action plan into the doing and living out my life with daily purpose.

As a young adult, I understand that life success adds up to learning from my mistakes. These experiences all help me move fluidly in my life—being resilient, shinning my light to assist others as I also help and develop my own life journey. I hope I make a positive impact on this generation and add my own success that will touch this generation.

Wright

Today we've been talking with Gabriella Contreras. Obviously, based on what she has said, she enjoys getting involved and making a positive difference in her community, from going on peace marches around her former school to participating in a variety of fundraisers to founding the BADDD. She has made a real difference in communities already. Even now, she's learned how to tap into resources and how to work with others to cause change instead of just looking across the street and feeling helpless.

Gabriella, thank you so much for being with us today on *Roadmap to Success.*

Contreras

Well, thank you.

ABOUT THE AUTHOR

GABRIELLA CONTRERAS is a vibrant, successful, and compassionate young woman, continuing to live from her heart while she takes the time to listen and develop herself in her personal journey, "To Live." Gabriella is currently studying Graphic Design at Lander University. She is a 2007 Premier Leadership Key Holder, and she completed the Tony Robbins University Life Mastery Leadership Series in 2001 as well as a dozen other educational trainings and workshops. She has been awarded the National Presidential Service Award, The National Points of Light Foundation Community Volunteer Award, The National JC Penney Golden Rule Award, and The National Prudential Volunteer of Community Service Award. These are just a few of the many acclamations and recognitions received in her youthful years of learning to fit into society regardless of her age. She is committed to assisting others to actively use the road map to success in learning and living their life's purpose. Miss Gabriella embraces life changes and assists others in adjusting to life changes in the application of sharing her young life experiences in many ways such as: keynote speeches at local and national conferences and facilitating and presenting workshops and consultations. She has learned to live her life's purpose in educating and nurturing herself, her family, and those around her in developing skills and tools to help live a progressive and positive life. At the age of nine, Gabriella founded a youth service club called Be Alert, Don't Do Drugs (BADDD) located in Tucson, Arizona, at Roskruge Elementary and Middle School, where she and other youth learned to take the time to care for themselves and others. Gabriella continues to discover and develop her skills and talents as she shares them with those around her to create a positive impact in homes, neighborhoods, and communities. Gabriella learned to take action at an early age in Tucson, Arizona. Along the way, she learned how to tap into resources and work with others to attain success.

Gabriella Contreras
PO Box 181
Due West, SC 29639
864-993-3895
gcontrer@student.lander.edu

CHAPTER

15

An interview with...

Grace V. Contreras

David Wright (Wright)

Today we're talking with Grace Contreras. Grace is a master life coach, facilitator, presenter, and consultant. She has more than twenty-eight years of progressive experience in a variety of projects and professional affiliations. She has experienced coaching men and women and youth on business development, strategic sales, financial accountability, customer relations, personal and professional image, and to live their passion. She also works with families and helps them through crisis situations. Grace has co-authored and published a manual and video for a workshop series focusing on youth and adults who volunteer to make a positive difference in the community. She raised fifty-two thousand dollars and coordinated twelve annual public education events in Tucson, Arizona. She raised twelve thousand dollars in South Carolina for the Red Cross.

Grace earned her Bachelor of Science Degree in Psychology, with an emphasis on counseling, from Lander University and she is an *International Coach Federation Master* Certified Coach *(MCC)*. She is a Certified Life Coach, a 2007 Premier Leadership Key Holder, and she has earned a number of certificates in several focused mastery classes. She was invited by Hillary Clinton to be a White House guest speaker in 2001 for resourceful youth, and participated in the "Presidents' Summit for America's Promise" held in late April 1997 in Philadelphia, by the Alliance for Youth. Colin Powell was chairman of the Conference and later became chairman of America's Promise Alliance, which was founded at that Conference. Grace is an image consultant for Progressive Communications.

Grace, welcome to *Roadmap to Success.*

Grace Contreras (Contreras)

Thank you, David. I'm looking forward to talking with you today.

Wright

So what is your personal map for traveling on the road to success?

Contreras

Well, what I learned at a very early age is to first focus on what life's purpose is. We recognize as individuals that there are so many road maps out there to create success, and success is different to each person.

I'm a parent—I have a daughter who is a young adult. What I'm passing on to her, I learned from my dad, Mr. Ben Montaño. He taught me to embrace who I am. At a very young age, I'd make mistakes and was confused about certain things in life. My dad introduced me to a life concept—that consciousness is God. My dad is very forgiving and has a lot of unconditional love, which is something I learned to take with me on my journey and in my daily life.

Along the way, I began to question what my skills and talents were and if I had any. I learned through the Bible that I actually do have some very specific talents and skills. I could identify those through what I was very passionate about in life, and I could choose to develop those talents and skills, so I focused on them. From there I learned that my life purpose is to sustain others and develop my skills and talents to assist my family, others, and myself in life.

My dad involved us very early in a community service project, the Jerry Lewis Telethon. I remember going door-to-door collecting donations for this organization. Once the neighbors asked, "Why are you doing this?" I had to come to an understanding from my father, my sisters, and me, why we were collecting funds for an organization. I learned that the organization helped fund research on finding a cure for muscular dystrophy. The organization was about caring for other people. I found that this concept resonated with me—I was very passionate about wanting to help other people. These actions also assisted me in making a positive difference.

Later I learned about the food bank, I volunteered at soup kitchens, and other community charitable organizations. I found I was very good at assisting other people and making connections with them.

From there, in my teen years, I began questioning how important was God in my life, and what direction did I really want to take? I remember going through geography class and looking at the maps, learning how to get from one place to another, and looking up different states. It came to me that this really is a lot like life—you can get lost quite easily or you can go in circles trying to find a place, never stopping to ask for directions. In my teen years, my dad taught me how to drive. I remember stopping along the way to ask along how to get from one place to another and arrive at my destination. I realized that the Bible had a lot of the same concepts; it had a lot of wisdom, and officered a lot of direction for me. I am not religious, but I embrace spiritual growth. The spiritual side pulls me through disappointments and dark days.

Wright

So what brought you to the point of stepping on the road to developing your life purpose?

Contreras

Well, I think what really got me there was my parents' divorce when I was in junior high school. It was then when I drew closer to growing spiritually. Then, when I continued on into high school, I recognized that many of my friends were making a lot of mistakes—premarital sex, dysfunctional family problems, pregnancy, and so on. I was confronted with a lot of those same issues, and I knew I had many choices to make. I learned to say no to a lot of temptations at an early age.

From that point on, I remember consciously making a decision to being committed to a future. I had to sit down and write out what I wanted to map out as my goals and accomplishments and what success looked like for me. What did success mean to me? I remember reading many books. I remember a particular book where a couple backpacked across America and then wrote a book about their experiences—that was success to them.

In school, I learned from my teachers that success for them was being able to fulfill their life purpose in teaching others. I looked around and saw very influential businesspeople and business success meant success to them. I had to identify what success was for me and realized that it was getting in tune with my spiritual side and what my heart was telling me. My heart was telling me to step up to the plate and be fully committed to my life, to take action, and develop my skills and talents. The road to success for me involved seven steps: 1) education, 2) training, 3) developing my spiritual growth, 4) family mentorship, 5) accountability for my personal choices, 6) recognize "I," and 7) apply love and forgiveness to others and myself.

So success meant saying no to a lot of temptations in life and staying on track. I learned throughout life that the journey has a lot of twists and turns and pit stops along the way, and big bumps in the road that you have to make detours around to stay on track to reach the destination. I learned that self-care and setting and staying within boundaries is honoring self—an act of self-love. The Bible tells us to love our neighbor *as we love ourselves* (Mark 12:31; Luke 10:27; Matt. 19:19 and 22:39 KJV).

Wright

So what things do you want to be remembered for as you leave behind a history of your life's results?

Contreras

I've thought a lot about that. Each person leaves a mark behind—perhaps it is a financial legacy or a plot of land or material goods or spirituals awakenings. Maybe they pass on their knowledge by writing books, journals, essays, or poems, and making donations. Perhaps their legacy is their children.

I was a virgin when I got married and I was married for ten years. During that time I had my daughter. Throughout life the road changes—life is about change. For me, divorce was part of that change. It brought me to another level, and life continues to develop for me. As a single person, I realized that what I really wanted to leave behind was a signature of loving others. I had to learn to forgive others and myself. I showed this in a passionate manner toward my daughter and those around me through consulting with other men and women through life coaching. I chose a worldly path for seven years after my divorce, and made a lot of mistakes.

So I think for me it's leaving behind my way of embracing life, living each day fully, and sharing that love. I learned to talk about my mistakes and move forward from them—to walk away from shame and learn to shine because I had grown beyond my mistakes along the way.

Wright

I know you're doing well, I've met your daughter—she's quite a tribute to your having raised her.

What are your map-reading skills that indicate you're on the right road and not traveling aimlessly to an unknown destination?

Contreras

I have learned that it takes a lot of dedication and time. I have to create a focused action plan. I have to sit down and look clearly at what I want to do in life. Ask yourself what your heart is telling you to do, and not just think from your head. So I evaluate where I am today and where I need to be for tomorrow. I look at each moment and determine what it takes. For me it's creating goals and actually writing them down. I then create a step-by-step action plan to make my vision a reality.

A few years ago, my daughter and I were given scholarships by Tony Robbins for the Tony Robbins Foundation's Life University Mastery Program. We took all five of his courses. In that process I learned to take action, get out of my comfort zone, and step forward into feeling that fear of change, then move forward into positive action. I also learned about walking across fifty feet of hot coals and jumping from a fifty-foot telephone pole in Hawaii while attending the Mastery program.

So for me, getting on the road to success and staying on track means writing out daily goals. It also means verbalizing what the Bible says: ask and you shall receive (Matthew 7:7). I must believe that I can have prosperity, happiness, and true love. From there I choose to stay focused and follow biblical principles. As I mentioned earlier, the biggest one is found in Matthew 22:39—the most powerful mission in life is to learn to love yourself as you love your neighbor.

Wright

What is one of the key elements and activities you use in map skills to map out your accountability of ownership in your focused destination?

Contreras

For me it's first knowing that my life is not my own—my life is to give a service to a higher calling, which is knowing that God is real and sharing that with those with whom I come into contact. My focused destination is to stand strong.

God has given each one of us talents. We must not be afraid of finding out what to do with them or of not doing it right. We must have the courage to apply what talents we have. Know that life is about making mistakes and creating opportunities to learn and make personal changes in ourselves by learning from our mistakes. We should learn from them and then move forward from there, focusing on the positive. We should focus on the optimistic side; failure and disappointment are part of life.

The Bible says to ask and you shall receive. So I ask these questions daily: What is my service? Where is the prosperity? Where is the joy? And I embrace those things. Yes, I make many mistakes, but I know not to linger on them. I look at them, reflect, and learn from my mistakes, and then move forward. I'm not beating myself up, but I am actually embracing the opportunity of learning about myself and make personal changes within myself from evaluating mistakes.

I've realized in life, going through school, trainings, education, being a parent, and having been married and divorced, that life is mostly about learning through mistakes. I've "been there done that," and then I've moved forward and embraced what was next in a positive perspective. This is my path to living my life. Formal teaching never includes how to handle disappointments or failure, yet this is a key detail to maneuver the changes that take place in life, just as Job did. The Bible records that Job took on his disappointments and stood strong. I can embrace that lesson.

Wright

So how do you know you're traveling on the right road to reach your destiny—success?

Contreras

First I hold onto the "I statement" and hold accountability in the I. I usually know—I can feel it. God gave each one of us an intuitive side—that gut feeling. I know when I am making a correct decision and if there's a doubt there, then go with that intuitive feeling. I whisper a small prayer and just breathe.

I do pray and ask God to give me direction and to give me wisdom; then I move forward. I do follow my God-given intuition. I apply it and develop it through reading the Bible and through embracing the values and the common morals it teaches. The book of Proverbs contains many wise sayings about morality. I will achieve prosperity along the way through following the basic principles of honoring self, loving self, and honoring and loving those around me. I do practice that. I recognize that I'm a powerful, playful, magical, spiritual, young woman of God, and I hold on to the knowledge that we really are precious individuals. This keeps me on track and helps me realize that yes, there are going to be many struggles in life, but at the end of the journey, I learn from the rough times as well as the prosperous times to grow and mature and create a stronger internal maturity within myself and through that to influence others around me.

I really do focus on not stating "they" or "we." I use "I" in the doing and being daily. There is where my accountability for my success is paved. I answer to God and can only be accountable for my actions. I can only change me.

Wright

Well, what a great conversation. I really appreciate all the time you've spent with me this afternoon to answer these questions. It's always great to talk with you—I always learn something.

Contreras

One thing I've learned is that when love and skill work together we can expect a masterpiece of miracles in our lives. I've recognized that embracing the road map to success is all about knowing up front that we're going to have many choices in life. We can choose to prepare ourselves early and rehearse what we are going to do when we meet temptation. We must prepare ourselves by learning to say no, and moving forward instead of remaining stagnant or getting detoured.

Life is like a car trip—we get in the car, we fill it with gas, and we make sure the car is running. We might end up with a flat tire, and a detour along the way, but at the end we've had some really wonderful, joyous experiences. I've learned to expect a masterpiece of God and miracles in our individual lives when love and skill work together.

Stand strong and persevere in moments of disappointment, tragedy, and feelings of fear. Press on forward. Create a circle of friends and mentors to assist you in the tough times. Speak to God and ask Him to guide you in the darkness. Ask Him to give you a renewed vision to embrace life.

Wright

Today we have been talking with Grace Contreras. Grace is a life coach, a facilitator, presenter, and consultant. She coaches men, women, and youth on business development, strategic sales, financial accountability, and customer relations. She coaches people on their personal as well as professional passion. She also works with families and helps them through crisis situations.

Grace, thank you so much for being with us today on *Roadmap to Success*.

Contreras

David, it's been a pleasure talking with you and sharing. I just want to thank you for this opportunity to share a little bit of my life in some small way. Maybe I can assist others in their growth also.

ABOUT THE AUTHOR

Grace V. Contreras earned her Master's International Certification in the field of Life Coach. She has in-depth life experience as a facilitator, presenter, and consultant. She is passionate in her field, applying more than twenty-eight years of progressive experience in a variety of projects and professional affiliations. She has experiences in her life journey in walking actively on the road to success. Grace attributes her success to actively committing her life to a focused daily behavioral spiritual development in her Christian faith. She coaches people in all walks of life in areas such as business development, strategic sales, financial accountability, customer relations, and personal/professional passion. She also works with families and coaches them through crisis situations, enabling them to building unity, healing, and family team accountability. She has openings for new clientele and speaking opportunities traveling in the United States and internationally. Grace has earned her BS degree in Psychology Counseling from Lander University. She was invited to the White House as a guest at the Raising Resourceful Youth Summit in 2001, and participated in the "Presidents' Summit for America's Promise" held in late April 1997 in Philadelphia by the Alliance for Youth. Colin Powell was chairman of the Conference and later became chairman of America's Promise Alliance, which was founded at that Conference. She has received several awards. She is committed to assisting others in actively using their map to success during their earthly journey. Grace uses the key resources in her coaching sessions and in her own personal lifestyle. Grace is referred to being, in the doing of Mastery in the direction of positive changes. Grace is creative and consistent in her methods of progressive communication. She enables others to walk the road of developing their life's purpose and realize that it is never too late to embrace their life and start now in making a positive difference. Love your life, love yourself, and create self-care as you give to others.

Grace V. Contreras
PO Box 181
Due West, SC 29639
864-993-3895
msgracenergy@hotmail.com

CHAPTER 16

Navigating the Sea of Possibility with Business Mentor/Coach...

Susan Ross

David Wright (Wright)

Today we're talking to business growth expert and Mentor-Coach Susan Ross.

Susan, How would you describe in 30 seconds what it is that you do?

Susan Ross (Ross)

You mean my "elevator pitch"—that's one of the first things we do in coaching, so of course I have several: You know how business owners and managers struggle to grow their profits and manage the multiple hats they wear while trying to compete in a changing economy? My passion is helping them define their dreams, clarify their vision and chart a course. I guide them through a process of building a better business and a better life that includes more time, more money, more balance and more joy; however, they might define those elements.

We build their "roadmap to success"— just as this book says.

Wright

Wow, I guess we will find out how you do that today. You will- it's funny that my chapter in this book is #16, which I will also explain later. There is a "Sweet 16" that's a must for business owners...

OK, I'll make sure you cover that! Can you explain your idea of Professional Business Coaching in relation to success, especially in today's economy?

Ross

There's a great little fable called *The Ant and the Elephant* whose message is *"You cannot be a leader to others until you are a leader unto yourself."* Successful people know themselves: their dreams, passions, goals and strengths. They work on those constantly, challenging themselves, taking risks and even scaring themselves a little.

Wright

Scare themselves?

Ross

Absolutely – when you ask successful people for their secrets, one of them is taking risks, scaring themselves a little in the spirit of living outside their comfort zone—where the opportunities are. That's what great coaching helps people to do. We've heard the coaching analogies of professional athletes and fortune 500 executives who credit part of their success or the speed and scope of their success to their relationship with a professional coach or mentor. In recent years, statistics and studies around the idea of coaching and mentoring have shown that those who engage in some kind of professional accountability partnership overwhelmingly accelerate and increase their results. (Ex: A study by the Lore Institute, found that 80% of large companies use executive coaches – a 550% ROI – return on investment was reported!) Accountability is a great investment in yourself and in your business. The question for many people is "How can I afford NOT to have a coach on my team to challenge and encourage me to stay on task, stay positive, creative and innovative?

Wright

Why do you think so many already successful, even famous people use coaches? They are already rich and famous!

Ross

It's not that successful people don't know what to do to reach their goals (Tiger knows how to putt), but they often rely on a coach or team of coach- mentors to help them brainstorm and prioritize, stay focused and on task, tell them the *truth*, and hold them accountable for results. It's like holding up a mirror and saying take a good long look! Leadership begins with leading ones self. As a mentor-coach, I supply an ongoing series of self-evaluation challenges, results assessments and personal challenges that clients use to stay sharp, stay focused and become increasingly aware of their own power to positively affect their situation and ultimately their world.

Wright

Accountability, that's a tough one for some, I imagine.

Ross

Ralph Waldo Emerson summed up great mentor-coaching long before there was such a thing. He said, *"Our chief want in life is somebody who shall make us do what we can."*

Accountability is a fundamentally big challenge for us all – we often crave the support we need to be our best. That's a big reason why business coaching is so popular. If success were easy, we'd all be accountable to ourselves- we'd all be rich, thin, popular, gym-going, non-smoking wonders! It's so easy to avoid the mindfulness and focus needed to manage the priorities at hand and follow through without getting distracted by the myriad "fires" that crop up in our daily work lives. I call it mindless autopilot vs. mindfully attracting possibilities. People know they need to look within and examine their strengths and weaknesses if they are going to stay on the cutting edge, keep up with technology and compete successfully. But the self-discipline to do it alone is rare. Once people engage in a successful coaching or mentoring relationship, they often find that doing it "on your own" with the help of a mentor-coach or accountability partner is a quicker path than doing it alone. It's a relief for most. They are often re-energized, able to charge ahead with renewed passion for their work, knowing they have a supportive accountability partner in their corner.

Wright

So how do you hold people accountable? It sounds kind of personal- almost intrusive.

Ross

Most successful people know the value of accountability regardless of how rigorously they avoid it at times. After all, it means we have to DO what we promise- that can be uncomfortable. How each person wishes to employ that principle is a matter of personal preference, something we discuss early on in the coaching process. It is personal in some respects, but many business decisions are based on personal preferences and needs, especially for business owners and managers. Choosing to be accountable to someone, dialing in to your vision, clarifying your goals, identifying the needed steps and anticipated obstacles is paramount. Then committing those dreams to another human being is a big step; but it's a vital one. A study by Brigham Young University found that our success multiplies exponentially each time we add an accountability step. For example- if we have goals in our mind, we increase our success by 10%. If we write them down, 20%, if we commit to a completion date, 30%, if we tell another person, follow up with that person etc. All the steps add up to a 90% chance of success vs. aimlessly thinking about success. It clearly illustrates the value of taking time to create a crystal clear vision of your dreams and goals, picture yourself there, as if you had reached them, percolate in that mindset for a short time daily- it's the science of mindset that is just now coming into the mainstream of business planning tools- now that science has caught up with philosophy, people are paying attention to the idea of working on your business vs. working in your business- this is a revolution for many. Dipping a toe into those waters can be a bit daunting for some which is why choosing mentor-coach that you value, trust and admire is very important to the success of the relationship. Don't spend time with someone you don't feel comfortable sharing your goals, fears or faults with. Results come faster when the relationship clicks and the coach and client are compatible and in-sync.

Wright

Do most people have a clear vision of their goals?

Ross

Often they do not. They might have an idea in their mind that they want to be successful, wealthy, the best in their field etc., but few have a clear vision, a specific written plan and the passion required to manifest their dream alone. They often are not aware of the fact that they are holding themselves back by working hard instead of smart, yet they don't exactly know where they are going or why. The "why" part – the vision, the passion, the purpose, the drive- precedes the how. In other words, the latest brain science has shown that the more clear our vision, the more emotionally connected we are to it, the more likely we are to succeed at the level that we envision. Those who have not been introduced to the notion that the pure energy power of our conscious and subconscious mind can propel us toward our goals, may find the idea a little "foo foo" at first glance. Once they understand that they are thinking too much and emotionalizing too little, they are amazed at how they can positively affect their results.

Wright

How do you emotionalize – in business?

Ross

For many clients it's first a matter of identifying their true passion and getting them to talk about it. Ideally, they have passion about their work. If they do not, we have to discover whether it's their family, their hobby, their charity work, their politics – whatever element of their life that really gets them excited and passionate. That's the emotion – that's the positive mindset and the feeling we want to connect to what they do to make a living. What would you do for free if you could? Often it's a matter of re-framing the value of what they do in a way that they can connect with and feel great about. There is value and meaning in most things if we look for it.

Then, depending upon their personality profile- something we examine early in the process, I often start by suggesting one of several great books on the subject such as *Change Your Brain, Change Your Life*, by Daniel G. Amen, *The Other 90%*, by Robert K. Cooper and *The Power of Appreciation* by Noelle Nelson PhD, and most recently The 4 Hour Workweek, by Timothy Ferris – a must-read. Most people are amazed at what they are missing by not tapping into their optimal mental frame when taking on new business challenges. It's the great business "secret edge" of our time.

Wright

How do they create a vision for their business if they don't have one?

Ross

It may start with a discussion of what the person chose as their business or career, what were their original ideas, what was the original dream? What do they want now or what they don't want is even easier to begin. If they feel they did not choose it and/or do not have a passion for it, that is an avenue we would explore. Once the client begins to really express their personal vision for their business and life, things begin to become clear. From there we work to define the why, (often based on a persons core values), clarify the vision, and lay out steps, processes, anticipate obstacles and solutions for same and help the client really see clearly what they want, why they want it and finally how they will achieve it and who will be on their team of advisors. Nobody succeeds in a vacuum!

A vision by the way should be clearly articulated and illustrated in your mind and viewed often. That's why it's called a VISION our brain needs to see it. Pictures, drawings, colorful vision board "triggers" that illustrate your dream goals are powerful too. My vision board is on a big blue shopping bag. Each time I see a picture of something I want to add I drop it in the bag. Every few weeks I update it. It's amazing the things that I have put "in the bag" that have materialized – with action and hard work of course. Napoleon Hill spoke of accountability to one's vision over 70 years ago. (Think and Grow Rich). It was a success tool explored in his original mastermind groups decades ago that are still considered the standard by many.

Wright

You mentioned "mindset" more than once. How important is that and how do you define it?

Ross

It's so important, especially now that science has given us so much data to support the idea that we can tap into powerful progress by simply re-programming our thoughts. It may be the one edge we still have: our mental energy laser-focused on a clear vision of our absolute success. Customers want to hear good news and inspiration, not doom and gloom. The ability to get up every day and program your mind to be positive, energetic and possibility-oriented is something the successful elite do every day. Millionaires think and act differently than average business people. T. Harv Eckert explained this brilliantly in his book "The Millionaire Mindset." So yes, I believe from personal and professional experience that we can make a big impact on our success by managing our "mental hygiene" as I call it, as part of our daily business rituals and habits. Having an open mind has always been the hallmark of greatness - now it's a requirement, a daily ritual that will change your life if you practice.

Wright

That sounds like a big job – managing your mental hygiene?

When you think about it, nearly everyone will tell you they talk to themselves often. If you ask what they are saying, much of it is negative- how often do we make a mistake and mutter something negative that we'd be offended by if someone else had said it. My theory is that we are all using affirmations daily- positive or negative, so why now just re-frame them a little and question our own thinking. If you kept track of now many negative thoughts or statements vs. positive ones you experience daily, you might be alarmed at the disparity. The negative usually wins – which is not the healthiest diet to feed our brains- it's like junk food for your mental health. Ask yourself; what am I feeding that thing- my brain? Is it junk-thoughts or healthy ones?

How do you suggest people stop thinking negative thoughts?

Ross

Author Byron Katie says that much of the source of our dis-ease or unhappiness is our own unquestioned thoughts. So often, we make over-generalization and create unfounded fears that not only don't usually materialize but we don't even question. Examples:

That's IMPOSSIBLE – is it? NOBODY is spending money, Nobody?

I could NEVER do that. Never? Are you sure? So the habit of questioning our own negative or limiting thoughts and beliefs is a powerfully life changing one to develop and a first step toward re-programming our negative thinking.

Wright

Why do you think most businesses ultimately fail?

Ross

Well, they are definitely not in the "Sweet 16" if they fail. Lots of research has been done and the numbers are staggering: Conservatively about 60% of *registered* small businesses fail within 5 years. Of the 40% that survive, only about 39% are profitable. That leaves roughly 40% of 40% of business start-ups or only 16% that survive and thrive after 5 years. I call it the sweet 16. My mission is to get clients into this elite group and keep them there. The reasons they fail are many, but the truth is that most run out of energy and ideas before they run out of money – they get stuck, they don't know what to do next or who to call. They did not anticipate the stress and demands of wearing what I call the 9 new hats, most of which are unfamiliar and uncomfortable- hats that someone else should be wearing. That's where the challenge of delegating begins along with becoming a leader instead of a technician as the the E-Myth (by Michael Gerber) explains. A great chef might be the worst restaurant owner, if he cannot clone himself, delegate and lead with a clearly communicated vision and plan. I see my mission as taking my clients to the "Sweet 16" and helping them stay there. A tall order!

Wright

So as a coach, you give them hope?

Ross

Although hope is not a strategy, it is an important reminder in the business growth process. HOPE means Hold Only Positive Expectations. And act accordingly. Adversity is part of the process and should be anticipated. We often discover untapped opportunities on the other side of adversity – *Thich* Nhat Hanh the famous Zen Master & Monk says that we should think of adversity as the fertilizer for our next beautiful garden – as it often is, if we think back on the adversity in our lives.

We can easily lose sight of the fact that there IS hope in every day in every situation if we look for it. We become mindful by simply tuning into things, the "frequencies" we may have been tuning out. We tend to brush aside our "wins" and "ya-but" ourselves instead of punctuating each victory and stacking it up on our tower of success. Mindfulness is the missing link for successful people who forget to take time to envision, reflect and allow their subconscious mind to work a little harder than their conscious brain in pursuit of their dreams. A coaching partnership is a great vehicle to keep ourselves mindful, hopeful, positive and focused on our passion, always in pursuit of our greater ideals while moving those forward via baby steps and bigger steps each day, not giving in to fear and uncertainty, which are always waiting to derail us. Celestine Chua aptly said, "Fear and uncertainty are your compasses toward growth." A great coach can help you manage fear and uncertainty and re-frame them into confident determination.

Wright

How would you explain your coaching philosophy?

Ross

Philosophically I believe we all have the answers within – if only we'd look and listen to the brain in our "gut" - our intuition, our inner voice that so often gets drowned out by the white noise of life. My role often is that of holding up the mirror and helping clients take a long hard look at themselves, their decisions, opinions, plans and paradigms and question them. We ask many questions – clients learn to ask self-coaching questions of themselves and their staff:

What is missing that could make all the difference?

What are my daily rituals that I use to stay on track?

What am I NOT doing that I know I must do?

How am I viewing myself in this situation?

What are my limiting beliefs and how are they holding me back?

What are my strengths and how are they serving me?

What would I do here if I knew I absolutely could not fail?

Wright

How do you think your relationship with your clients impacts their success?

Like any life-changing partnership, the level of one's commitment directly affects the outcome. Just as 2 horses can pull a load 250 times what one horse can pull, two people, working in tandem, create a powerful synergy that can impact results in a highly accelerated manner. That's the essence of great coaching: creating synergy. The way I experience and define a professional coaching relationship is illustrated in my C.O.A.C.H. Acronym:

Co-Active Thinking Partner – Impacts quality/quantity of solutions

Objective Set of Eyes on Your Business – Impacts client's perceptions

Accountability Mentor (czar!) – Impacts client focus, resolve & results

Collaborator – Impacts creativity, broadens the view & possibilities

Honest, judgment free facilitator of your success – Impacts client awareness, outlook and results.

Wright

I read about your "MOORF" system- what exactly is that?

Ross

M.O.O.R.F. Metamorphosis is transformation- ideally into something better, which is what we are all doing- like it or not, know it or not, every moment of every day from our skin cells to our brain cells. Why not "Moorf" consciously into something grand?

Wright

So how does one MOORF into something grand?

Ross

You simply by apply the MOORF principles to your day or to a specific situation. It's a little tool to help re-frame things and put them in perspective. I use it as a daily ritual, a framework to plan my priorities for the day beginning with quiet reflection and visualization time, also known as mindset. The MOORF daily ritual challenge is:

Mindset - Before I begin my day, I will pause to reflect and create a positive outlook.

Organization - I will prioritize & manage my day with a written system for success. Visualize positive outcomes and resolve to inspire one person today.

On Purpose - I will reach out to new and past clients, and practice accountability in my production activities and commitments.

Review/Revise - I will gratefully acknowledge and review my wins and challenges.

Focus - I will work to maintain my focus, using my positive "triggers" as guides.

If you look at any challenge you face in business and apply these 5 principles, the job will quickly feel more manageable. When I do consulting with business owners and their staffs, we demonstrate and implement this tool to help simplify, prioritize and organize. We print it on the back of little cards to keep as a visual trigger to remember that you can MOORF into something grand each day.

Wright

How would you describe coaching vs. consulting?

Ross

I believe that a professional business coach operates as a supportive challenger to the client, expecting and encouraging him/her to reach for more through the coaching partnership than they might do of their own volition. A consultant does more in the way of hands-on solution implementation. In coaching, we often find the client has the answers, and simply needs an expert, intuitive and experienced executive coach to brainstorm the issues and bring forth the solutions.

A consultant or trainer may focus on one or more issues such as sales, marketing, building a team, etc., and should have extensive expertise in the area of business development, whereas a coach may not, but is a trained expert in developing the discipline, commitment and planning required for the client to execute for the desired results.

Wright

How would you define what you as a coach experience with your ideal client and what is the payoff for you?

Ross

Coaching for me is a wonderfully integrated partnership of brainstorming, collaborating and defining with people their goals, purpose, passions and priorities; then helping them to hold themselves accountable in the pursuit of those goals. It's a simple but challenging process. It requires courage and fortitude – from coach and client. Great coaching is not for the faint of heart- it requires reaching and challenging yourself in new ways that you might not have experienced before as well as a willingness to re-frame and re-think some often long-held beliefs. It boils down to behavioral change on several levels, something that takes Passion, Practice and Persistence. The demands and requirements of great mentor-coaching require that I as coach practice and model the principles I am preaching – we teach what we need to learn. The great payoff is participating in the success of others. It's what I am passionate about – what I live for.

Wright

What do you think are the biggest measurable benefits of coaching or mentoring and the impact a person's success?

Ross

Self-knowledge is a big one that is often overlooked as a leadership tool. But leadership is born of a deep sense of self, which requires constant reflection and personal development. Clients are asked to take a hard look in the mirror and ask themselves: Am I ready and willing to push myself to step outside of my comfort zone? Examine my results vs. my goals?

That's the measurable part. We often do monthly or annual reviews of the "measure-ables" - the results vs. goals in a variety of areas from financial to operational to professional and personal goals, depending upon the client's needs.

As they become adept at this questioning, the change is remarkable. Challenges begin to be viewed as opportunities, from a higher altitude, with more clarity and a determined sense of curiosity about the many possible solutions. Dreams become bigger and more confident. The ability to focus on strengths, delegate the rest and carve out more time for friends, family, balance, life and love becomes a priority along with working on the business instead of working in it with your hair on fire! It's a positive philosophical change at nearly every level that illustrates the endless possibilities that many people miss in life.

Wright

What are the important things to look for in a Mentor-Coach?

Ross

In my 18 years of experience, I would say the best, most effective coaches have some similarities. A great coach is a gifted, intuitive listener, prober and challenger. They have a solid business background, good references and training, often including coaching-specific certification. Great coaches are creative and curious as well as voracious readers. They serve as a resource for you. They are supremely interested in YOUR story, your progress and success and are not prone to discussing their story, but share related experience when appropriate. They need to mesh with you and be someone you feel comfortable and connected with you in a way that allows you to lay it all out there. There is no use in sustaining a relationship that will not challenge you to complete honesty and fearless acceptance of the challenges you will confront together. Big challenges/big rewards.

Wright

What type of person benefits most from coaching?

Ross

Anyone who is willing to take the step and really commit to examining their success and making the changes they want but have not been able to do alone. Leaders are often the most in "need" due to the isolation and even lonely factor- many report having nobody to really unload on or bounce things off of who will: 1. Tell them the truth without fear of reprisal, and 2. Have the experience and background needed to be a formidable sparring and collaborating partner. But need does not constitute "want." Coaching is sometimes a little like going to the dentist- you have to want to take care of your "mental hygiene" and find a coaching practitioner with great "chair-side" manner, good listening skills and ample training and experience to inspire and motivate you to become your best on many levels.

Wright

So what is the ideal client profile for you as a coach?

Ross

My ideal client is a business owner or manager who is ready, willing and able to identify needed change, clarify their vision and move toward their goals, regardless of the perceived obstacles. That's where the courage and the HOW part comes in. HOW meaning honest, open and willing. Change is the foundation of progress and the essence of successful coaching. But "some things have to be believed to be seen". Faith in ones ability, in the process and in the coach is paramount. It's not a magic bullet, you have to surrender to it, believe in your ability to exceed your own expectations and maybe allow your coach to believe in you before you do!

Any business person who wants to stretch and push themselves to accelerate their success can benefit from a supportive, challenger with a fresh pair of eyes and no emotional investment in our business. Each client is different in how they learn, how they want to be challenged or accountable and at what pace they want to work. Each has their own definition of success too. For most it hovers around more time, more money, more balance- those seem to be the 3 big umbrellas. There's an old Japanese Proverb that illustrates the dilemma of many leaders: "Vision without action is a daydream. Action without vision is a nightmare." There's a delicate balance between vision and strategic action. Often people have either a vision OR an action plan, but not both. Clearly, they work best in tandem which again is where an accountability partner and supportive challenger can help you push through the blockage that is keeping you from creating, defining and implementing both.

Wright

What kinds of industries are your clients involved in?

Ross

My client's are mostly business owners and managers or sales and marketing people. I've worked with a clothing designer, international travel planner, retail owners, business colleges, service providers and consultants, doctors and mortgage, finance and real estate people. Corporations know that often their answers come from people outside their own industry - Jay Abrahamson, (a $5000 per hour coach) works on the premise that his experience with 400 diverse companies around the world gives him a vast pool of ideas that could help you. I'm sort of a "Junior Jay" in my approach- but more affordable! I've owned businesses, bought and sold them and consulted with hundreds of business people through my business college, consulting and coaching. I've enlisted a coach myself- since 1995- who is now a best friend and trusted advisor. She's become ultra successful in the time we've known each other and a fabulous mentor to me who collaborated on nearly every major decision from the time I launched my business college in 1995 through the sale of that business 10 years later. We still talk or meet often. It's a long term relationship, similar to what I have with many of my own clients. I have experienced first hand the huge impact that a dynamic coaching relationship can have – it made all the difference for me. So I aspire to provide that same exclusive success partnership for my clients.

Wright

Does each client go into a specific coaching program?

Ross

That depends on their situation and needs. I am an avid ANTI-cookie cutter coach. To each his own, but my experience has been that the variables are so great from person to person that a certain amount of customization is required for best results- but that requires a coach with some background and/or experience and education in business psychology and behavioral change, learning styles etc. Coaching is not for the faint of heart- coaches have to be as strong in their convictions and authority as they are in intuition and deep listening skills. You can't do that well without the background and the back bone to "back" you up, in my opinion. I usually require a 6 month commitment because behavioral change takes that long to implement once it is defined, expanded and implemented- then tweaked. If it didn't take time, focus and persistence, we'd all follow through on our own, from our gym memberships to our diets exercise and other life commitments that so often fall away when we are busy doing other things. Having personally lost 80 lbs and maintained that for nearly 10 years is a constant lesson and reminder that mindset, daily disciplines/rituals and accountability partners are part of a larger behavioral change mentality that requires the 3 P's of Passion, Practice and Persistence.

After 6-12 months, the coaching relationship often evolves into an ongoing consulting arrangement- monthly or more often depending on the client's need and style. I often become part of the team of advisors, and often do sales meetings, seminars or project management.

Wright

What happens during your coaching sessions?

Ross

Over the course of months: Miracles! During the actual meeting- anything is possible. But, the premise is simple. I use an agenda outline that begins with current HOT items or issues that may have come up since our last conversation. It's important to know what's going on now before diving into a set agenda in case the person has a burning issue or circumstance on their mind that will distract them or keep them from getting anything out of the meeting. There are coaches who believe in strictly following the coach's agenda or script- I'm not one of those. It's not about me- I'm the facilitator and challenger.

I've had a lot of interesting bombshells in that first hot potato minute! That is another book I think – an anonymous one of course. Once, a person's cat had died and was in the freezer awaiting shipment to be stuffed- she was devastated- so we did a coaching call on loss and change and dealing with reality. Other hot-potato moments included a client's drug-addicted adult child had relapsed; an abusive, marriage blow-up; a client who crashed her $150K Porsche on a race track and nearly died, births, deaths, and the occasional rant from a client who has just reached the end of his or her rope and needs you to just take it for a few minutes. That is the supreme test of a coaches listening ability. When it's over, there is inevitable relief, maybe a little chagrin but always gratitude from the client. Did I mention that coaching is not for the faint of heart?! Reality comes first during a coaching session. It's tough to ask the client how many sales calls they made when the beloved cat is in the freezer! Life eventually collides with business – and it IS sometimes personal. If life at home is unhappy, who wants to go to work and make sales calls? A coach has to be sensitive, intuitive and confident in dealing with such things. There are times when a coach stops coaching and suggests therapy or other resources before coaching can be resumed effectively. I have done that too. Again, training and experience in the signs of trouble are important coach characteristics.

Wright

Wow, coaching can be intense it seems. What would an average Susan Ross coaching session look like?

Ross

In a 60-minute meeting, the goal is for the coach to do a lot of listening, drawing out, challenging and collaborating. Often we help the client identify a grey area among the obvious black and white. I'm there to hold up the mirror, present challenges, ask for a different frame of reference from the client and together we often come up with some genius ideas- two heads (2 anchors) are always better than one.

We review and document Wins, Challenges, Focus Items, Stats and results. We set goals for next month's actions, commitments and focus. I ask them for one "Impress yourself" goal and one ASTONISH yourself goal. We may examine specific issues in depth. The idea is to tackle and make an impact on 1 or 2 key points rather than gloss over too much information and not feel like progress was made. At the end we review the call, evaluate the progress and how the client feels about the key issues now vs. when the call began. It's an energy- packed hour!

Wright

Do most clients have specific outcomes from coaching that they request?

Ross

Absolutely – we identify those in the first "discovery" session, reviewing and revising as we go. Right out of the shoot the first thing for many clients at the onset of coaching is more business. I know that there are not too many problems that can't be managed better with a few more deals in the pipeline or a little more money in the bank. In other words, if someone can't see where the rent check is coming from next month, they're not too motivated to start creating new systems. But once we get some momentum, which is born of action, things move pretty fast. Action creates momentum which builds motivation. Many people are better spurred into action when they are mentally prepared, organized, reviewed and focused. Remember MOORF? Mindset, Organization, Outreach, Review, Focus.

My format is built around the client's agenda- it is their responsibility to determine what is important now and why. They might be able to sell it to me and might not- they might be challenged on a specific priority and asked to question it, but we begin with their chosen agenda and brainstorm from there.

Wright

Is there a specific take-away from each session?

Ross

Yes—at least one or two! The broad goal is for the client to feel measurably better: more clear, confident, relaxed, relieved, rejuvenated and focused. They most often make strides in at least one or 2 key areas of focus. Constant feedback is important to our mutual success so outcomes and results are a reviewed during the call and a written set of agreed-upon Action items is created by the coach and given to the client after each session. The other take aways would be the priorities and plans we developed and agreed to during the session which they set out to conquer after our meeting.

Wright

How often do you communicate or follow-up with your clients?

Ross

It depends on the client of course and how they have agreed to be held accountable for results. I do occasional "pop calls" and emails, often with an idea or item of value to share. In the spirit of accountability they are asked to email a weekly update- some are more diligent than others, but some will fly through all of their focus and action items without an update. My policy is that they can email me as much and as often as they like. I will return the email within the business day if possible, which is the norm. Nobody has every abused the "unlimited" part, although some famous long winded folks have earned coaching sessions on the beauty of brevity...

Wright

What has your success looked like, how would your clients describe their coaching success?

Ross

It's been overwhelmingly good- the long term relationships and renewals often tell the story. Clients would say, and the have, that when I am not working with them, I am thinking about them and how I might connect them with resources, people, ideas and challenges that will help them to build a better business and a better life. Early in my career I taught Kindergarten, then I taught college, then I launched a private college where I taught and consulted with many business people in a 10 year period. I learned that coaching and teaching are 2 different things – coaching is a co-creative relationship, while teaching is also interactive I believe, it implies more of a telling/sharing of ones knowledge and is more linear. The results people get from just being accountable to a coaching relationship, and in touch, focused and clear on their goals are incredible, in any market or economy. When times are tight, the last thing to delete is your ongoing development and growth. It's like stopping your sales and marketing- it's the opposite of what you should do: go deeper into exploration, planning, re-visiting and revamping the plan. Sometimes people think they need to dismantle their business when what they really need is to dismantle their thinking. The Japanese theory of Kaizen taught me that. Their approach (think Toyota) is a complete 360 degree analysis and dismantling of any challenge with 3 rules in mind: No judgment or blame- that's considered a waste of time; 2. Process and results - vision and action are what matters. 3. Systemic Thinking: Big picture thinking while addressing the details at hand.

I think my clients would agree that a great coach can help you dismantle your thinking and reconstruct it in a more full and balanced way, much like the Kaizen theory. No judgment, just looking forward, creating a vision, a process and a system with a focus on the now and an eye on the destination. You CAN paint a new picture - write your own story. You just have to take time to envision it, define it, set a course and write it or it will be written for you. Having a good editor helps. My clients would agree that I am a good editor – for your copy and your life.

Wright

I want to try coaching. Where do I start?

Ross

A Test Drive- Once you identify a coach you might want to work with, ask for a consultation to determine if you and the coach are a match. Ask them for details on their philosophy and approach. What is their style? Will they challenge you enough or just chat with you about their story- a red flag. Coaching is about the client's story and what the next chapters will be.

Find out who the coach is – what's their background, experience and education related to coaching and behavioral change, not just training in your particular industry. If you want someone to train you in the things they did, marketing tools they used etc. – you can do that too, or get their materials from a website. In either case ask for referrals, testimonials and examples of their client's successes.

Does the coach have a coach? It is surprising how many coaches have never been coached by a professional mentor or coach. In psychology you have to go through extensive counseling before they turn you loose on clients- so you can see how I feel about coaching the coach. We all need to keep our saws sharpened- coaches included.

Don't' just shop price- it's important - but compare the product, accessibility of the coach and how much homework their might be in terms of your time investment. Is the approach personalized to your needs and strengths or is it a cookie cutter, pre formatted program. A new business owner may do well with a basic pre-formatted approach, but a more seasoned manager or owner will require more skills from an experience from a mentor-coach.

Success is something we each define it for ourselves – and redefine over time. A good way to test your coach-ability and better define your goals and purpose may also be a group coaching experience Group coaching teams meet monthly in a facilitated round-table format. It's another great tool the high rollers of all industries have used for decades (since Napoleon Hill) to tap into the power of "group think" with like minded passionate people. The skills of the facilitator are important to the process of keeping the group on task and moving forward.

Wright

Do you have a personal definition of success?

Ross

Great question! Yes I do, and I have been so fortunate in my life to have experienced success on so many levels- enough to realize that the one big mistake I made as a young person was NOT dreaming big enough. I dream really big now because I know that anything is possible – I am living proof. Since success is defined differently over time by each of us but in the end we are all looking to say we lived a good life, touched some people, and left the world a little better.

Did we find joy in this life?
Did we bring joy in this life?

That's what the ancient Egyptians asked themselves as they prepared to leave this earth. They believed the answers to those questions determined your place in the after-life. I try to ask those 2 questions of myself often, as I believe they really define success at its core. They sum it up simply and beautifully. Working hard, making a living, and paying the bills sounds pretty basic when compared to asking myself, "Am I bringing JOY to the world?" Now that's a lofty and worthy goal.

There's a great 2-minute video called "The Dash" which beautifully illustrates the point. We all come into this world alone and we all go out the same way. "Ant none of us getting out of here alive" as Chef Paula Dean says. We all will have a tombstone with a "born" date and a "done" date. In between is a little tiny *dash*. How we use that dash and what will be left of our work and earthly endeavors will be reduced to that tiny little symbol. However you define success, we now know that the power of our own minds to get us there is far greater than ever imagined. The power of 2 minds focused on your dream will dramatically, exponentially increase it's manifestation. Everyone can dream big, bring that dream into focus see it, envision it and ACT it into reality. Those are the first simple steps to success. Allowing it to take shape and become more real by sharing it with a mentor coach will help you hold yourself accountable to your life's purpose-and your DASH! www.thedashmovie.com.

Wright

Sounds powerful. Summarize for us: how do we build a better business and life?

Ross

Remember the Cheshire cat from Alice I Wonderland? He was prophetic:

"If you don't know where you're going, any road will get you there."

It turns out that our habits are thousands of times more powerful than our goals and desires combined! Best Selling author Gary Harpst (Six Disciplines for Excellence) states that "accountability coaching" outside your organization is essential and perhaps the most insightful way in which to learn to deliver and execute a great strategy. Most leaders fail to understand the human barrier component in them and in those they lead. Our tendency as humans is to do what we want, instead of what we should, despite our goals and desires, unless and until we are compelled to do so by virtue of our willingness to stretch and spend some time outside of our cozy, comfort zone.

Simply put, to challenge ourselves to live up to our greatest potential we need a *roadmap to success* including a vision, a plan, a compass to keep us on course, a steady navigator to keep us focused, and a great destination to stay determined along the way. A great mentor- coach will encourage you, help you adjust course and even challenge your direction at times. You just have to be willing to invest in your accountability, grab the wheel, and trust yourself to be the captain of your own ship and leader of your crew. The adventure is often in the journey and worth the bumps encountered along the way to becoming a balanced, successful and joyful you.

ABOUT THE AUTHOR

SUSAN ROSS HAS DEVOTED 20 YEARS to the study and practice of her passion for growing small businesses as an owner, developer, consultant, sales trainer and business growth coach. She helps business owners to define their dreams, clarify their vision and chart a course. Susan offers her expertise through a mentoring process in which clients build a better business and a better life that includes more time, more money, more balance, and more joy, however they might define those elements.

Susan M. Ross
Certified Business Mentor-Coach
Ventura California
877. MCOACH 1
susan@blueoceancoaching.com
www.blueoceancoaching.com